The Courage to Rise Again

⇠ by ⇢
Bertha Cooper Harris

A Journey from Tears to Testimony

To: Lari

Best wishes!
Bertha Cooper Harris
2017

The Courage to Rise Again:
A Journey from
Tears to Testimony

Copyright © 2012 by Bertha Cooper Harris

All rights reserved.

No part of this book may be reproduced or utilized in any form
or by any means electronic or mechanical, including photocopying, recording,
or by any information storage and retrieval system without permission in writing.

Inquiries should be addressed to:

Glad2b4u Press

7004 Wheeler Branch Trail
Austin, TX 78749

Glad2b4u@gmail.com

First Edition

First Printing: September, 2012

Cataloguing-in-Publication Data

Cooper, Bertha Harris
The Courage to Rise Again: From Tears to Testimony

185 *pp.*   1.0795 cm. (0.425")

1. Personal Journey   2. Domestic Violence   3. Folk Art   4. Southern Literature

I. Title   II. Author

ISBN 978-0-9828476-4-0 Pbk

Paintings by Bertha Cooper Harris

Cover Design by Bertha Cooper Harris (background painting), MMCC (text layout)

OneTouchPoint/Ginny's
Austin, Texas

Printed in the United States of America

To the many people who have blessed my life, especially:

- My Husband — Alce Harris
- My Daughter — C.C.
- My God-daughters — Reneé and Evelyn
- My Grandsons — Rodney, Jonathan, and Roderick
- My Brother — Odell
- My Sisters — Ella and Ann
- My God-grandchildren — Antrevious, De'Kenzy, and Tahlor N. Jackson
- My Great-grandchildren — Tina, Bonica, Rahquel, Naomi, Trika, Trevion, Bethany

May they never have to ask, "How can I smile tomorrow if I cannot laugh today?"

My loved ones who are no longer with me:

- My Daughter — Jennifer
- My Father — Jim
- My Mama — Annie Bell Young Edwards
- My Sisters — Peggie and Clara
- My Brothers — Jimmy, James, John, Sam, and Eddie.
- My Niece — Cecilia Faye

I know that you're smiling down on me from Above.

To my Mother, **Annie Bell Young Edwards**

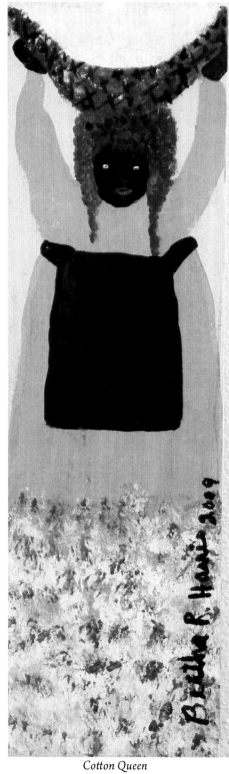

Cotton Queen

Contents

Foreword	vii
Preface	ix
Acknowledgments	xi
Introduction	xiii
1. Cooper Hill	1
2. Mr. Hunter's Place	3
3. Granpa Young	13
4. Separation of Sisters	17
5. Beene's Plantation	21
6. Race Relations	29
7. Early Teens	33
8. Charles	35
9. A New Lesson, Teenage Pregnancy	39
10. Albert	45
11. Employment	51
12. Guy	53
13. Court Date	57
14. Nightmares Come to Pass	61
15. Guy is Unfaithful	65
16. Downward Spiral	71
17. Even More Pain and Confusion	75
18. The Beast Hits Home	81
19. Our Home	89
20. Mama	91
21. Shut Down	93
22. On My Way	97
23. Moving	101
24. Death Strikes	103
25. Regression	107
26. Goodbye to the Past	109
27. Racial Healing	113
28. Yorkstone Insurance Company	115
29. Return to Yorkstone	121
30. The Transfer	123
31. The Godfather	127
32. Carter Loses Control	129
33. Carter Tries to Rape Me	131
34. Searching for an Out	135
35. No Enthusiasm	137
36. Carter's Behavior Worsens	139
37. The Turning Point	141
38. History Repeats Itself	149
39. The Depositions	151
40. P.S. Loved & Cherished	155
Conclusion	163
Sexual Abuse	164
Sexual Harassment — Know Your Rights!	164
Incest	165
Unforgivness	167

Angels watching over the Church

Foreword

THE *COURAGE TO RISE AGAIN* IS A RIVETING ACCOUNT OF THE LIFE OF ARTIST BERTHA HARRIS.

This masterfully written book unveils struggles, laughter, relationships, secrets, and triumphs. No matter what we face, God is able to bring us through it and give us victory, regardless of how hard the tests and challenges.

Psalm 46:1 reminds us, "God *is* our refuge and strength, a very present help in trouble."

Bertha's autobiography will keep you on the edge of your seat while bringing healing to your soul as it encourages every reader to have *the courage to rise again.*

— *Bishop L. Lawrence Brandon*
Praise Temple Full Gospel Cathedral Baptist Church
Shreveport, Louisiana

Mary, Joseph, and Baby Jesus

Two Mamas

Preface

My motivation to write this book stems from first hand experiences of horrors that the strong can inflict on the weak.

Growing up as a black child, driven by poverty in the South, living the life of a battered wife just to prevent my daughter from having to grow up in the same poverty I knew so well, I have battled the avenue of sexual harassment and any abuse possible. Yet I have risen above the pitfalls and the pain to share my experiences, in hope that some way I can help others who may still find themselves in this predicament.

I call Sexual Harassment and sexual and domestic violence the "Beast." Why do I call it the Beast? How did I know it existed? Those are the easy questions.

As a youth I was brought up in the church, and Sunday was a time for strengthening your beliefs. The messages they preached were uplifting, and no matter what faced me during the following week, I had always drawn strength in the knowledge that I was not alone.

That was, until the awakening of the Beast within. Then, I no longer attended church. Anger and depression kept me weighted down. If I did make it there, I found it impossible to focus on the message. I was constantly wondering why. This so-called man of God had never talked about the Beast in any of his messages. Could he not detect that some of us women were not crying because we were so holy, but because we were hurting and needed healing? The church was supposed to be a spiritual hospital. Why are such subjects taboo in some churches?

Later, on my journey in search of spiritual healing, I found Praise Temple Full Gospel Baptist Church. There I found out that God was a forgiving God from a true man of God who preached with boldness on every subject possible to get us saved and healed. Thank you, Pastor Brandon — you helped save my life and gave me the courage I needed to rise again.

In case you have not understood who the "Beast" is, allow me to introduce him. He is any thing or anyone that uses his believed power that he may have had over you to manipulate, demean, isolate, humiliate, and terrify you. He leaves you powerless. You become aware of pain so intense and overwhelming that it consumes all that you are and every dream you ever had and nullifies every prayer you ever uttered.

By telling my story and the battle I had with the Beast I hope that other women may find the courage and the determination to not only defeat the Beast, but conquer the devastating effect of the battle waged against him.

Sincerely,

Bertha Cooper Harris

JUBILEE 2008

Patterns, Pictures and Poetry - the Art of Claiborne Parish

featuring parish native

BERTHA COOPER HARRIS

and her depictions of Claiborne Parish during a bygone era

10 A.M. May 10th on the Courthouse Square

Quilt Show —Friday & Saturday, May 9-10 (judging Thursday May 8)

Sidewalk Art Show — Saturday, May 10th

POETRY CONTEST — READING — MAY 10TH

Poets of all ages are encouraged to submit a maximum of three works prior to April 2

Acknowledgments

THIS BOOK WOULD NOT HAVE BEEN POSSIBLE without the encouragement and support from my nieces Lois Johnson, Jackie Harris, Dewana Smith, Trisa Gee, Von Smith, Linda Turner, and Dorothy Turner, who always believed I could fly and cared deeply about me getting my story told.

To my nephew Dorsey Washington, you hardly ever miss a day from calling me and saying some type of encouraging words.

Thanks to my editor Marion Marks, who told me, "this book will walk on its own!"

A very special note of gratitude and appreciation is owed to my Pastor, Larry Brandon, and his wife Co-Pastor Wanda Brandon, of the Praise Temple Full Gospel Baptist Church. Thanks for preaching the truth without condemning.

Thanks to Cynthia Steele who got me known in Claiborne Parish by getting an article published in the Homer newspaper about me. She believed in me enough to have me as the guest visual artist in the Claiborne Parish Jubilee in 2008. She continues to support me in all my work. Love you my Sister!

Thanks to Trish Holland, Cynthia's sister, who drove all the way from Austin, Texas to offer her expertise in getting me published. Your kindness will never be forgotten. Love you!

Thanks to Nina Kelly Avant for assisting in proofreading.

Thanks to Pam Sloan and Tracey Prator for supporting me and calling me their "Chocolate Momma." Love you Girls!

Thanks to Laura Curtis; I couldn't ask for a better friend. You are always there for me. Love you!

Thanks to the Law Office of Attorney Nelson Cameron, and Staff: Bonnie, Christine, and Deana. Your cooperation and kindness will never be forgotten.

To all my family members that I did not name, I love you all dearly. Remember, we are family.

And not least, to my Church members and friends Clara Vance and Mimmie Thompson. Thank you for encouraged me to keep painting.

All the encouragement of my big family of supporters keeps me moving every day.

Special thanks to the publisher & Trish Holland, principal at Glad2b4u Press, for all the encouragement along the way with this project. The regular communication, coaxing and recommendations allowed me the freedom to express myself and my convictions regarding issues I needed to address.

As an artist, I see the world through my experiences and hope that my struggle will make the next artist's journey more enriching. My journey has become more meaningful and the load more bearable through our personal connection.

Sharing our experiences, both joyous and unpleasant, allows us to become more understanding of those whose lives we strive to enrich.

Introduction

I HAVE BEEN RIPPED APART BY THIS THING THAT GROWS INSIDE ME. I am waiting for the day when I no longer have to fight off his power in my life. It is a fight I must continue, and one that I cannot lose. He's waiting for me just beyond each heartache in my life. He's waiting for the time when I no longer have the strength to fight. He's the thing I call the Beast.

There was a time when he had taken over my life and took me to a darker place than I've ever imagined existed. He was my deepest secret. But, as I write this, I cast him into the light of day.

I will no longer give this Beast power over my life. I will be strong, and I will become stronger as I write. I suffered the loss of my mother, and the accidental drowning of my seventeen-year-old daughter. I endured the battery of a former husband. But I'm still here to face the sunrise of another day.

Friday, Nov. 20, 2009 — The Dallas Morning News

Lakewood home tour raises money for area schools

BY KENDALL KIRKHAM
kekirkham@neighborsgo.com

It was a big weekend for Lakewood Nov. 13-15, as approximately $125,000 was raised for Lakewood Elementary, J.L. Long Middle School and Woodrow Wilson High School at the 33rd annual Lakewood Home Festival.

The home tour, auction, market and cafe drew more than 3,000 people with the help of 459 volunteers over the span of three days.

Meredith Manak, president of Lakewood Early Childhood PTA, said this year was a huge success, especially considering the current state of the economy.

"We broke records from what we can tell," Manak said.

Last year, the event raised about $100,000.

According to the vendors and artists that participated in the market, this year's tour has been the best yet, Manak said, and she thinks the added publicity efforts helped make the weekend a profitable one.

The festival kicked off Friday night with a candlelight tour and an auction party and casino themed "Caddyshack: Gopher the fun, gopher the schools."

Among the items was a piece of artwork created by 87 Lakewood Elementary fifth graders. Each child painted a small segment of the Lakewood Theater Tower using their own styles and techniques, and the pieces were then assembled together to build a large image. The final artwork sold for $5,300.

The home tour, market and café continued the weekend Saturday through Sunday.

The tour featured six Lakewood houses that ranged from ultra contemporary to ranch style to French Hutsell, and each home was sketched by a Dallas area artist, Dahlia Woods. Other artwork by Woods is painted on the walls of Lakewood Elementary.

As the LECPTA's only philanthropy, the funds raised from the tour are being concentrated on the implementation of the International Baccalaureate program for the schools.

For more information on the LECPTA, visit lecpta.org.

Photographer Nick Mann at his booth in the market. Nick works with fractured lighting, color and glass. "Glass is like a sponge with lights – it works with everything," he said. Originally from San Antonio, this is Mann's first year to be a part of the Lakewood Home Tour weekend.

Bertha Harris of Shreveport, LA shows off her booth in the market. Bertha's artistic style is southern folk art; she paints about life experiences and things her grandparents used to talk about. "I recapture the history of my family," she said. More of her work is featured in the photo below.

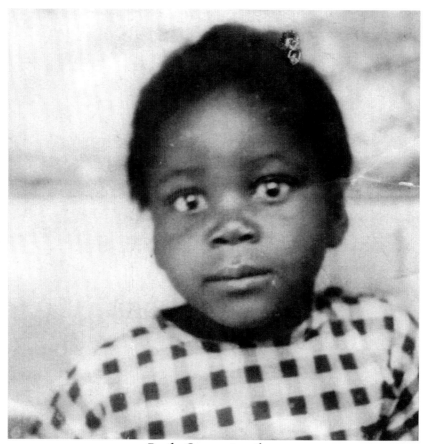

Bertha Cooper *at age three*

Cooper Hill

1. Cooper Hill

THE COMMUNITY WHERE I WAS BORN AND RAISED WAS KNOWN AS COOPER HILL. Today people know it as the St. John Community, but we knew it as Cooper Hill because Granpa Riley Cooper owned the land of our homestead on the hill by the main road. It was just a few miles outside the city limits of Homer, Louisiana, and it was our home. The road up that hill was so steep that many horse drawn wagons could barely make it up the hill. Many travelers had to get out of their wagons and walk or push their wagon up the steep hill.

Years later the hill was lowered to make way for a paved road. And since Granpa Cooper no longer owned all the land, it was renamed Spring Lake Road. That's the way we know it today.

One of my most distinct memories about Cooper Hill was that it was all inhabited mostly by Cooper families, hence the name, I suppose. I wish I could say that we were a close family, but we were not. There was a beast that rambled over Cooper Hill — a beast marked by greed, prejudice, and evil.

Cooper Hill reminded you of a colony divided. There was a light-skinned group who tended to be an educated group, and the darker-skinned group. Unfortunate for us, we fit in the dark-skin group. My father was not as educated as some of his brother and sisters, therefore he was looked down on and referred to as the black sheep of the family. He was light-skinned but, he married a dark-skinned woman, who was my mama. The why wasn't for me to know, I guess he just loved her.

I was the eighth child of nine born to Jim and Annie Bell Cooper. My father died when I was around seven. But, just before his death, my family and I lived in Granpa Riley's house. My father didn't have his own house. He just started out living with Granpa Riley.

Granpa was generous enough to let us live with him. The ones that had houses there on Cooper Hill just owned the houses, they didn't own the land. Granpa Riley had more than enough land to go round. He owned more than two hundred and fifty acres, but down through the years he sold most of it off when he needed money. My father and most of his brothers were farmers, just as their father, Granpa Riley Cooper, before them.

The road that led to Granpa's house went up a steep hill. So steep, in fact, that the many horses and wagons that traveled that way could barely make it to the top without stalling in the middle. Usually, anyone unfortunate enough to be driving that way would be forced to guide the horses and the wagon down to the bottom of the hill on foot. There were times when women and children would have to get out of the wagon to help the driver push until the wagon finally rolled to the bottom of the hill. Normally that would be the end of their journey.

As if these deplorable conditions weren't bad enough, add to that the road leading to our home. It was red clay and sand. When the road was dry, red sand would saturate our clothes and cover our feet, making a bad situation even worse. Many days we used a whiskbroom to brush the sand off our clothing and we used the wet towel we kept to wipe it away. The red clay and sand seemed a part of our lives.

Granpa Riley had lost one of his legs in an accident in his younger days, but he never let it slow him down. In its place, he had an artificial leg, made out of wood, the best most folks could afford in those days. Usually, he dressed in a black suit, and wore a top hat. His straight sable hair fell softly around his warm, olive complexioned face, giving him the noble look of his Native American ancestor.

Besides being neat and handsome, Granpa Riley was an honorable man. I loved to see him riding around in his shiny new buggy with his shiny white horses, as he drove through Cooper Hill.

Giddy up, horse, he'd yell to his faithful horse, he'd say with unchallenged authority. I loved mostly the times when he'd allow my brothers Sam and Odell to ride in the back seat of his buggy as he drove through Cooper Hill. Then he was off to check on his many tracks of cotton and corn. I can't remember a time that he didn't have peppermint sticks in his coat pocket to give to the children he met on his journey. It was like a magic ride when we were allowed to go along.

Our home on Cooper Hill was a two-story log cabin surrounded by vast amounts of wooded property, and was situated in the middle of Cooper Hill. Granpa, along with a few other men from the area, built our home long before we were born. But we got to hear stories about the olden days when it was built.

The flooring was crafted from oak. The house had long halls that lead out to the huge kitchen, where a cast-iron stove stood in the corner of the room. Granpa even had running water in the kitchen, which was pumped in from the well outside, a luxury that I would soon come to appreciate. The dining-room table had plenty of chairs surrounding it, their craftsmanship adding an understated touch of elegance to the otherwise masculine decor of the room. Many of our family meals were eaten there, listening to the older people reminisce about their life's experiences. These were happy times for all of us children.

There was a fireplace in the sitting room, and believe me, it was really appreciated during the winter months. This room was most likely where all of us could be found during the winter months, except, of course, Mama.

Regardless of how much she did daily, it seemed Mama's work was never done. She always seemed to have something to do. Whether in the kitchen cooking, washing dishes, or whatever she could find to do, she would work diligently until bedtime.

Mama was about medium height, with the darkest, smoothest skin. Her hair was thick and jet-black, and her eyes were the warmest brown. I've always believed she resembled Granpa Seaborne Young, her father.

But I digress as I was telling you about our home. Anyway, the second story of our home at that time was where Granpa spent most of his time. We always knew when he was coming, because of the distinctive thump of his wooden leg on the stair steps. My brothers and I found it a welcome sound. We would simply wait for him to throw his seemingly endless supply of peppermints down to us. "Here is something to make your bellies sweet," he'd say with a warm grin. And it always made us smile with him. Our Father died before Granpa did, so Granpa made sure that we were taken care of. When Granpa died, there went our breadwinner.

2. Mr. Hunter's Place

Much of my childhood, until the age of seven, would be vague impressions of what I supposed were better days. At any rate, over the passage of time, they have faded somewhat and are not as clear as those that followed.

It was about that time that our mama moved to the Hunter chicken and dairy farm, taking with her my brothers Jimmy and James, my sister Annie, and of course me. Mama's primary goal was to work hard and take care of us the best she could. Back then I never understood why we had to leave Cooper Hill and I suppose, because I was a child, no one felt it important enough to explain it to me.

My sister Ella went to live with my father's sister, Aunt Lena. Brother Odell was sent to live with Aunt Molly, my father's aunt. Finally, Eddie, John, and Sam, the remaining brothers, went to live with other relatives. Through a child's eyes, my Mama's decision might have been painful and unfair. But today, I realize it was the best she could do for us.

Not until meeting Mr. Hunter had I ever encountered white men. He was a tall man with reddish brown hair, and his eyes were the coldest I'd ever seen, or hoped to see again. He acted as if he'd known Mama for years. He began calling her "Auntie." I never did know why, but I'm more than certain it had been an offhanded derogatory remark, especially coming from him. This man also had the most irritating habit of acting as if he owned my brothers. I suppose you could say he was a throwback from the days of slavery. If it had been left up to him, my brothers would definitely have lost their right to freedom. Those cold, almost soulless eyes of his left us feeling that we meant less than nothing to him, as servants or human beings. I remember times when Annie and I looked into the dark abyss of his eyes and made it a point to cleave closer to Mama.

Living on Mr. Hunter's farm was an experience quite unlike any I had ever encountered, in the seven years of my little experience. He was generous enough to allow us to live free of charge, in return for the labor we all did around the farm.

One evening, much like the ones since we'd moved to the Hunter farm, we were playing round the porch, with Mama sitting in her favorite chair, rocking back and forth; when Mr. Hunter decided to pay us an unexpected visit, placing his feet on the bottom step. He began to give Mama all of our job descriptions. He let Mama know right away that the boys had to work out in the chicken house and dairy.

"Auntie," he said in his demanding tone, "You and the girls are to work in the house and help my mother. Your girls can also help watch after Sherry."

Mama parted her lips as if to say, "My girls are not going to be watching anybody's children." Instead, she rose from her chair and walked slowly into the house. Her internal anguish was obvious to us all, 'cause Mama had never been one to like being told what to do as if she was a child — by white folks in particular.

Our home on the farm, which, to be honest, was more like a shack, was nothing compared to the house on Cooper Hill. There were two bedrooms and a small kitchen. Ann and I were forced to sleep with Mama, for lack of other suitable accommodations. There was absolutely no inside plumbing or electricity to illuminate the dark shadows of the room. For light, we used an oil lamp.

During the winter months, when it grew cold, we had to build a fire in the old wood-burning heater that stood in the corner near the blistered, peeling wall of the old shack. Mama cooked what little food was available to us on an old wood-burning stove that sat in the middle of the wretched old kitchen. Worst of all, at least for me, we were forced to use an old outhouse as our toilet facilities. We even had to use old newspaper to wipe ourselves — talk about a lesson in harsh reality.

Sometimes when I look back, I ponder what constitutes child abuse, and I'm pretty certain that by today's standards, we were definitely abused. If she'd ever been investigated by child welfare, they probably would have escorted her to jail.

Taking a bath was another one of those laborious chores. In order for us to have enough water to bathe, we had to fetch the water from the spring located deep down in the darkest abyss of the woods. We reluctantly fetched the water from the spring just as we had been ordered.

This water had to serve several purposes. It was used for drinking, cooking, cleaning, and washing as well. Mama established what we called "washday." Washday was every Saturday morning. It was not a day any of us looked forward to, but then of course, I can't think anyone in his or her right mind would contemplate washday with pleasure. So off we went, trotting down to that spring and carrying water in a tin bucket to fill the two or three tubs that sat on the end of the ragged old front porch.

Mama scrubbed and rinsed her towels and pillowcases until they were white. Not a blemish remained on them. Her soap was made of Eagle Lye, a foul substance consisting of old grease, which she would cook in a huge pot over a smoldering fire. Of course, for the soap to be useful it had to be made weeks in advance. There were times it would set overnight, and by morning it would be thick enough to cut into bars. Once it was ready for use, it was used for everything, including bathing, which as you can imagine was an experience in itself.

Saturday nights around our house were designated for ironing, which as you can imagine was faced with about as much enthusiasm as hauling water from the spring. We used one of those antiquated irons that were so popular in those days. Because there were no cords attached, we would use the fire in the stove to heat it, and once it was hot enough, Mama would iron the dresses, pants, sheets, and pillowcases. Thank God those days are over.

As if the day hadn't been laborious enough, before we were allowed to rest our tired, haggard bodies, we'd have to scrub the unfinished wooden floor with the same hot eagle lye water, so they would be sanitized by Sunday. I'm sure you can guess from my dissertation that the weekends were not an occasion to celebrate in our home.

As for the Hunters, well, they lived in a big white house with a lovely porch that wrapped all the way around their beautiful home. They had more room in that big house than they could ever use themselves. But of course, it never occurred to them to share. I wondered at times, what it would be like to live in a house such as theirs.

Only three people actually lived in that sprawling house: Mr. Hunter, of course, and his mother, and Sherry. I gathered Mr. Hunter's father must have died when Mr. Hunter was very young. Mr. Hunter had never married. But he was such an arrogant, cruel, and derogatory monster, who would have him?

Mama spent her days at the Hunter's cooking and cleaning for them. Most of Annie's and my time was spent playing with Sherry, Mrs. Hunter's granddaughter.

Sherry and Annie were both six years old at the time. Sherry had long, red curly hair. Most of her face was covered with freckles. She told us that she lived in South Louisiana. Her mother was Mrs. Hunter's daughter. Sherry lived with her grandmother because her mother was ill.

During lunchtime, we helped Mama set the Hunter's extravagant table that sat in the middle of the dining room, covered with the most beautiful linens, china, and silver that I had ever seen.

Mama, Annie and I had been relegated to the Hunter's screened in back porch. Instead of beautiful china plates to eat on, our meals were served on old tin plates. We drank from old fruit jars. Our flatware was a tarnished spoon, not forks. Annie and I would watch Sherry eating through the small window in the room where we ate. Imitating her, we would eat with one hand and place the other under the table, as proper etiquette demanded. After a while, it became second nature to eat that way. As children, Annie and I didn't understand why the Hunter's insisted that we take our meals on the back porch in the heat, alone.

One day Mrs. Hunter walked out on the porch and saw us eating, using proper table manners. To say she was utterly stunned would be putting it mildly. It was as if she thought we were incapable of such behavior.

"Annie Bell, your girls sure do have good table manners," I overheard her telling Mama.

Mama thanked her and continued washing dishes, glancing sharply toward us to let us know that she needed our help before we went back out to play with Sherry. Usually, any food that was left over from the Hunter's dinner was taken to our home to be eaten later.

Whenever Annie and I played with Sherry, she loved for us to ride her on our backs, and we did it often. However, one day we asked her to ride us on her back. Why not; it seemed a logical request to us. Apparently, Sherry didn't share that view.

"I am not going to ride no niggers on my back," she replied adamantly.

"Then we aren't going to ride no niggers on our back, either," we retorted just as adamantly. To tell you the truth, at the time, Annie and I had no idea what a "nigger" was, but we figured as long as she called us "nigger," that she should be one too.

Sherry, however, must have had some idea of what it meant; she was furious. Right before our very eyes, she turned beet red and ran screaming into the house as if she'd just been slapped, stomping her feet as she went along. Once inside, she told her grandmother that we had called her a nigger, and you know that infuriated the old lady.

I suppose, in her defense, she believed that Annie and I knew what the word meant, hence her irrational outburst. But we didn't understand her anger — you can believe that.

Later that evening, after we returned home, we asked Mama why everyone was so upset. She never really answered us, though. Instead, she just looked at us with a bewildered look, as she continued her quilting.

Our brothers, however, were not so closed mouthed. In fact, they thought the whole incident was hilarious. Once we completed our tale, in full detail to them, they laughed so hard they nearly fell off the porch.

"Lord, girls, y'all trying to get us killed?" my brother, Jimmy, asked trying to control his hysterical laughter. "You don't call white people niggers. That's what they call us!" he finished breaking into another bout of hysterical laughter.

"Well," I thought to myself still not fully comprehending the problem," I guess that's why they got so mad."

My brothers, James and Jimmy were expected to report to Mr. Hunter at four o'clock every morning, and worked until sundown each day. There was very little time for us to spend time with them. Basically, we only saw them from a distance, and whenever we did, Mr. Hunter would be yelling at them.

"For God's sake," he yells, "don't let them cows get out of that pasture to eat them bitter weeds. If y'all do, your asses belong to me." (Bitter weeds grew in clusters in the pasture and had pretty yellow blooms, but if eaten by cows, it would make their milk taste bitter.)

I was so afraid for my brothers. Mr. Hunter would yell at them all day, as if he were speaking to some kind of ignorant animal, which, in his eyes, was exactly how he saw them. There were many times I felt he would actually beat them, without much provocation on their part.

While we lived there, a big truck with a long silver tank would pull into the yard to collect the milk from the dairy. It was James and Jimmy's responsibility to pack the eggs in their containers in preparation for Mr. Hunter to take into town to the local merchants and sell them. Most of the time, he would take them along with him, bringing them home late at night.

Many times Mama would sit around, worrying about their safety until she heard their footstep on the porch. Most of the time I felt she had nothing to worry about. After all, what could possibly happen to them? They were with Mr. Hunter. Surely he would take care of them. But I couldn't have been more wrong. Mama must have sensed the evil that lurked within the man's heart, for she spent many nights sitting up quilting until she knew with certainty that her sons were safe. However, her overwhelming fear could have been a direct result of Jimmy telling her that Mr. Hunter got drunk sometimes and left them outside in his jeep. They weren't permitted inside with Mr. Hunter. In those days colored folk weren't permitted to eat or drink in white-owned cafés.

Sometimes Mr. Hunter would stagger outside with his girl friend in tow, and bring them some food to the jeep. That is, whenever he remembered he'd left them there.

"Betty, he'd say, these here are my colored boys. I brought y'all some of this stew. Now go on and eat it before it gets cold," he'd order them just before staggering back inside the café.

I suspect Jimmy was afraid of sitting out there in the dark for so long. If he were, there had been no way to hide that fact. Jimmy's skin tone was of the darkest black and he had the biggest, whitest eyes, I have yet to see. Whenever he was talking to Mama about Mr. Hunter, his eyes would bulge out of his head just like a frog's, an unmistakable sign of his fear.

My brother James, on the other hand, had a rich brown skin tone. His eyes, for reasons we have yet to figure out, were more slanted than the rest of us. Whenever he was frightened, it seemed his eyes simply disappeared, retreating to the back of his head.

Though you may not believe this, the Hunter's *chicken* house was much better equipped than our house. At least they were fortunate enough to have electricity to keep them warm. In better days, Annie, Sherry, and I made the chicken house one of our favorite playgrounds. That is until the day we decided to have an egg fight.

I have to admit, at the time it sounded like a wonderful idea; at least I didn't see any flaws in the theory. What was the harm? The three of us had a blast, hitting each other in the face and head until we could no longer see where we were throwing them. But we didn't stop there, oh no. When we were finished, we took our little game one step farther. By the time our game was over, there were eggs on the walls, inside and out, we even smelled like eggs.

I must confess, though, of the three of us, I came out the worse for wear. My hair had shrunken into a ball like a poodle's hair, and I probably looked like one as well. Annie's hair was straight like grandfather Riley's hair. Therefore, her hair wasn't nearly as nappy as mine. Sherry's long curly red hair just lay plastered to her scalp and face. My hair, on the other hand, presented Mama with a whole new set of problems, as if she didn't already have enough.

When Mama and Mrs. Hunter glanced out the window and saw the mess we had made of the chicken house (not to mention ourselves), they came running, and you can bet it wasn't to give us a hug. Both of them were angry, and we didn't have to wait until they reached us, to figure out that little tidbit. For the rest of my life, I'll remember the whipping that Mama gave us that day. And on top of that, we were forbidden to play with Sherry again, and banned from the Hunter's house for good.

As time went on, the Hunters refused to change their minds about us, so we could only wave at Sherry from a distance. We truly missed our friend, and I don't think it presumptuous to say she missed us as well.

With the fall season upon us, Annie fully six and myself seven, we were sent to school. In those days it wasn't too unusual for children of color to begin their formal education much later than those today; some were forced to miss school altogether. Those unable to attend school at all were required to work instead, to help support their families. Fortunately, Ann (as I now called my sister) and I were not among them. Jimmy and James weren't so fortunate. Though nine and ten years old, they were only allowed to go to school when they were not required to work for Mr. Hunter.

Rising Star Baptist Church, where we attended school, was quite a distance from where we lived. Ann and I walked for miles and miles down an isolated dirt road, through thick eerie woods to reach the old church.

Rising Star served two purposes. Colored families attended church services on Sundays, and weekdays the sanctuary was used for classes attended by colored students of all ages. It didn't offer much in the way of comfort, and the only restroom available was the old outhouse in the back. The only other school that colored kids could attend that wasn't located in a church was the Bill Chatman Colored School, located outside of Homer. Mr. Chatman, a wealthy colored man, built the school in 1922, seventeen years before I was born. The school had living quarters for the teachers to live, but was long gone by the time I was old enough to attend school.

There was a large open area that our teacher, Mrs. Smith, would section off, dividing her students into groups by grade level. There were no kitchen facilities available to us, so we were forced to bring our lunches with us, carrying them in brown paper bags.

In the middle of the room sat a large, wood-burning stove, which gave off the only heat available against the cold. Only a few boys attended class with us and it was always their job to cut wood to be burned in the old heater.

I thought Mrs. Smith was a beautiful woman. She was a light-skinned woman with long brown hair. Actually, truth be told, she resembled a white woman more than a black one. From my earliest childhood, it seemed that people who were in authority, in any capacity, were either white or as close to white as they could possibly get. I'm sure that it didn't hurt either that Mrs. Smith's father was a white man, which is probably what propelled her to an uppity stature.

Sadie, Mrs. Smith's daughter, also looked white. She had long, brown braids, and always wore the most brightly colored and starched dresses, trimmed with lace and ribbons. The plain dresses Mama made for Ann and me by hand seemed dull and outdated when compared to those worn by the other girls that attended class with us.

Recess was our social time. We'd run out on the white sandy, church grounds and play ring around the roses, hide and seek, and jump rope. The see-saw, which was only a six-by-four-foot plank placed over a wooden sawhorse, served as our only real playground equipment. Ropes back in those days were plentiful, but then they would have had to be. They were used for everything from drawing water from the well, to hanging colored men by the neck.

After school was out for the day, Ann and I walked home with white sand all over our shoes, clothing, and hair. Every day as we walked home, a big yellow bus carrying the white children home from school passed us by, blowing even more sand on us.

The white children on the bus would taunt us, throwing things out of the windows, trying to hit us, then yell at us, "niggers, niggers!" Still unaware of what the word meant, exactly, I knew enough to realize it was a derogatory word. Even so, I didn't understand why we couldn't play with them, or go to school with them. As a child, unaware of the hatred harbored against my race, I couldn't understand why. Somehow, it just didn't seem fair.

Many times I found myself saddened and confused by the cruel hatred directed at me for no apparent reason. I just couldn't comprehend why children we had never met wanted to insult us and call us ugly names.

"Mama," I asked one day in frustration, "why can't we move back to Cooper Hill?"

As usual, I received the same answer; she simply refused to discuss Cooper Hill, to me or anyone else for that matter. But to be honest, Mama never really did much talking about anything. She did a lot of humming and smiling though. Mama had the prettiest smile. I remember looking at her when she smiled at something said or done by one of us, and it seemed the whole room would be illuminated by that simple gesture. Her beautiful black face seemed to transform with radiance, and genuine warmth flowed freely from within her very soul, warming the hearts of those she granted a smile.

Earlier, I believe I mentioned that no matter what happened, Mama would sit by the window and wait for James and Jimmy, my brothers, to come home after a day with Mr. Hunter.

Well, finally, I discovered why her fear was so overwhelming, and how very real it was. The happenings of that particular day, and the terror we all felt will remain with me forever.

On this night Ann and I were doing our homework, as usual, by the old oil lamp. Mama, as usual, was sitting in the corner by the window sewing her quilting pieces together. I can still hear the sounds of the wood popping and crackling in the old heater. The evening had turned cold, and the wind outside the old, rundown house we called home was roaring through the open cracks in the floors and the walls.

To keep out some of the cold, and retain more of the heat, Mama pasted the old newspapers on the walls, not that they did much to help. Actually, what I've been politely calling cracks in the walls and floors were more like holes. Mama sometimes tried to close them off by stuffing rags and paper in them, but the wind that particular evening refused to be stilled. There just didn't seem to be enough paper and rags available to keep the cold wind from blowing cold air throughout the house.

Suddenly out of the darkness, we heard loud shouting coming from the direction of Mr. Hunter's milk dairy. At first, I thought it might have been the wind. But from the stark look of terror Mama wore as she jumped from her chair, throwing the shutters open wide, I knew without a doubt serious trouble was brewing.

I stood frozen, watching panic in my mother eyes, wondering what could possibly have happened. I grew more and more frightened by the moment. The force of the wind jerked the old shutters from Mama's hands, slamming them repeatedly against the outside of the house, making sounds as if they were about to be ripped from their hinges.

Unmistakable sounds from the dairy grew louder and louder through the open window. Over the roaring wind sounds became more distinct and we began to understand what was going on. When the second cry sounded, there was no longer any doubt in our minds that the voices we heard were James, Jimmy, and Mr. Hunter.

"Don't you run from me, you niggers," Mr. Hunter yelled. Through the cries we heard James and Jimmy begging Mr. Hunter not to hit them. Evidently, they were struggling to get away from him, because we later heard Mr. Hunter yelling at them to come back.

Mama, Ann, and I stood in stunned silence, listening attentively to the slaps of leather against bared skin. Devastated by what Mr. Hunter might be doing to her sons, Mama closed the shutters and returned to her seat. The tensions in the lines of her body were evident to Ann and me. It was obvious to us that what she'd heard outside was more than just troubling. The concern for her sons' safety was certainly paramount in her thoughts. Mama felt the sounds of leather tearing flesh as deeply as if she were being beaten.

When silence once again reigned, Mama began pacing form room to room, tears streaming unchecked down her face. Ann and I were terrified and ran over to her for what little comfort she could give us amidst her own turmoil. We wrapped our arms around her legs so tightly she couldn't move.

Finally, after God only knew how much time had passed, we heard footsteps coming from the porch. I thought at first it that it was James and Jimmy having escaped Mr. Hunter's tirade, but unfortunately, it wasn't. It was, as you have already guessed, Mr. Hunter himself.

I guess he felt that he hadn't beaten them nearly enough because here he was, big as life, looking for them, so he could beat and humiliate them even more. He was so angry, he didn't even give Mama a chance to open the door before he kicked it in and walked in as if he lived there, smelling like alcohol, his face as red as fire, eyes resembling the devil's own. He strolled past each of us, and then walked through each room, searching the darkened interiors with a flashlight.

"Where are the damn heathens?" he roared at Mama. "They let every one of them damn cows out in the bitter weeds and they ate them all! Now, my milk will taste bitter and I can't sell it. I am going to kill them niggers," he continued screaming at Mama as if she could snap her fingers and tell him where to find her sons.

Satisfied that they weren't there, he turned to walk out, shining his light under the porch as if to search for them there, which is probably where he believed they would hide. Had he bothered asking, we could have told him they were not under there. Finally he left, leaving Ann and me frightened and confused.

"Mama," I whispered, looking up at her, "please don't let Mr. Hunter kill my brothers."

We slept very little that night, as you might imagine. Throughout the night we dozed and prayed fervently ever waking minute that James and Jimmy would be all right.

By morning, when there was still no sign of them, Mama, finally at her wits end, left to go up and down the road searching for them. When she returned, she told Ann and me to get more clothes on for the walk over to the house where my Uncle Raymond, her brother, lived on the Homer Road.

She was desperate to find my brothers and hoped, I'm sure, that they had made it safely there. I wanted to tell Mama that I doubted they would go there, because they didn't like Aunt Pearlie, Uncle Raymond's wife that much, but I simply couldn't break her heart like that. She'd endured enough in the last twenty-four hours and I refused to add to her pain and frustration.

Once, a while back, Mama had left us in Aunt Pearlie's care for about two weeks, while she went to visit her mother in Little Rock. Aunt Pearlie fed us leftovers most of the time, while she and Uncle Raymond ate fresh hot biscuits for breakfast. However, we were given the day old, cold, hard ones to eat, but not before she made a hole in them with her finger and poured syrup in them. We retaliated by throwing the food under the house for the dogs to eat. To be honest, I really don't believe Uncle Raymond had any idea what she'd been doing to us. Usually, he left for work long before we were up for the day. We never told Mama about it, either. Mama believed her sister-in-law loved us, so we allowed her that illusion.

The walk to Uncle Raymond's house was one of the longest and coldest walks I can ever remember taking. We wore dresses over our jeans, and then covered ourselves with coats and sweaters. To protect our heads, we wrapped scarves around them. I can still recall how the ground was so frozen and hard that day as we walked the road. I kept looking back, almost falling in my haste, for fear that Mr. Hunter had somehow found out what we were doing, following closely behind us, hiding in the shadows cast by the woods surrounding us, trying to catch us unaware.

By the time we arrived at Uncle Raymond's house, Mama was a wreck, consumed by worry, exhausted, almost frozen and frantic about the loss of her sons. Cold to the very core of her, and shivering so badly, Mama could hardly relay the events that had led us to Uncle Raymond's.

"My children, Raymond, my children!" she cried desperately.

"What about your children, Annie Bell?" Uncle Raymond asked trying to make sense of her rambling.

"I can whip my own children!" she stated adamantly, Uncle Raymond still confused. "I don't need no white man to do it for me," she finally managed to get out. "That man act like he own my boys," Mama finished, her worry turning into anger and fury. Exhausted after having spent all the pent up emotion that had kept her going thus far, she slumped down in the nearest chair, and an endless stream of tears continued to fall, streaking her beautiful, saddened face.

"You girls go on in the house and tell Pearlie to bring Annie Bell some water," Uncle Raymond instructed us, which we did happily. As soon as we walked in, we placed ourselves in front of the warm fireplace. After that walk in what felt like sub-zero temperatures any heat would have felt good, even Aunt Pearlie's.

Mama was finally able to pull herself together enough for Uncle Raymond to understand what was going on. We heard her tell him what had happened, emphasizing that she'd held out hope that the boys would have come to him for help.

"I tell you what, Annie Bell," Uncle Raymond began, "we better try and find them boys, before Mr. Hunter does. These white people around here will kill you," Uncle Raymond informed her needlessly, glancing over at the old run down barn, where the mules and wagons were kept. After a few minutes of silence he said, "I'll hitch up the wagon and we can ride around and look for them."

After they'd gone, Auntie Pearlie put a blanket down in front of the fireplace so Ann and I could lie down. We were so tired after that freezing walk and everything that had happened between Mr. Hunter and my brothers. We didn't even try to argue with her. We were too glad to have a warm place to sleep, and sleep claimed us immediately.

Some time later, I'm not sure how much later, I was awakened by voices coming from outside. I aroused myself to be fully awake, realizing it was Mama and Uncle Raymond. And thank God Almighty my brothers were with them. Jim was cold and frightened; I could tell by the way his eyes were bulging out of his head. But this time they were also red from crying. As for James, his slanted eyes were almost invisible; he'd been crying too.

I can't begin to tell you how glad I was to see them safe. I hurriedly ran out to greet them. "Where have y'all been?" I asked, throwing myself toward them in my excitement.

"We found them over on Cooper Hill," Uncle said sadly. "Why they went back there, I don't know. The Cooper's offspring are still feuding over Riley's land."

"Did Mr. Hunter hurt y'all?" I asked anxiously. I could care less at this point what the Coopers were up too.

"Yes, he just got to hit me one time before I got away," Jimmy said as he pulled up his shirt, showing us the bruises on his back.

James, who up until this point had remained silent said, "We got tired of doing all that work for Mr. Hunter, while he was always sitting around drunk," he said, anger reeking from every word. It was then that he turned around so we could see the bruises inflicted on him by Mr. Hunter. "We didn't mean to let them cows out," he said adamantly. We were just tired," he finished. The need to explain to his family what had happened to cause such anger in Mr. Hunter toward them was uppermost in his mind.

Frightened by all that had taken place, Ann and I started crying. We wanted to know for certain that Mama would never take us back to live on Mr. Hunter's farm.

"You'll just stay here tonight, and in the morning, I'll go over and talk to Mr. Hunter. I'll see if we can work things out," Uncle Raymond told Mama, as she stood in one spot, unmoving.

"Okay, brother," she said finally. "Whatever you say."

Early the following morning my uncle went over to see Mr. Hunter, alone. When he returned, he had some of our things thrown in the back of his wagon. Apparently Mr. Hunter had decided that we were more trouble than we were worth. I overheard Uncle Raymond telling Mama that Mr. Hunter wanted us to move. It seems that he felt my brothers were responsible for the loss of hundreds of dollars. Therefore, he was washing his hands of us all.

Uncle Raymond went back later to gather the rest of our things. This time he took James and Jimmy with him. When they returned, they had our furniture, which they put in Uncle Raymond's barn to store until we had a place of our own.

"We don't even have a place to live," Mama cried pitifully then, as if the full impact of our reality had only just occurred to her, as she shook her head side to side mourning the loss of her home, such as it was.

"Ah, Annie Bell, y'all just stay here until you can get back on your feet," Uncle Raymond said, trying to console his distraught sister.

"Raymond, y'all don't have enough room for us. I have four children of my own, and y'all have two of your own," Mama pointed out. She was grateful for the offer, but she was reluctant to inconvenience them.

"Just go on in. We'll just have to make room for y'all," Uncle replied, unwilling to take no for an answer. And so we did. We slept on the floor, or wherever we could find a spot. Some nights I would wake to hear Mama sobbing

It would literally break my heart. And even though I no longer mentioned it to her. I couldn't help wondering why we just didn't return to Cooper Hill. As far as I was concerned, that would have solved all of our problems, at least that's what I believed. But then, I was only a child; what did I know?

Granpa Young at ***Joe Tuggle***'s place on "White Lightning Road"

3. Granpa Young

Early one morning Mama got up and without saying a word about where she was going, left the house. When she returned, she told us we would be moving in with Granpa Seaborn Young.

Granpa Young, as we affectionately called him, lived on the Joe Tuggle Place located off Louisiana Highway 146. This was also known as the "White Lightning Road." Anyone who has lived in Claiborne Parish since the 1950s and 60s knows why LA146 is called the White Lightning Road.

As to how the White Lightning Road got its name, a couple of generations ago brewing one's own liquor (making moonshine or "white lightening" or "corn liquor") was common. However, *making* moonshine wasn't illegal, but *selling* it was! Selling it was called "bootlegging." In the 1920s the convicts that were in jail for bootlegging were put to work cleaning and laying out the route of the White Lightning Road.

As for back as I can remember my grandpa Young talked about the White Lightning Road and the Tuggles and Ramseys who were bootleggers. They were always in a family feud that escalated around the bootleggers and their "tufters" or enforcers. Their feud really escalated when Joe Tuggle's Brother shot and killed William Ramsey in a desperate street duel in the downtown of Homer, Louisiana. Hamp Tuggle was shot in the hand and his brother Henry was shot in the shoulder. Sometime later John Ramsey emptied a load of buckshot into Joe Tuggle as he was getting on his horse to leave home. After that, the two families were constantly at odds with each other. It was the Homer version of the Hatfields and the McCoys.

As far as Granpa Young knew, the sheriffs didn't make an arrest in either incident. The Sheriff and everybody around that area were afraid of the Tuggles and Ramseys. Even the revenue men a few times a year would make a country break though that hill and woods trying to catch them, but they never did. "Those men" he said to me and several others "had look-out men loaded with 'wapers and ammo' that meant they were armed. We had a secret sound we made to alert them." The Tuggles and Ramseys would just as soon to kill you as look at you.

Granpa Young's job was to help make the white lightning and be a look-out man for any trouble.

Everyone that drank alcohol from far and near was acquainted with my Granpa Young. I guess you could say he was smart enough to have his own whiskey stills. Granpa had whiskey stills strung out all through them woods around the old place. I guess Granpa just raised enough hogs, chickens, corn, and greens to camouflage his true occupation.

Granpa was so adamant about not having children hanging around while he makes his whiskey that he made sure Mama sent us all to school every day. You see, he didn't want us kids hanging around messing up his business.

Granpa was stocky, with coarse, white hair that offset his smooth, jet-black skin. His eyes and teeth were so white they actually appeared to be artificial. His usual attire, for what reason no one ever knew, was a pair of overalls worn over a pair of pants. The house wasn't larger than the one we lived in on the Hunter's place, but nevertheless, we were grateful to Granpa Young for giving us a place to live. He always made sure we had plenty of food to eat, and for that alone we were eternally grateful.

Whenever his customers came to buy their whiskey, he'd go down in the woods, and then come out about fifteen minutes later. He'd look around to see if the law was anywhere in sight.

When he was certain that the coast was clear, he'd pull out his bottles of whiskey, hidden somewhere deep into his pants, and hand them over to his customer.

There were times when we were sure he wouldn't notice us that we would follow him and watch him pouring the whiskey into glass bottles. I still remember vividly the still that he used, sitting like a big tank up off the ground on a couple of blocks, leaving just enough room to have a fire under it. Granpa would let the whiskey sit awhile, allowing it to cook the fermented mash and all the other unknown ingredients. Then the alcohol would rise to the top, ready to pour into bottles and be sold.

When he was finally finished bottling the whiskey, he'd hide the bottles under the leaves in the woods so the revenue men wouldn't find them, if they ever had a mind to search for them. In all that time, he never once forgot where he'd hidden them.

Granpa seldom if ever used his wagon to go anywhere. Instead he chose to walk around, as you might have guessed, with his pockets full of moonshine. Jimmy and James always accompanied him on his excursions. Once, when Ann and I asked if we could come along, he just ordered us back to the house in that stern, no-nonsense voice of his, and we never asked again. I could only guess at his reasons. Perhaps he felt girls didn't need to be around the moonshine, so that we wouldn't be tempted later in life. If he'd known what I knew, he could have put that worry to rest.

One day, Jim decided to open a bottle of Granpa's moonshine and let the rest of us taste it. I remember my mouth feeling as if I'd just swallowed fire. That one taste erased any lingering doubt that I would one day want to repeat my mistake, believe me. As far as I was concerned, Granpa could have left a jar open around me twenty -four seven, and I wouldn't have been tempted to taste it.

That same day, we were playing in the woods near the whiskey still. Ann got her leg burned. But we never told anyone, not even Granpa or Mama, how it really happened:

While Mama and Granpa were gone to town to gather supplies, Mama always wanted to leave enough food cooked for us. But Jimmy killed a chicken, and told Granpa that a fox had done the deed. Finally he took the chicken, built a fire in the woods, and roasted the chicken over an open fire. After we'd all tasted the whiskey, Ann stood there with her hands in her pockets, moving around as she laughed and imitated Granpa. Her antics were so funny we rolled on the ground laughing.

The next thing we knew, one of the patches on her jeans caught fire. Immediately she broke into a run, screaming, "I'm on fire, I'm on fire!"

"Don't run, Ann!" we yelled trying to reach her. We tried to put out the flames with a pine tree branch, and when that failed, we threw her into a hole filled with water — not the smartest thing to do, I admit, but we were quickly running out of options.

When we got home with Ann, and pulled her jeans downs so we could examine the burned area, Jimmy's big eyes flew wide open. "Lords have mercy, girl. Why did you stand so close to that heater?" he asked, the harshness of his voice caused more by his fear for her safety than anger. "That's right, you got burned in that old heater," he kept repeating, as if he thought she hadn't heard him the other twenty times he'd said it. "Y'all know what's gonna' happen when Granpa finds out us was down there near that whiskey still, don't you?" he whispered as if afraid the walls had ears.

"We sure do," we all answered in unison.

"So, we better tell Granpa just that! Annie got burned on the heater," he kept repeating, again and again. Surely, he would have, though. We understood him by them.

I for one knew how that ol' whisk standing in the corner felt when applied. I still hadn't forgotten the day I'd been introduced to its stinging power a week earlier. I had been playing in the loft of the barn when Granpa called out for me. Instead of answering, which would have been the correct choice of action, I said not a word as he continued calling out to me, "Bertha…"

During a temporary moment of insanity, I still can't explain, I decide to peek out of the loft and yell, "Hi, Seaborne."

To his credit, he never missed a step, nor did he turn around to find me, he just kept walking as if he hadn't heard me. When he reached the porch, he pulled out his pocketknife and began carving a stick.

When I finally did find the courage to come out of hiding, I was certain he had forgotten — he was an old man, after all. As I approached him, he never looked up, he simply continued carving on his stick, as if he didn't know I was drawing nearer. Boy, was I wrong. No sooner had I closed the distance between us, when he grabbed my arm. That was it, then, there was absolutely no escape.

"What did you call me?" he asked in that no nonsense tone of voice that let you know what was about to happen. Believe me when I tell you, that man tore my behind up.

"Please, Granpa," I pleaded when I couldn't take anymore. "I won't say that no more," I wept pitifully, praying for mercy. To tell you the truth, I was actually surprised that he would whip me. I never dreamed he would ever do it, but once again, I was wrong.

One thing could be said about my grandfather, during the entire time we lived with him, we never knew a dull moment. Every Friday or Saturday night, he would have what was called a supper. Tables would be placed across the length of the kitchen door, blocking it off. He would sell fried chicken and fish dinners, but he'd also sell beer and whiskey, too.

Around the corner from my grandfather, lived a little old gray man everyone called Beanstalk. He would bring his guitar and play those down home blues, much better than that we hear today. Everyone would gather around, stomping their feet to the beat of the music, anxious to get out on the floor and dance. There were so many people that some of the couples were forced to dance outside on the front porch.

Later, as the night progressed, Beanstalk would sing, "Lardy, Lardy, Miss Claude, whys don't you bring your fine self home?" For every note he played, he would stomp his feet to the rhythm. When he played "Midnight Train,"everyone came to their feet, including Mama, who up until that time had been in the kitchen.

Ann and I were too young to be invited, but we would peek through a hole in the door. We knew sooner or later our brothers, Eddie, and Seaborne would show. John and Odell would arrive, and we always looked forward to seeing them.

Whenever the brothers were around, it never failed that the party would take on new dimensions, and really come alive.

Eddie would always pull Ann and me out of the shadows to dance with him, he always knew we were hiding there. He taught us how to do a dance called "Ballin' the Jack," which, for those of you who don't know, is a dance where you made two steps back, two forward and then jump to the center and "Ballin' the Jack," shaking your booty.

Eddie could always be counted on to be the life of the party, and women vied for his attention. It wasn't just because he was a good dancer that the women flocked to him, but more likely because he was tall and handsome. Wherever you saw him, he walked around with a key chain hanging out of his pocket and a bebop cap on his head.

Those Saturday nights at Granpa's were more than just entertainment for the neighbors, though they were quite entertaining, to say the least. But they were held for a more important reason: that of ensuring the family had extra money should hard times befall us. If you'll remember in the forties, especially in Louisiana, there were no clubs for coloreds, so everyone would take a Friday or Saturday night to have supper at their place and take on the responsibility of entertaining at different times of the month.

Three weeks before the Christmas holiday, Mama, along with the other ladies in her group, started baking in preparation for the holiday season. Mama kept her cakes in a big antique trunk, choosing to keep her pies stored in a pantry.

On Christmas Eve, Mama and Granpa would cut a slice out of one of the cakes, and tell us that Santa Claus had been there and had thoroughly enjoyed the dessert we'd so kindly left for him.

Granpa always made sure each of us had some great big peppermint sticks, with lots of oranges and apples. Mama would give Ann and me the dresses she'd made for us. It never failed, year after year we always got dresses, and a pair of shoes. As for toys, my sister and I received dolls and the boys would get BB guns. On the table that day was more food than I'd ever thought it was possible to eat in a lifetime. Ironically, there would come a time in the future, I would look back on those times and realize how fortunate I had been, and remember them as the good ole days.

As much as I loved Granpa Young, and even when I was happiest being there with him, no matter what new memories formed in my mind, I was never able to forget the early days spent at Cooper Hill. Somewhere in the back of my childish memories, Cooper Hill always remained the only safe haven I had ever known.

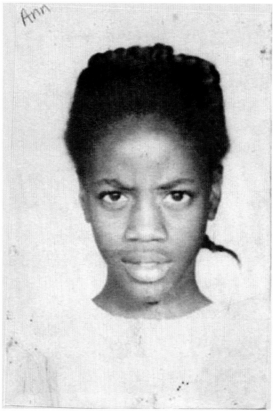

*My sister **Annie***

4. Separation of Sisters

MY SISTER AND I HAD A RELATIVELY HAPPY CHILDHOOD — THAT IS UNTIL WE WERE SEPARATED. After that, things for me were never the same again. For that, I lay the blame at my Auntie Callie's door. Aunt Callie was Mama's aunt who had come for a visit.

She suddenly appeared out of nowhere. Ann and I arrived home from school that day to find a well-dressed woman sitting across the table from Mama. There was something vaguely familiar about her. After a few minutes longer as I stared at her, trying to decide what it was about her, it suddenly dawned on me: she looked just like Mama. It was her smile, I suppose. They were so much alike, the only difference being the quality of clothes they wore.

Aunt Callie was dressed in the most stylish fashion. I had seen clothes like those only in fashion magazines, and then they were only worn by white folk. Aunt Callie's hair was parted down the middle in a pageboy style. There wasn't a hair out of place, the color was as black as the darkest night. Her skin was smooth and the color of mahogany. When she smiled at us, I noticed how white her teeth were, pearly white, I guess is the best way to describe them.

"Girls, this is my Aunt Callie," Mama told us. "She lives in Junction City."

Ann, always able to make friends easily, ran to Aunt Callie and gave her a big hug. Not me though. I went over and stood near my mother. I never did take to strangers well. Ann bounced around, blending right in, full of confidence, looking Aunt Callie directly in the eye. Turning away from her never crossed Ann's mind, not for even a second.

I'd always been on the shy side, talking only to people I felt comfortable around. As far as I was concerned, I was just a homely girl with nappy black hair, skinny as a beanpole. Believe me. I had no grandiose illusions about my lack of beauty in comparison to Ann's flawless beauty.

Now, one thing I can say about my Mama, she definitely knew her way around the kitchen. The aroma from the simmering pots made your mouth water. She was cooking greens, hot water corn bread, fried chicken, and rice and gravy.

After dinner Aunt Callie asked Mama if she would allow Ann to come live with her. How she actually convinced Mama to let Ann go home with her, I will never know. Only the pain that I felt at the idea of being separated from the only friend I'd ever truly had occupied my every thought and emotion. One thing I did recall clearly was hanging under my mother's dress tail, but she acted as if I wasn't there. The pain and rejection I felt at Aunt Callie's slight meant no more to her than a convenience, one that wasn't worth considering. Desperately clinging to my mother, desperately praying that she wouldn't send away the only friend I'd ever had, the one person whom I knew truly loved me. I felt abandoned.

After Aunt Callie left, taking Annie with her, I went into the woods and hid there until nightfall. I was upset, but certainly not stupid, and the woods were definitely not a place I wanted to be after sundown, even if my feelings were hurt.

Never one to be outgoing, but mostly introverted, I'd always relied on Ann to be a buffer between me and anyone I didn't feel quite comfortable with. Whenever I was around strangers, I always said very little. Ann was my voice.

My insecurities only worsened after Ann left. So overcome with grief, I became depressed. I literally could not function on any level. I missed Ann so much. My memories of her followed me into the classroom, and whenever Mrs. Smith, our teacher, called on me, I couldn't say a word. "What's wrong, Bertha?" she would ask. "Cats got your tongue?" And I guess she was right.

Even when asked simple math questions, I was incapable of answering. I knew that two plus two equaled four, but my mouth refused to convey that message. I was too afraid of answering any question she asked, mostly because I was certain that if I did, I would pee on myself. I was just that shy. It's ironic that I'd been shy all of my life, but not until Ann was gone did I come to realize it. The depth of my shyness was so intense, I was terrified I would suffer a panic attack if I so much as uttered a word to strangers.

My brothers James and Jimmy weren't much help either. Some nights they would actually sit around in the corner of the room, near the oil lamp and call out, "Hey, Bertha," then they would show me the silhouettes they had made on the wall in front of the light with their hands. They would have me looking as if I had long ears, big lips, and hair that stood on my head like buckwheat. How's that for promoting self-esteem? They would merely burst out laughing at their jokes, never realizing the pain and anguish they caused me. Both Ann and my sister Ella had long wavy hair, perhaps to my brothers they represented what beauty should entail.

I was told once that I'd inherited hair from my father's mother. She had short, stubby hair, and maybe I did. I remember Mama pressing my hair, and an hour later, it looked as if it had never been combed, let alone pressed.

One morning, after Ann had been gone awhile, I woke to hear a puppy barking. Granpa was trying to make him go away. I ran to the window to see a beautiful, brown, German Shepherd puppy standing on its hind legs, wagging its tail. I knew right away I wanted to keep it. More to the point, I needed him in my life.

"Granpa, Granpa, could I please have the puppy?" I begged relentlessly.

"No, that dog ain't going to be nothing but trouble!" he declared.

Before he could utter another word, I was on my way outside. Mama stopped me, before I made it out the door.

"Where do you think you're going, young lady?" she asked. "Running like a bat out of hell," she continued in a no nonsense tone of voice. "You just get back here and wash your face and hands," she demanded. I reluctantly walked over to the washbasin and threw a few drops of water on each eye, then dashed out the door.

"Granpa, where is the puppy?" I asked as soon as I spotted my grandpa.

"I ran that mutt off, and don't you go bringing him back. He ain't gonna be nuthin' but trouble no way."

"But, Granpa, please, he won't be no trouble," I swore, as my eyes filled with tears, though I had no idea how I would go about keeping my words.

"He down yonder in them woods," Granpa finally said, his fingers pointing to where the dog romped and played a little farther from where we were standing. "If you bring him back, you'll be the one to feed and take care of him, you hear me?" he shouted to my back, I'd already stopped listening as I sought out to find my new friend.

I ran into the woods, "here doggie, here doggie," I called after him, but I suppose he didn't hear me, or maybe he didn't want to be bothered. After giving up on ever finding him, he popped up out of some weeds, wagging his tail as if he'd just made some great discovery.

When I got home, I gave him a bath and fed him. I thought about a name for him. Right off the bat, the name "Trouble" came up. *That'll be his name,* I thought. *Trouble.*

Trouble and I came to be good friends. I made believed he was Ann. We went everywhere together. We often played under the house, in my playhouse. Trouble never had to worry about being fed, I gave him most of my food. He was, after all, my best friend.

About a year later, James and Jimmy asked me to walk with them down by Granpa's whiskey still. Trouble and I strolled on ahead of them, not really paying attention to just how deep into the woods we had gone. When I looked back to find them running back toward the same direction we'd just come, I began yelling after them. I didn't understand what had happened. *What had happened to frighten them so,* I wondered.

"Wait for me," I yelled when it seemed as if they'd forgotten about me. They never stopped. They turned in unison to look at us, but they kept running, and laughing. Laughing?

That's when I finally realized what they'd done. It had never been their intention that Trouble and I should walk with them. They wanted to get us lost in the woods, knowing that I would be terrified in the dark.

Trouble and I wandered around the woods until almost dark. I was terrified by the least little sound. Every step I took, seemed as if something was snapping at my heels. The woods were thick, brimming over with all forms of trees that only seemed to make the darkness even darker. The heat was smoldering, my clothes wet with sweat, my hair rising high on my head, the sweat sinking to the roots, making it even thicker.

As darkness crept around us, the sounds of wild animals came alive. Hoot owls hooting, foxes hollering and frogs, croaking seemed to intensify the darkness surrounding me. Trouble came over to me and licked my face. I can't really say how long I'd been sitting there crying before Trouble joined me there, but I guess he must have sensed my fear, and wanted to reassure me, he knew his way home.

I let Trouble lead the way. When we finally wondered out of the woods, I could barely see anything ahead of us. The stickers from the vines and branches had brutally torn my dress, held literally together by mere thread. In the distance a light was shining, reflecting in a window ahead. I could hear Granpa's and Mama's voices calling out my name.

Trouble and I ran as fast as we could toward the sound of those welcoming voices. I made certain that Mama and Granpa knew James and Jimmy's roles in our nightmare, which earned them both a whipping, but I'm sure it did nothing to enlighten them to the horrifying experience I'd just had in the woods.

Beene Plantaton

5. Beene's Plantation

Mama was happier than I had ever seen her, for awhile. For some strange reason, she'd begun humming, cleaning, and smiling all the time.

It was about that time that a little short man knocked on the door. I assumed he was there to see my grandpa, but I was wrong. Instead of asking for Granpa Young, the man asked to see Mama. She stopped what she was doing at the time and dashed to the door to greet the man I would soon come to know as "John."

"John, how are you doing?" she asked, her voice somewhat hushed as she shook his hand.

"Just a little tired from that long walk," he answered her with a grin.

"Bertha, come out here. I want you to meet someone," she ordered as the big, short man extended his ashy hand out to me.

"My name is John Edward," he said with a twinkle in his eye.

"Pleased to meet you, sir. My name is Bertha," I informed him, as if he didn't already know.

I had looked him over by then. It wasn't so much that I didn't like him. I didn't know him well enough to say that. I guess I just didn't like his thick lips that looked as if they were about to fall off his face. Then again, it could have been that I resented this strange man calling on my mother. In all my eleven years, I could recall my mama keeping company with no man, other than my father, of course. Mr. John was the first.

He best get on somewhere, I thought to myself as I stood there looking at him, just short of out-and-out rebellion in my eyes. I looked then at Mama and realized that I would be the one who would have to change. I'd have to start looking at him as Mama's new husband cause that was what he turned out to be.

I can't say when their courtship began. I don't even remember Mama mentioning him to any of us, as if she would need to. Sometimes, as you can see, I had a little trouble remembering that she was the grownup, not me.

About a week later, Mama and Mr. John were married, and Mr. John took us to meet his eight children. I learned then that Mr. John had been married before and his wife had died; that's where the eight children came from. They were older than I was. The older children cared for the youngest of them. They were all well-mannered, and I really did enjoy meeting them.

It was nice to have them around of course, but I still missed Annie. The only time I got to see her these days was during the summer months when she would visit, or I'd be allowed to visit her.

Three months after Mama and Mr. John married, he came home, riding in a truck with a strange man, and informed us that he had found a place for us to live in Bossier City, Louisiana. Granpa and I were shocked. I had no idea moving was an option, and here he was telling us he'd found a place. I wasn't quite sure how Mama felt, I guess she was surprised too. None of our things had been packed. She must have thought it was the right thing to do cause the next thing I knew she was putting our stuff together with Mr. John's, what few we had.

Granpa didn't say much of anything. He just went along on his daily stroll, I suppose to keep from being there when we left.

Mama and Mr. John finished loading our stuff and just as we were about to leave, I was informed that there was no room for Trouble, we'd have to come for him later. That news was almost as bad as the news that Annie was leaving. I didn't want to leave my Trouble.

I begged Mama to let me stay with Granpa until they come back for Trouble, but she informed me that that was totally out of the question. She wouldn't even consider leaving me behind.

James, Jimmy, and Mr. John sat on the back of the truck, while Mama and I sat in the front with the driver. I could see Trouble running alongside the truck, barking and whining his heart out. He didn't understand why we were leaving him behind, either. As the truck picked up speed and he could no longer keep up, I hung my head out the window and watched until he was out of sight. Deep in my heart, I felt I would never see my dog again.

The Beene's Plantation was almost like a city on its own. For miles ahead one could see the white fleeces hovering above the sandy covered grounds, as silvery clouds hung insidiously melding with the green of grass and ferns. Undoubtedly, this was one of the cotton capitals of Louisiana.

The plantation grounds were like a city within the plantation proper. It had a cotton gin, dairy, pecan trees, machine shops, cars, tractors, and trucks. A big general store supplied the sharecroppers with various necessities, and anything in between.

Little white houses lined in neat little rows, each of them equipped with two or more bedrooms, and all had electrical wiring. I suppose plumbing would have been too much to ask for: we still had to use an outhouse, and a tub for washing.

However, the fact that there was running water near the front porch alone offered more luxury than that we'd had at the Hunter's place.

Over a hundred families lived and worked on the Beene's Plantation. I had never seen so many colored people and white people all in one place before in my life. The white people lived on one side of the railroad tracks, and the coloreds lived on the other.

The Beene family lived in a large, white, Victorian house on the lower end of the plantation. Mr. Beene was a tall man with salt and pepper hair, with a ruddy complexion. He wasn't much of a talker, not to us, anyway. He wore fancy western clothing, cowboy boots and hat, and sported a fancy white Ford sedan. It's only fair for me to add here that Mr. Beene was a handsome man, for truly he was. Although he didn't have direct contact with us on a daily basis, we were fortunate enough to glimpse him now and again. He left no contact between the colored folks and his folk. He left us to answer to a white overseer.

Colored people served the Beene family in numerous ways. Some of them were delegated to work around the Beene's house as housekeepers, chauffeurs, and groundskeepers, while the others, the lesser of the bunch, were left to do the work needed on the plantation. As a rule, it seemed that those who worked within the house and grounds were treated better than those who worked in the scalding, heat of the plantation.

Before we settled in, one of the old-timers, Joe, came over to welcome us. Naturally, he informed us of the rules and regulations those of us living within the plantation's arms were subject to.

Joe walked with a limp that made him appear to be somewhat shorter than he actually was. Whenever he'd open his mouth to speak, his teeth were covered with the grotesque stains of snuff. His white hair shown from under his old steward's crumbled hat that he constantly wore, and his jet-black skin appeared rough, like old, cracked leather that had spent a lifetime working in the sun.

Joe had nine children, and they were all born and raised there on the plantation. "Ole Mr. Beene, a good white man," he informed us. "Mr. Beene give us a free place to live, and we can get anything we want at the store on credit. Don't worry about bein' in trouble. Mr. Beene keep his colored from being incarcerated. Naw, don't go killin' no white man, though, that's another story," he added with a snuff stained grin. Your ass gon' probably be hang then," he explained.

"See dese three cut off fingers on dis' hand?" he asked raising the injured hand to the light. "I didn' get no money, but Mr. Beene gonna make sho' I have a place to live fur the rest of my life," he hailed proudly, as if Mr. Beene represented the Second Coming. I listened as he went on to say, "On Saturday, us ride dee truck into Shreveport, which is right down over the bridge, and us stay all day. They got juke joints and stores under de bridge, where us coloreds get drunk and dance all day, til time to come home. Coloreds from everywhere come down under there."

"Oh yeah," he said, taking a quick breath between words, "dey have a school for colored right across the tracks in the Ole Church. Now, Mr. Beene only lets dee girls go to school all day. De boys have to work all day since this is cotton pikin' time. Now de girls come to work after school."

The expression Mama wore as she heard those words spoke volumes of how she felt about Mr. Beene's educational values. "You mean, my boys can't attend school, now!?" she shouted.

"Naw, yore boy can attend schools all day in de winter time," he explained, clearly not seeing a problem with the way Mr. Beene ran his business.

"I am sendin' my boy to school, tomorrow," Mama said adamantly, angrier than I could ever remember seeing her before.

"Annie Bell, you heard what that man say," Mr. John replied.

Mama must have been paralyzed by the anger infusing her body at that moment; she looked as if she'd been transformed into an uncontrollable force. Nothing Mr. John said to her seemed to make a difference, she was determined to see her boys go to school. Mama knew in her heart that Mr. John was powerless to say or do anything against Mr. Beene's decision to keep James and Jim out of school, but that didn't calm her down, not one bit.

This was the fifties, and even though blacks were no longer called slaves, their status hadn't been elevated much above slavery. Although they were free to move from place to place, they were, for all intents and purposes, still in bondage. This made it virtually impossible for some coloreds to benefit from the existing power structures, especially if they were poor and uneducated. Plantation owners provided them with free housing, but very little money, and even less education, if they were unfortunate enough to be born male.

The school was located in a little church that was smaller than Rising Star, the church/school we'd attended previously. Other than its size, there was little difference. They both held to the same basic rules, whites didn't mingle with the coloreds.

Our teacher, Mrs. Brown, met us at the door. She said, "Y'all must be the Cooper children? Mr. Beene don't let boys go to school until winter," she replied, as if we hadn't heard that before. Pulling her long black, silky hair away from her olive-toned face, she stepped back, her hand outward. "You can sit right here, next to Emma and Sue Mae," she instructed.

Sue Mae held her head down, and didn't look up until I was seated next to her. Finally, she looked at me, rolling the large whites of her eyes and turning her nose up at me, as if she were socially above me. The irony was lost on me. I couldn't understand why she wanted to be so uppity, it wasn't like she had a whole lot more than I did. She was obviously considered just as black, cause here she was, right along with the rest of us colored kids.

Not to be mean, or anything, but Sue Mae wore the ugliest ole cotton stocking and high-top shoes I'd ever seen. She was a thin, homely girl of eleven, with dark brown skin and thick, hard hair. (Some of you may have a little trouble going there, but I understand.)

Emma, the other girl, was dark-skinned with bright eyes. She wore her hair pulled back in a ponytail, and just looked at me and smiled. I found my way to my seat and sat down next to them. Emma wore a fresh starched and ironed dress, with a pair of penny loafers and white socks. She lived two doors down from us with her mother, father, and older sister. I had waved at her from a distance, but had never really met her. They had moved in a few weeks after we moved in. Her father moved on the plantation from a small town outside of Bossier. Emma and I had more in common than Sue Mae and me.

Sue Mae lived down the end of the road from our house. We all began walking to school together, after awhile, I guess you can say we all got to be buddies. But Sue Mae and I didn't have much to do with each other because of her being naïve and so attached to the plantation.

After school, we were all sent straight to the cotton fields. It was not, however, one of mine and Mama's favorite things to do. We'd never had to work in the cotton fields before Mr. John, and so far, there wasn't much to commend the process favorably, for either of us.

Of course, Jimmy and James hadn't picked cotton before either, and they didn't like it any better than we did. I often heard them talking about leaving to go to Texas, they'd had their fill of working on white folk's farms. Mama was afraid they would manage to land themselves in trouble with the overseer, who always sat in the middle of the field on a horse, watching to make sure the field workers kept their backs bent. (Wouldn't want any of them too straight up, might upset the massah).

After their earlier encounter with Mr. Hunter, Jim and James had often said they would rather die before letting another white man hit them, and Mama was afraid they just might. It was no secret to anyone that they both had bad blood with white folks.

My older brother Odell, Seaborne, Eddie, and my sister Ella had long since moved to Texas. They all had jobs working in factories. As far as Mr. John was concerned, it seemed he knew his way around in a cotton field, sometimes picking rows at a time with glee, sweating and puffing, trying to beat the heat.

One evening Mama stopped picking cotton for a few seconds and looked across the field with dismay written in all the weathered lines of her face. "Bertha!" she said frantically, "I want you to get your education. I don't want you having to work in these cotton fields all your life," she stressed with every fiber of her being, wiping the sweat from her beautiful, black face.

Needless to say, she could have put that thought to rest. Before anyone else, I had no aspirations or desire to make picking cotton a lifetime career, so she could certainly allow her mind to have peace on that one subject. As soon as I came of age, I planned to take the next thing smoking out of there.

When I told Sue Mae my plans to leave the plantation, she looked at me with humor, sniggered and said, "Where do you think you going?"

Her attitude infuriated me, it wasn't as if this was the last place on earth for any of us to be. "Girl, I could go back and live with my Granpa Young, or back to Cooper Hill," I shouted adamantly. "Don't no white folk live on Cooper Hill. My Granpa Riley owned Cooper Hill," I explained to her, with no avail.

"Girl, don't no colored people own no land," she swore, the authority on the subject I assume.

"They do too! Plus, I got a white friend named Sherry," I boasted, really stepping out there then.

"Girl, don't tell me no more. You just done totally loss yore mine," she snapped back with indignation, abruptly bringing an end to the matter. Good thing too, I was quickly running out of boasts that even sounded true. The next one would have surely sounded like something out of a fairy tale.

There was very little to do on the plantation in the way of recreation. We didn't have no televisions, but sometimes we gathered around the radio and listened to music while we ate popped field corn. Of course, the best you could hope for was country and western music. Some evenings Sue Mae, Emma, and me played in the hay barn at the end of the road, often fantasizing about what we were going to do when we grew up.

"Well, girl, I am gonna marry me a man and stay right here on the plantation," Sue Mae announced one day.

"Not me, girl," I popped in, "I'm gonna marry me a city man, and we going to live in a big white house, jus like the one the Beenes live in," I assured her.

"Me too, girl," Emma added.

"You must be gonna marry a white man?" Sue Mae asked gleefully.

"Girl, there's a lots of colored men in town we can marry," Emma shouted, clearly becoming frustrated with the effort of convincing Sue Mae that there was more to life than Beene's Plantation.

"Sure is, girl," I swore, as if I was the authority.

"Well, how do y'all expect to get all that then?" she asked, her mind finally trying to grasp the possibility.

"Me and my husband both gonna be college graduates," I told her. "Besides, Mama always told me to keep dreaming and one day it would happen."

"Girl, you need to get your mind off staying on this plantation," Emma and I tried to tell Sue. However, Sue continued talking as if she hadn't heard a thing we said.

Mrs. Louise, Sue Mae's mama, was a weird critter. She wore a red rag on her head, her cold beady eyes going around in her head as she moved her short little body around half stooped. The hunch in her back reminded me of the Hunchback Of Notre Dame. Her mere presence gave me the creeps. Most of the people on the plantation believed she could cast spells on you. She had voodoo bags and dolls hanging in her house.

Her house had a funny smell that emanated from the many different colored candles she kept burning. Sometimes she would sit around the old fireplace at night and tell Emma, Sue Mae, and me tall tales about the people who had gotten killed in the swamps during the earlier years, when her mother lived on the plantation.

"Don't ever try to run away," Mama used to warn me. "Them night riders will kill you!"

At night you could hear some of them run away spirits that died at the hands of the nightriders screaming out pleading for their lives.

Mrs. Louise went on to say that her mother also told her that spirits walked the plantations on rainy nights. Sometimes she could see them outside the house, walking around without heads.

I'm not saying she was telling the truth, but if I had all those images running around in my head, I'd probably be a little weird, too.

One night the wind was blowing so loud, Mrs. Louise said, "Listen to 'em spirits, hollering! They still live," she whispered as she looked through her beady little eyes.

All of the children on the plantation was afraid of Mrs. Louise. One night some kids stood outside her house yelling, "You leave from here, you creepy old lady," they shouted, throwing rocks at her house.

Mrs. Louise ran out the house and shook her black doll at them, yelling, "If y'all don't get away from here, my friends from the swamps gonna get you!" With scary looks on their faces, they took off running down the road.

After a visit to Sue Mae's house, I never got a full night of sleep again. I stayed under the cover with my head covered up and I believe Emma did pretty much the same thing. Of course, it wasn't something we discussed.

Mama didn't make many friends with the women on the plantation. Other than working for the Hunters, Mama hadn't worked and lived under these conditions before. I always assumed it would probably be fair to say she was somewhat uppity, though I'm sure she didn't mean to be. Most of the other women, other than Emma's mama, hadn't had a life beyond the plantation. Mama was trying to reconstruct her life, as we did as children after leaving Cooper Hill.

James, Jim, and Mr. John took up a weekly habit of going over the tracks on Saturday nights. Ms. Hattie who lived over there sold beer and whiskey. Mr. John, my stepfather, would come home late some nights staggering after he had gone there.

Mama would ask, "John, what all them men doing over at that house?"

"Ah, Bell, we just be over there drinking and having a little fun," he answered.

"Well, I don't want my husband going over there. That woman Hattie don't even speak to me," she said with barely concealed anger in her voice.

"Do you speak to her?" he asked. "People say you and that girl of yourn, think y'all more than them. Y'all need to cut that shit out," he demanded, certainly not thinking clearly any longer.

Undoubtedly, Mama seen she wasn't gonna change him much, so she just left it alone.

The plantation workers had to rise early to catch the trucks for a ride to the cotton fields. They would arrive at the fields before sunup, and stay late in the evenings. The women prepared breakfast along with lunch for the day, and the workers usually took a break at noon and sat around under the trees to eat their meals. Other than lunch, the men got a very short break in between, and the rest of the time was spent working. They didn't even get to break for a sip of water. There was a young colored boy named Jack who ran over the fields with a bucket of water to quench their thirst.

Picking cotton was hard work, and the hot sun didn't make it any easier. Although most of the workers wore straw hats to shield them from the sun, it still didn't help much. The cotton rows were over a quarter mile long, and it was so high you could barely see the top of some of the people ahead of you.

One day, Sue Mae, Emma and myself dragged our sacks almost to the end of the row. Thinking we deserved a little rest from our labors, we sat down, but instead of just resting, we fell asleep. We were so hot and tired that we forgot where we were, and the overseer found us.

"Get up from there and get back to work," his voice cracked as loud as a whip. "You lazy niggas will try anything to get out of workin" he shouted.

Our bodies drenched with sweat from the heat, we stood there with the cotton sacks hanging about six feet long, with straps the hung over our shoulder, the stickers on the cotton bulbs making our fingers sore and our backs breaking.

To help endure the hard labor, some of the older folks would begin singing the old Negro spirituals, harmonizing the words, "Come by here, my Lordy, come by here…" Or, when even that was too much, they would sing, "Precious Lord take my hand…." When the Holy Spirit would come over them, and this is the truth, they would stop working, and begin clapping their hands and shouting, right there in the middle of the fields.

"You niggas cut out that hollering, and get back to work," the overseer's cruel voice would soon erupt around them. The old folks paid him no attention, right away and just kept on shouting. Stunned beyond belief, he just sat there and looked at them for a few minutes longer and moved on.

Some of the men pulled two sacks and picked two rows at a time, trying to earn enough money. After the sacks were filled with cotton, it had to be taken to a truck in the middle of the field to be weighed. We were paid to pick cotton by the pound. The pay was very little, considering the amount of labor required to make a pound, not even enough for "luxuries" such as food and clothing. Every year the plantation worker found out they were deeper in debt at the end of the year than they were at the beginning, regardless of how much extra work they'd done. The cost of food, clothing and supplies were taken out of the workers salaries, long before they ever saw them. They were never given a receipt for the items bought. They had to pay Mr. Beene whatever they were told they owed.

One night I overheard Mr. John, James, and Jim telling Mama when they went to ask for the money they'd earned, they were told they owed it all for the food and clothes we had gotten from the Beene's store.

"John, we only got a few things, a little salt meat, flour and beans from that store. There's got to be a mistake with all of us working. How much did we get paid for all that cotton we picked?" Mama shouted, fury in her every word.

"Mama, me and James are leaving this place," Jim informed her. "When we get to town this Saturday, we are not coming back. We are going to Texas and find work."

"Jim, I don't really want you boys to leave, but I don't want y'all wasting your lives working on this plantation for nothing," she said with tears of regret in her eyes as she gazed upon her sons with love.

"I tell you what. If this situation don't get no better, me and Annie Bell will be moving too," Mr. John said adamantly.

Mr. Beene had all of his bases covered. Keeping the workers' money was just one of many. The trick of the game was, they never let them get out of debt. Some of the workers' were so deep in debt, they risked their lives trying to run away, without paying. Whenever that happened, the poor souls who didn't get away got the beating of their lives.

"Get Up!"

6. Race Relations

When the truck arrived to pick up Sue Mae, Emma, and me on Saturday, there was standing room only. I was so excited, I didn't really want to sit down. I liked watching the beautiful scenery as we sped along. Most of the streets that ran along the highway were lined with tall oak trees that led up to big beautiful, white Victorian homes. Those beautiful homes had magnificent polished lawns, and within a few feet of them, I could see the duck ponds, with white ducks riding the blue waves, as free as you please.

The fresh breeze blowing, caressing my face with its chilling fingers, as we topped the Texas Street Bridge, thrilled me through and through. The Bridge somehow reminded me of Cooper Hill as we ascended it on our journey to the other side. The only difference I could see then was that there weren't any wagons lined along the Texas Street Bridge.

A few weeks earlier, Granpa Young had been rushed to the hospital with eighty percent of his body burned after one of his stills had exploded and hot whiskey had blown all over him. When I was allowed to visit him at the hospital, I couldn't hold back the tears. Seeing him lying there, helpless, white gauze wrapped around his painfully scarred body, nearly broke my heart.

My once strong grandfather never said a word the whole time I was there visiting him. He simply slept the whole time. A week later, he died. We only got to visit him a few times after we moved to Mr. Beene's plantation, and when we did, my dog Trouble was no place to be found. Granpa said that Trouble had wandered off one day, and never came back.

When we pulled into the parking lots under the Texas Street Bridge in downtown Shreveport, colored folks were standing everywhere. Someone yelled out of the group, "That's the Beene's plantation pulling in now."

Boy, truck loads of women, men, and children from all the surrounding plantations got off the truck beneath the Texas Street Bridge. This was an all-day event on Saturdays. They would not return home until dark.

Shreveport, though not the largest city in Louisiana, was a large city with many tall buildings. It was the largest that many of us had ever, and probably would ever, see. As we walked through the streets, looking up and down, I almost tripped over my feet. People were standing all on the sidewalks, eating and drinking. The sound of music came out of the brick buildings that stood in rows along the length of the street. Those were the juke joints, the ole timers told us. They were so closely built that people could dangle out one door into the next.

The juke joints had swing doors that put you in mind of the ones seen in western movies. Whites, of course, owned these juke joints. The colored people who lived in the city came under the bridge on Saturday to shop and party.

We went inside a big store that had everything, from clothing, groceries, and washtubs, to rub boards, baby chickens, and feed for cows and hogs. Folks stood in line to get what they needed to buy. After standing in line for awhile, I finally made my way up front. A big white man behind the counter reminded me of Mr. Hunter by calling all the women "Auntie" and the men "Uncle." He asked me in a loud, booming voice, "What do you need, gal?"

"My name is Bertha, and I want some cookies and a root beer," I replied nervously.

He hurriedly gave me what I asked for, and threw my change back to me. His face was red as fire, and it was one of the angriest faces I had ever seen. I was puzzled by the magnitude of his anger. I'd only told him my name. I remember leaving there with the strangest feeling that day.

Of course that wasn't the only thing that confused me that day. There were also signs along the walkway, and over the dime store, the diner, and water fountains, practically everywhere, and they all said "**colored only**" or "**white only**."

When we went inside one of the stores, the white sales people hung around us as if they thought we wanted to steal something. When we tried to buy blouses and skirts, we were told colored folks couldn't try clothing on before buying them, but the whites could. Of course they didn't say why. Maybe they thought our color would rub off on their clothes and get them permanently dirty, I don't know. What I do know is, it was a stupid and painful lesson that I learned that day.

For the first time in my life I understood this thing my mother could never talk to us about. It was race. I finally understood why Sherry's grandmother, Mrs. Hunter, was so angry at Annie and me. It was simply because of our race, that simple. But, for a child, that was complicated. Simply put, they were white and we were colored. I understood that fact, but the question still lingered, why? We were all children, the only difference was our skin color.

Prejudice is a sick, saddening emotion. Through the years whites and blacks alike have taught their children hatred. Back then, it was mostly whites who taught their children we were less than nothing beneath their feet. Most white children weren't taught anything positive about coloreds, nothing about our traditions or our culture. Most whites didn't own a book with colored people or pictures of us around their homes. Back then and today very few black families are invited to a white family's table for dinner. Sadly, even today very little has changed about prejudice, the basic fact is that until it does race relations will not heal.

That same evening, as we were approaching the spot where the trucks were parked, I heard a colored woman shouting out, "Please, don't hit me." When I got in view of her. I could tell from the way she was staggering to and fro that she'd been drinking too much alcohol. The bag she was carrying had items falling out of it.

A big, white man with a gun on his side, and holding a black nightstick in his hand pushed her hard. He as saying, "Nigger, gal, don't you talk back to me. I'll knock your damn brains out." Her items went one way and she tripped, falling to the sidewalk.

The big angry, white man slammed his foot down on her neck. Holding her down until a police car arrived and another white man got out. They snatched her up and pushed her into the car. I stood there, petrified, I couldn't move. Someone in the crowd said simply, "they're policemen," as if that explained everything, but it didn't.

As I stood there, my mind flashed back to the man in the store, then to Mr. Hunter, the colored signs, and the swamp runaways, pleading for their lives and I felt as if I were seven again. I was there, overhearing my brothers and my uncle saying white people would kill us. This day, at age eleven, it devastated me, and all that I'd held true. Although what that was, I still don't know.

I didn't understand any of it. Was this the way it was supposed to be? Was it okay for me to feel resentment for white folks? Something was fundamentally wrong with a "yes" answer, and even then I knew it. It simply didn't make sense that all the colored people that day were standing around as if nothing wrong was going on. Seeing that poor woman get beaten by two white men, regardless of who they were. Was this what humans did to each other? Why didn't these conditions stir any of the colored folk standing around that day? Was I the only one who felt her pain and fear? Later I realized that it wasn't so much that they didn't see anything wrong, it was simply that they'd known no other way of life.

I got very little sleep that night. Every time that I closed my eyes, I saw that poor battered woman, lying on the sidewalk, helpless and beaten. It made me realize something that night: I didn't want no white people to have power over me for the rest of my life. It wasn't just white folks. I knew I didn't want *nobody* to have power over me, nobody but *me!*

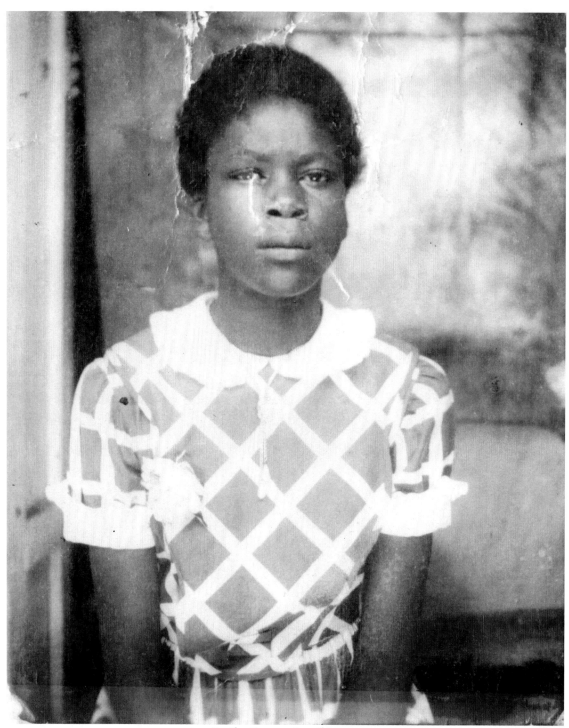

Bertha Cooper *at age thirteens*

7. Early Teens

I WAS THIRTEEN YEARS OLD WHEN I TRANSFERRED TO BUTLER ELEMENTARY SCHOOL IN BOSSIER CITY. Although it probably doesn't seem like a big deal to any of you, to me it was. You see, Butler was a real school, built of red bricks. Over the years it was kept well manicured, with beautiful flowers and green plants. Each teacher had his or her own classroom, and when we ate lunch, we did it in a real lunchroom, set up for just that: lunch.

Mrs. Lavera Smith, my teacher, truly loved children, and it showed. She inspired us to be the best at whatever we chose to do. Her smile and her manner let me know she truly cared, really cared, about me and what I wanted and what I was feeling. Somehow, she knew instinctively that I was shy. Whenever I was attempting to stammer through the next page of my reading assignment, she never once lost her patience. She would simply say, "Bertha, there is no hurry," and she'd flash that sympathetic smile of hers, and erase the fear of my feeling stupid.

Butler was where all the children who lived in Bossier City attended school. The children from the city dressed differently from those of us on the plantation. The girls wore gathered skirts with "*can-can*" slips under them, and pretty sweaters. They also wore oxford shoes and all-star tennis shoes.

Of course, I wore the dresses and blouses mama had brought me in different colors, all made from cotton. I thought, at first, they were pretty. Consequently, the city girls did not. They made fun of me and said I looked "country." Believe it or not, they made fun of my hair, and where I lived. Sometimes they would stand outside as we got on the bus, shouting out, "Go home to **Massah** Beene."

I'd be so humiliated by their remarks. I'd play sick for days, so I wouldn't have to go to school. Mama finally figured out that something was wrong with me, other than being sick, and it didn't take her long to find out what it was.

"Mama," I began, "the city kids poke fun at my hair, clothes, and where I live," I finally sobbed the whole story to her as she sat next to me on my bed.

"Always remember, baby, that you are a decent human being, no matter what they say about you," she said softly. The pain I felt was audible in the tone of her voice.

The next day Mama took me over to Ms. Alma's, a beautician on the plantation. We sat in the waiting section, and finally Ms. Alma beckoned for me.

"Bertha, have a seat over here. I'll just sit on this stool, look like this going to be a hard damn row to hoe," she said in a matter of fact tone.

When I heard those words, tears began streaming down my face. There were a lot of things about myself that I was very sensitive about, my hair was the number one thing.

In 1954, I enrolled in Mitchell High School. My goal was to get my education and become a teacher. The following year, I made the basketball team. Playing ball helped me to forget about my hair, and the type of clothes I wore. I still missed my brothers, but I knew they had a better life in Texas than they ever would have had at Mr. Beene's.

Soon, after we enrolled at Mitchell, Sue Mae, Emma, and I went our separate ways because we simply had different interests.

Lovers at tree swing

8. Charles

I WAS JUMPING AROUND IN THE END ZONE ONE NIGHT AT A SCHOOL GAME WHEN I NOTICED HIM. He was supposed to be trying to catch the football that was being thrown in his direction. Instead, of catching the football he ran straight into me, almost knocking me down in the process. Naturally, he held me within his strong arms, helping me to keep my balance, and his smile was a knockout. He smiled right at me! I stood there, dumb-founded. Watching him as he ran back on the football field, his smile was still on me.

That was our "Homecoming Game," and we were wearing C.H. High School out that night. I was wearing my blue and gold cheerleader outfit, and I knew I was looking good. How's that for self-confidence? I knew I was looking good, you see mostly because all the boys had already told me how pretty my legs were. By then I'd figured out it must be true.

It was that night after the game, as I stood on the outside of the gym waiting for my bus, when I saw that beautiful smile again. Lordy, something was happening, chemistry wise, you know. For the first time in my life I was actually feeling something for the opposite sex. Up until that moment, I had been too busy with school activities and studying for boys. To tell the truth, getting out of that cotton field meant far more to me than most anything else.

"Hi," he said in the most beautiful baritone I had ever heard, as if I'd heard a lot of them. "My name is Charles Brakefield. It sure was a tight game tonight, wasn't it?" he asked.

"Yes, it sure was," I replied, barely above a whisper.

"I'm glad we won," he bragged. "By the way, what is your name?"

"My name is Bertha Cooper," I answered shyly. This experience was way out of my league. I can't remember having a conversation, in life, with any male that wasn't related to me, which, I'm afraid, left me sadly lacking. By the time I got my name out, my bus pulled up and I thought I had blown it. As I got on, though, he yelled out, "You sure do have some pretty legs."

The ride home passed in heavenly oblivion. Thank God I wasn't driving; we wouldn't have made it. I sat there thinking about his smile and his beautiful white teeth. He must have been a new student. I was sure I would have remembered a smile like his. I assumed I knew all the boys on the football team.

The next day, as I walked down the old familiar hallways of my school, there he stood, as if I'd somehow created his presence by intense concentration. I didn't know if he'd noticed me or not, but I pretended that I hadn't noticed him. I went straight to my first period class, as if nothing out of the ordinary was taking place in my hormones.

When the bell rang, he was there again. It was strange that someone I had never seen before, I was seeing quite frequently today. When I saw him this time, he was standing at my classroom door. Walking past him as if I hadn't seen him was out of the question this time.

"Why don't you have lunch with me today?" he asked flashing that beautiful smile of his.

"Are you talking to me?" I asked, as if he were standing there talking to someone else.

"Yes, you!" he answered, this time with a wide grin.

"Okay," I said quickly. *Forget coy,* I thought as I walked to my next class with a pretty wide grin of my own.

Although my self-confidence had risen quite a bit by this time, I still couldn't believe he wanted to have lunch with me. There were plenty of pretty girls on campus. This was a fact and had absolutely nothing to do with self-confidence. I might not have thought I was the ugliest thing alive any longer, but I wasn't a fool either. These girls wore clothes, which were much prettier than mine, and their parents allowed them to drive their cars to school each day. Some of them were even light skinned, and had long, pretty hair. You might think this last thought, a bit strange. Ironically, most colored men just didn't date or marry women who were darker skin toned, unless they were professionals or their parents were well off, neither of which I could claim to. There were some who might have wanted to, but their parents would tell them right off. "Don't bring me no black-ass grandchildren around here." In some families, you were actually penalized for being darker complexioned. Isn't it ironic that not only was I disliked by whites because I was black, there was a stigma within my own race?

They even had a saying for their ignorance, "ain't nothing a black, nappy-head ass woman can do for me, but tell where I can find me a lighter-skin woman," some men would proudly say.

Even job status improved the lighter your skin tone was. Most of them had parents who worked on the railroads. My parents could barely feed and clothe me. The things they had, I felt I could only dream about.

When the bell rang to announce lunch period, I glanced nervously at the clock. It was eleven thirty, and there he was, standing at the door as I walked out. He was the perfect gentleman. He opened the door of the lunchroom for me, and the pulled out a seat for me to sit. I was impressed. When he smiled at me then, I noticed he had gold on two of his side teeth. I was even more impressed.

Charles, I found out, lived in the city with his mother and two sisters, one older and one younger, who was only about four months old. He was eighteen and a junior. His mother and father had been divorced for years. After talking to him, I learned that his plans were to attend college, just as mine were.

The more we talked, the more I liked him. I liked how his brown eyes lit up, and I loved his sense of humor. His black skin was as smooth as a baby's behind, and I thought he was gorgeous. He stood about five-foot seven, and wore his clothes well. The man wore sex appeal effortlessly. It wasn't an act with him .It was simply who he was.

After we'd sat looking across the table at each other, he finally asked, "Are you allowed to receive company?" I had to do some fast thinking then. How would I know? This was something Mama and I had never discussed. What the heck, I'll take a risk here, I thought to myself. "Yes, why?"

"I would like to take you to the movies sometime," he replied.

"I'll have to let you know," I told him honestly this time. I wasn't about to step out that far on the limb.

After we'd finished lunch and were on our way back to class, I finally actually had the nerve to accept his invitation to the movies. God only knows what I was thinking. I'd work it out, though — I'd have to. I told him I would meet him at the Star Theater that Saturday. I know it was shallow. I really didn't want him to know that I had to ride on the back of a truck into town. I did, however, inform him that I lived on a plantation. I suppose I did it mostly to see what his reaction to me would be then.

"I know where you live," he informed without missing a beat. "What that got to do with you going to the movies with me?" he asked as if it really didn't matter to him. I could have shouted 'Hallelujah' right then and there.

The movie was our first real date, and my first date. I'd had no earlier intention of dating any of the guys on the plantation, I was too afraid they'd want to keep on living there, and that was not an option for me.

After the movies, Charles and I went to the drugstore downtown and had ice cream. Needless to say, that was not our last date. In fact, he and I had gone out a few more times before I told Mama anything about the nice boy I had met at school that I wanted her to meet.

My announcement seemed to take her by surprise. At the time she was at the sink washing dishes when I sat down at the table doing my homework. The plate she was holding in her hands at the time, she gently slid back into the dishwater and came over to take a seat next to me.

"Bertha, you need to keep your eyes on your books and off them boys," she said quietly.

"He is a nice boy, Mama. You'll see, you will like him," I said with enough enthusiasm for both of us.

But Mama wasn't having it. "I don't doubt he is," she said. "Baby, you are fifteen, and I am going to trust you to do the right thing," she said without further argument as if she sensed already it would do no good. Although she didn't say it, Mama's right thing,' was "keeping your dress down and getting your education."

I had no intention of disappointing her, either. I had no intention of disappointing either of us. I was a good student, and I made good grades. I was just as enthusiastic about getting my education as she was, and the incentive hadn't changed. I wanted off that plantation. My motivation was like a slave boy by the name of Booker T. Washington, whom I'd read about. I kept my eyes in some type of book.

Without really realizing it, Charles and I became steadies. We enjoyed each other's company, and naturally began gravitating toward each other at barbecues and parties. As for my family, they loved him. He was always respectful, and made sure I got home at a respectable hour.

We loved hugging and kissing, and just having nice clean, teenage fun. For a full year, we enjoyed our relationship just as it was, but somewhere, during our courtship, the naïveté and innocence of our kissing and hugging turned to heavy necking. This was a dangerous graduation for two young people who were becoming sexually aroused and didn't have a clue how far to go, or the sense to use the knowledge even if we had. It was like lighting a stick of dynamite and not expecting it to blow. It was becoming harder and harder to reach that point of, whatever it was we were on the brink of and simply pull back. Realizing that there was even more just beyond our grasp.

I suppose at sometime a red light with "STOP" was flashing furiously in the back of my mind somewhere, but it was quickly getting dimmer and dimmer. I suppose that at some point I even considered the fact that Charles only wanted me for sex, because as handsome as he was, he could have had any girl he'd wanted. To be honest, one day, I just out right asked him, "Charles, why do you like me when there are so many girls prettier at school?"

"I like you because you are sweet, lovely, smart, and you don't pretend to be somebody you're not. I also feel comfortable around you," he explained one day as he walked away from me. That was it, I was lost.

The turning point in our relationship ironically was initiated because we were babysitting his little sister, alone. While she slept, Charles and I settled down on the sofa in the front room, to music, pretending, for a moment, we were grown and the owners of the castle. A real sexy song came on and we got up to dance. Immediately, he began showering me with kisses and slowly backing me toward the sofa. It was a dream, we were in love and crazy with desire. I wanted him, and he wanted me, so naturally, we made love for the very first time.

When it was over, I thought about what mama had said, but this couldn't be wrong. Charles and I loved each other, but way back there, where the red light used to be, was the thought, "We shouldn't have let it happen."

Family fun time on Cooper Hill

9. A New Lesson, Teenage Pregnancy

At the time Charles and I were dating, I was naïve, not stupid. I'd learned in hygiene class that there were three reasons a woman didn't have her period: she hadn't begun yet, she was in menopause, or she was pregnant. Two of those possibilities could easily be ruled out. I was pregnant, I knew it, and I was scared to death. There was only one person I could share this dark secret with, my sister Annie.

When I told her, she freaked out, "Girl, how you gonna tell Mama?" she asked, inadvertently adding to my distress.

The truth was, I had no idea how I was going to tell Mama. She'd held such high hopes for me. I knew, when she found out, it was going to break her heart. How I thought I could keep it secret from her, I don't know. Sooner or later she would figure it out, because she counted my sanitary napkins. I was trapped in a nightmare. I couldn't sleep. Having a baby would surely stop my chances of getting off the plantation, and that terrified me.

One morning, the inevitable happened, Mama walked in on me vomiting, a dead give away, but I tried. I told her I had a virus or something and followed her to the kitchen to get a glass of juice. Mama entered the kitchen and went straight to the sink, attempting to pull a dish from a pile only to allow it to slide back in the sink. Suddenly, she turned and looked at me, "Are you pregnant?" she asked quietly.

I almost choked on the cup of juice I was valiantly trying to force down my throat. "No, Mama," I lied avoiding eye contact.

"Well, the way you are having morning sickness, indicates to me you are. Besides, I been counting your sanitary napkins. When the last time you had a period?" she asked.

The game was over, I couldn't think fast enough to respond. "This was horrible," my brain screamed. This was beyond a disaster, my brain and mouth couldn't begin to coordinate fast enough to be convincing. As a matter of fact, I couldn't even move.

"You go on to school today," Mama said finally. "I'll see if I can find someone to take you to the clinic tomorrow," she said seemingly making a decision. I suppose it was obvious enough I wouldn't be able to do it.

After school, I met Charles. "Have you? Have you seen anything yet?" he asked nervously.

"No," I answered sadly. "Mama is going to take me to the clinic tomorrow."

"Everything is going to be alright," he sighed.

I'd thought telling mama would be the worse part of my ordeal, I was wrong again. The clinic was the first time since I'd become a teenager that I'd had to take my clothes off from the waist down for a doctor to examine me. I was so embarrassed having to get up on that table, spreading my legs to put my feet up in the stirrups. As if my humiliation weren't complete, a big light was positioned down at the end of the table, so the doctor could see how to do the examination, I suppose. After that, they made me go pee in a jar then bring it back to the nurse. After another excruciating hour, the doctor finally called us back in and told mama I was going on two months pregnant.

Mama remained silent on the ride home, simply staring forward out the window. Her mind, I'm sure, was reeling. My worst fear was that she was blaming herself, and God knows, she shouldn't have. Mama had done the best she knew how to steer my life in the right direction, never once thinking that she needed a life of her own. Personally, I doubt if she'd ever had a selfish thought in her life, she simply wasn't built that way.

Mama was married because of us, her children, certainly not because of Mr. John's love and devotion, though she pretended to be happy despite the fact that he continued to visit Ms. Hattie's even after the vehement objections. He did help to keep bread on the table, I will give him that. However, I can't really say he ever showed any real interest in our welfare. The significant cost of food was a constant complaint.

By the time we arrived home, Mama still hadn't said anything, she remained as silent at the end of our journey as she'd been at the beginning. I kept sitting there, wishing she would say something, anything. I wouldn't have cared if she'd beat me. Maybe that would have helped rid me of the ever increasing weight of the over burdening feelings of pain and shame that I was feeling.

It wasn't until later that day that she finally spoke to me, "Child, what are you going to do?" she asked with anguish, both of us finally giving in to the despair and allowing the tears to flow. We cried together for life's cruelties, and for the seeming end to our dreams of my education.

That weekend, when Charles came, Mama lit into him. "What are you going to do, young man?" she shouted.

"I love Bertha, and I want to marry her," her replied nervously.

"Child, how are you going to take care of a wife and child off a part-time job?" she asked pointedly.

Though he meant well, he couldn't honestly answer her. He didn't know himself how he would manage. I loved Charles, and I knew he loved me, but we were smart enough to know we were in trouble. Like most teenagers who have found and will find themselves in our situation, we didn't have a plan and absolutely no money.

When the news spread around campus that I was pregnant, you'd have thought that I had suddenly contracted the plague. Many of the girls began pulling away from me, their parents didn't want them associating with me. Who knew, I might have been a bad influence on them. Not all of them were so cruel, though. Half way through the tenth grade, I had to drop out of school.

There were very few alternatives for colored girls like myself in the fifties. Opportunities granted to the young ladies of today who make such mistakes would never have been offered to the women of my generation. The only alternative school we had was home, and for me, the plantation. Birth control was unheard of. Back then, birth control was commonly known as abstinence, a state I had already relinquished. Some of the more unfortunate girls back then were sent to relatives that lived far away to have their babies so their families could be spared the shame. Sometime later, after the baby had been born, she would return and the baby would become a brother or sister to her, rather than her offspring.

Not that I wanted to, but after four months I began prenatal care. It wasn't my choice really, Mama just took the bull by the horns and made me go. There was only one clinic available to us and it was located at the State Charity Hospital. By the time I finally did go, the doctors and nurses there were alarmed because I had waited so long to begin care. One nurse blatantly told me, "You look as if you're about to have your baby, now."

Five other teenage girls — a couple my age, a few even younger — attended the clinic together. It wasn't hard to recognize the expressions of shame they wore when confronted with their big bellies, evidence of their sins. I'm sure I wore the same one, constantly. To hide my belly, I wore my coat, or a large sweater most of the time.

I was so grateful that Mama attended my appointments with me. However, when I appealed to her to accompany into the restroom for my urine test, the nurse halted her half way. "You're mama wasn't with you when you got this baby, was she?" she asked viciously, her lip carved upward in hatred and venom.

"How did I get myself in this mess?" I groaned, for the first time realizing the full magnitude of what I had done to my mother, the shame and humiliation I had inadvertently cast on her. I was so embarrassed. I was just a child, having a child. Yet at fifteen years of age, I was about to become a mother.

As for my stepfather, he said nothing to me about being pregnant. In fact, he barely looked at me. I assume he was thinking about the cost of another mouth to feed.

Prenatal care was good for one thing, I learned a few things there that I had never known about my body, about babies, but most importantly, I learned that even at age fifteen, I had become a woman. Yet, I was torn. There was still the childish part of me that yearned to be at school, playing with my friends, going to parties, being young, but there was now an alternate being within, making herself known. The woman flowering within me, screamed at me to get a grip and take responsibility for what I had done and the child that I had created within.

The nurses reminded me constantly that my body was going to change, but couldn't they see, it already had. I was now trapped inside a body I no longer recognized as my own. My breasts began swelling first and continued, then my feet joined in the fray. As if that weren't enough, after a few months, my belly got larger and larger making me even more awkward and uncomfortable.

I no longer wanted anyone to see me, least of all Charles, not that that fact stopped him from coming. Dear Charles, he was so wonderful, he continued to want to take me places with him, but I could no longer agree to accompany him.

Around three o'clock one morning, I awoke with pain in my lower abdomen, real pain. When I attempted to use the night pot, I suddenly felt something warm running down my leg. I became frightened then and yelled out, "Mama, something is happening!"

As I looked down there was all of this pink stuff running down my legs. Needless to say, I was quickly becoming hysterical. Mama ran into the room with her eyes only half opened. She took one look at me and said, "Child, your water done broke," she said calmly, reaching forward to pull a drawer open and retrieve and sanitary pad. "Put this on," she ordered. "Let me get John up so he can run down the road to find someone to take you to the hospital," she said leaving the room again.

Around four thirty that morning, our small party arrived at the admitting room of the hospital. A nurse noticed me waddling down the hall and rushed toward me with a stretcher. By this time the pains had practically become unbearable. "How far apart are your pains, Mom?" she asked.

"I don't know," I gasped through the contractions.

"Is this your first baby, Mother?"

"Yes," I gasped, fervently wishing she would shut up.

"Don't push down," she instructed me, "the doctor will be here shortly."

When the doctor arrived, he instructed the nurses to take me to the maternity ward, which she did as Mama walked along beside the stretcher, silently holding my hand until we got to the ward.

"Mama, can't you stay?" I asked forlornly.

"No, child," she replied softly, only then letting go of my hand.

With the loss of Mama's comforting touch, I became even more afraid and the pain was becoming even worse. A nurse came in the room then with a basin full of soapy water and a razor to shave my vagina. The good news is, the pain was much too fierce for there to be any thought of lingering humiliation.

When she was finished, the doctor came in and examined me again. "It's almost time," he announced when he was finished. "Nurse, take her to the holding room," he instructed.

The first thing I heard when the door to the holding room opened was the sound of mothers in waiting, screaming and yelling. This room was located just outside of the delivery room. All of the beds here had rails on both sides, to keep the distressed mothers from tumbling out, I suppose.

"Oh shit, these pains are killing me," the mother in the next bed suddenly shouted. "You must not be having any?" she asked, of whom I don't know. "I told my damn husband I didn't want any more babies," she continued, crying out again in pain.

When my pains became too severe, I called for Mama. Who else would a child call? Around seven that morning, they rolled me into the delivery room and placed me on a table, a big light hanging down over it.

"Stop pushing, Mother, you're going to tear yourself!" the doctor ordered abruptly. By this time, the doctors and nurses were yelling, and when he looked again, I felt absolutely no shame, none at all. I just wanted it over!

The very next thing I remember is my baby lying in my arms. I'd just delivered a six-pound baby girl. When I got home, I could barely sit, I was so sore from all of the stitches.

Charles visited us almost every day after school to see his daughter, Lois, and me. Like most men of that era, regardless of their age, he didn't have a clue about the trauma I had just endured to bring that child into this world. The only reality for him was his daughter and the fact that she was here.

He did, however, take on the responsibility of trying to take care of her with the little money he earned from his part-time job. It wasn't nearly enough. Taking care of a baby, even then, was expensive.

When Charles graduated from High School, he moved to Texas to find work for the summer. Our intentions were that he would send for us later to join him and visit a while with him. His plans to go to college that fall fell through.

I really missed him. I felt so alone and confused, and I wasn't nearly ready to be a mother at fifteen, mentally or physically. It was tough. I had no money or job to take care of either my baby or myself, not to mention the new set of problems my situation made for my mama and my stepfather, as if they didn't have enough as it was. They had no money, and were barely surviving themselves.

As for me, not only was I broke, but I didn't even know how to feed a baby. Mama did the best she could to prepare me to care for my child and trained me to change her diapers, bathe, and feed her, which was vital for her survival. I still missed Charles, though. He wrote me daily, but that simply wasn't enough. I needed him to be with us.

One morning during this period, I overheard Mama telling Mr. John, "I am fed up with living on this plantation. I'm going to the city and look for me a job at a house," she shouted.

"Bell, you know we still owe Mr. Beene. I can't leave," Mr. John replied.

"Well, you better get up there and make an arrangement to pay him on time, if you want to go with me, because I have had it. As soon as I get a place, I am taking my child and my granddaughter with me," she announced firmly.

That was the best news I'd heard in years. James and Jim were both doing well in Texas. Both had found jobs as truck drivers.

After Mr. John returned from seeing Mr. Beene, he informed Mama that Mr. Beene told him he could move, but he had to pay the money he owed, or he could move and continue working for him.

We moved to the inner city of Bossier, but living in the city wasn't much different from living on the plantation. The only real difference I could see was that our housing had a bathroom with running water, but Mama and Mr. John had to pay rent, which made things even harder.

Mama found a job doing housekeeping for some white people that lived in the city, which is what most colored people who lived in the city did. Most of all, the colored people that lived in the city still had daily connections with the plantation. There were no other choices for those who were uneducated for other employment.

After a few years went by, someone reported Mr. Beene to the labor board and he was forced to pay quite a large amount of back pay to his workers, finally freeing Mr. John of his debt and allowing him to find work elsewhere.

Charles did come home for Christmas. I was thrilled to see him, as he was to see the two of us. He bought gifts for the baby and me, and had dinner at his mother's house, and that evening we took in a movie. We held hands as usual, but it seemed as if his mind was elsewhere. Later that night I confronted him about it.

"Bertha, I have something to tell you," he said looking away. "I met someone in Texas and we are going to get married," he said finally.

"How could you?" I shouted, devastated.

"It just happened," he said calmly. "If I'm hurting you, I'm sorry."

I stood there as my mouth dropped with disbelief. I felt as if my whole life had suddenly been shattered.

This man was the father of my child, I loved him, and he was standing here telling me he was marrying someone else. *This couldn't be happening,* I thought. *How could I have been so dumb?*

He left to be happy with another woman, and I became depressed and stopped eating. After only the first month, I'd lost twenty pounds. I still loved him, no matter what, but he didn't love me anymore.

Brother Jim hauling cotton on Beene's Plantation

10. Albert

AFTER THE BREAKUP WITH CHARLES, I WAS ANGRY. As far as I was concerned, I didn't want anything else to do with him, or any other man. Stine, my next door neighbor had other ideas.

Stine was a year older than I was, and sometimes I'd visit her and we'd listen to music, or go to a movie. She had already finished high school and had plans to marry Bill, the young man she was dating at the time.

One evening, the phone rang and it was Stine. "Girl, this guy named Albert want to talk to you. He's a friend of Bill's."

"Stine, I don't want to meet him," I snapped.

"How long are you going to continue grieving over Charles?" she asked. "You need to get out and do something. Bill say he's a nice guy," she tried again.

"Stine, I already told you, I don't want to meet him," I said, hanging up the phone. I picked up a book from the table to read. I'd been thinking wholeheartedly about returning to school when Lois got older, if I could get someone to care for her.

Charles still infrequently sent money to buy milk and diapers. Of course, I was pretty sure I needed to try getting a job, if I could find anyone to hire me at age fifteen. My stepfather still wasn't real happy about the baby and me, and I knew I needed a job.

A month later someone knocked on the door. It was Stine. When I opened the door, I found, to my surprise, that there was a guy with her.

"Hi, girl," she said nonchalantly, as if we hadn't already had this discussion a mere thirty days ago. Yet here she stood at my door, grinning, all three of her gold teeth apparent through her thick lips. "This is Albert Miller," she said, still smiling.

Stine was pretty in her own way, I suppose. She wore nice clothes and kept her hair neat all of the time. Her mother had a good job working at the phone company, and she was as nice as could be.

"My name is Bertha," I said finally, trying to be courteous.

"My name is Albert Miller," he repeated again needlessly. "Stine talked to me about you all the time, but she didn't tell me you were this pretty," he said.

"Pleased to meet you," I lied, trying to maintain the façade.

"We are going out tonight, girl. Why don't you come with us?" Stine asked, effectively putting me on the spot.

"Yes, why don't you?" Albert joined in.

"Sure, why not?" I finally said, deciding I might as well go and get this over with. *This girl makes me sick!* I thought silently.

"I will pick you up around eight-thirty," Stine said as they walked out.

Maybe it will be good to get out, I thought finally. Rambling through my clothes, I found a red blouse and a black skirt I thought would look good on me.

Albert wore his clothes well. The brown shirt and black pants draped his brown, tall body nicely, and his black hat and well-shined shoes really topped them off. His smile made his large eyes seem larger. We went to a club in the west part of town that had a live band playing. Albert was a good dancer: he could split, and come right back to a standing position with ease.

During breaks from the dance floor, I learned that he was two years older than me. He and his sister shared a home with their mother and father. He had a brother who was married and out on his own. Albert worked as a pastry chef at a restaurant. He told me he'd been working there since he was a small boy. I gathered he must have made a good salary; he drove his own car.

"You're a good dancer, Bertha," he complimented me.

"Not as good as you, I'm afraid," I replied honestly. "How did you learn to do a split like that?"

"It just came naturally, I guess," he replied with a smile. "I understand that your boyfriend lives in Texas," he said cautiously.

"Yes," I sighed, reliving the old pain.

"He must have been out of his mind to leave a pretty girl like you here alone," he stated.

I looked at him without commenting.

Stine and Bill came off the dance floor to catch a breather. I found out that Bill worked at the same restaurant as Albert, but his plans were to move to Texas when he and Stine got married. I admired them, they seemed to be so much in love, and Bill appeared to be very ambitious.

"Seems like you guys are having a great time," Stine said.

"Man, I wish y'all had met sooner, maybe you could have come to Texas with us," Bill said. Neither Albert nor I commented.

We did double date for a while, off and on, then gradually it was just the two of us. After a while with Albert, I began to feel like my old self again. I could tell Albert was falling in love with me, but I didn't share his feelings. Deep down within, I knew I was still in love with Charles.

Albert finally popped the question after a few months of dating. We were having dinner at one of our favorite eating-places one night when he approached the subject.

"Bertha, will you marry me?" he asked.

"I don't know, Albert," I answered, not wanting to hurt him.

"I love you, Bertha," he declared.

Here was a man saying all of the things I had hoped Charles would have said to me when he came home for Christmas that year. He had gotten married, but not to me, so that dream was out of the question.

I asked myself, why not marry this man? Charles was married. But I couldn't make myself believe that that was a good enough reason to do the same, not unless I was in love with Albert, although, maybe love would come later.

Albert took me to meet his family. They lived in a middle class neighborhood. When we met, his mother looked me over real good. Mrs. Miller wore no make-up on her brown skin, nor did she wear lipstick, and she was dressed in a long dress that hung to her ankles.

"Where do you attend church?" she asked when she'd finally completed her perusal of me.

"I attend Pine Grove Baptist Church," I said proudly.

"We are members of the Church of God in Christ, and we don't wear make-up. That's too worldly."

"Neal, that's enough," Albert said intervening.

I was shocked that he'd called her by her name, but I found out later that they all called her that.

"Neal," he continued, "Bertha and I are getting married, and we want your blessing," he finished.

His sister wasn't home; she was at work. Mr. Miller, his father, never came out of the back of the house. Neal did all the talking. Three months later, Albert and I were married. We had a small wedding at his mother's. Just a few friends and family were invited. Mama wasn't too please about me getting married.

We found a one-bedroom apartment in west Shreveport, within a few blocks of Mama. We used part of the living room for Lois's bed, and went to Schorr Furniture Company and got a house full of furniture for three hundred dollars. The furniture was so fragile that by the time it was paid for, we needed more. Schorr was about the only store that poor, colored folks could get credit.

A month after we were married, I discovered that I was going to have another baby. Rather than feeling happy and elated about the news, I actually became more depressed. I was having a hard enough time as it was taking care of Lois. I had to wash cloth diapers in a bathtub instead of a washing machine. I hadn't heard of Pampers — I don't even know if they existed at the time. I used cloth diapers and washed them out after each use.

The baby was born on June 18, 1957. She weighed six pounds, and we named her "Jennifer." I really tried to be a good mother and wife. But somehow, I felt trapped and hopeless. Albert was a good husband to me and father to the girls.

I suppose he was better prepared as a husband than I was as a wife. Usually, he would come home and find dishes in the sink from the night before, and no food cooked that night.

"Bertha, why are you so lazy?" he asked one night, after this pattern had gone on for a while. "Is something wrong with you?" he asked concerned.

"I just don't feel that good," I shouted in my defense.

"Why don't you go see a doctor?" he asked frustrated.

I wasn't lazy, I was just depressed. I simply was not doing a good job of coping with my role as wife and mother.

Finally, when Albert couldn't put up with me any longer, he asked Neal, his mother, to come over and help.

"You shouldn't have married this lazy, un-saved girl," I overheard her saying to him.

"Neal, you stay out of my business," he said through clenched teeth. "Her being lazy has nothing to do with her being saved," he shouted.

"Albert, you make sure she bring that baby to our church," she said.

"Neal… Neal, please just go," he said finally, he'd had enough.

We had been married almost a year when Albert came home one day and ordered me to start packing.

"For what?" I asked shocked.

"We are moving in with Neal. My daddy is sick, and she needs me to help her out, since my sister moved out.

I wanted to move in with Neal, I'm sure, about as much as she wanted me to move in with her. But I didn't have a choice with two children and no job. No sooner had we moved in before Neal drew the boundaries. She informed me in no uncertain terms who was going to be the boss here. I would have no say in what we ate, or how things were ran. She even shopped for the food. One day, I was permitted to get a loaf of bread from the store that I preferred to eat. She never touched it. A day later, I saw it in the trash.

"We don't eat Holsum bread," she snapped, rolling her eyes at me.

"Well, I do," I informed her.

"We'll see about that," she shouted.

That evening when Albert got home, I told him I wished to do the shopping for our food. He then informed me that Neal would do it.

"Why does she have to buy food for us?" I asked dismayed by his answer.

"But Albert, you are my husband! You can teach me. I want to eat some of the food I like."

"Bertha, Neal will do the shopping," he shouted with finality.

His message to me was clear, either I would eat what Neal cooked, or I wouldn't eat.

Neal soon took over Jennifer's care, from feeding to bathing and church on Sunday mornings. She acted as if Lois and I weren't there. One day as I was dressing to go see Mama, she stormed into my room.

"Where do you think you're going, looking like Jezebel with that on?" she asked. "I don't know why Albert married an unsaved woman in the first place," she snapped, not waiting on any response from me at all.

"Neal, I am a Baptist and I will most likely be one until the day I die," I shouted back, finally having enough of her venom. Neal's mouth flew wide open.

In February, Albert took me out to dinner for my birthday. When we returned, Neal jumped all over him.

"Why are you throwing your money away running to them clubs?" she asked seething.

I thought maybe he would speak up, but he didn't. Albert just went to his room as if he were a child.

"Why can't we move out?" I asked later that night.

"That's just impossible, Bertha. I promised Neal when she got this house, I would help her pay for it," he said. After that, I knew it was useless talking to him about moving. We were there to stay.

I was a virtual prisoner. I couldn't even go to the store. Neal would sit on the porch, stretching her neck, watching until I returned, if I did. If I made a phone call, she would listen in on my conversation. She never wanted my family to visit, and when they did, she pretended to be busy just to avoid having to entertain them.

I soon fell into a deeper depression. I had asked Albert I could go back to school, just to get out of the house. He asked Neal if she would watch Lois and Jennifer. As I expected, she said no. "She don't need to go back to school."

Mr. Miller, Albert's father, was an alcoholic. He drank every day and when he went to the store, I would ask him to bring me a beer back. Neal was so hellish I could understand why he drank. She treated him like dirt, and then called herself a saved woman. I adored Mr. Miller, he treated me with nothing but kindness.

"Bertha, Neal ain't gonna let Albert grow up. I wish you would take these kids and get the hell up out of here," he said one day as he staggered trying to embrace his weak body.

Mr. Miller just lived there. He had no control whatsoever. Neal always called him a good-for-nothing drunk. We became good friends and drinking buddies. We'd bring each other beer from the store. I kept it hid out in my room. Some days I would get drunk and sleep all day. Mr. Miller would watch Lois for me.

Albert had reached the point where he stopped taking me any place altogether. It was out of the question for me to go out alone. One day when I went to the store, I stopped in the juke joint around the corner. It sounded as if there were actually people there having fun, something

I no longer did. I ordered me a beer and sat at a table, watching people talking and dancing. I'd reminisce about how much fun Albert and I used to have.

I had come to love Albert, just as I thought I would, but I had lost respect for him as a man. I hated the fact that he couldn't seem to stop his mother from interfering in our lives.

I enjoyed myself so much that I lost track of time. It would soon be time for Albert to get home. As I rushed toward the door, I bumped into someone, it was Albert. By the expression he wore, I knew he was angry.

"Neal told me you been coming around here." He yelled at me before I could say a word, drawing back his hand as he spoke, as if he wanted to hit me. Instead, he pushed me out the door. I was embarrassed, not to mention shocked, by his attitude.

"When you get home, you pack your shit and get the hell out! You are not taking my baby either," he roared.

He walked behind me all the way to the house, shouting and cursing as we walked. When we got inside of the house, Neal had Jennifer in her room with the door locked. I banged on the door, but she would not come out. "Let me have my baby," I yelled desperately.

"Get the hell away from that door, and get the hell out of here. I told you, that baby is not going anywhere," he ranted.

Lois was in our room on the floor, crying her eyes out. Mr. Miller staggered out of his room trying to see what was going on.

"Albert, you let that girl have that baby," Mr. Miller ordered. Bless his heart. But his aid was too little, too late.

"Daddy, you just get back in your room and stay out of this," Albert roared at him.

"Albert, you just like you damn mama, crazy as a bessie bug," Mr. Miller said.

I suppose I hadn't started packing fast enough. Albert walked into the room and began going through my drawer, throwing my clothes on the bed. I grabbed up what I could and put them in whatever I could find and called a cab.

I was so downhearted and horrified, I couldn't think straight. I was young and inexperienced, and I didn't know at the time that they couldn't lawfully take my baby, not until it was too late.

I was nineteen years old and unprepared to do anything for the future of myself, or my children. Back at home with my mama, feeling as frightened as I had that day in the woods, wandering around lost. Only this time, I didn't have ole Trouble to help me find my way out of this mess. Losing Jennifer to Albert, Neal made me realize I had to take control of my life. I could no longer keep running home to Mama. It was time for me to grow up.

Cotton gin *(painted directly on wooden cabinet door)*

11. Employment

I FINALLY DID FIND A JOB. I worked as a dishwasher and bus girl for one of the luxury hotels in downtown Shreveport. The pay was thirty-two dollars, every two weeks. The pay wasn't that much, but it was better than welfare. When I'd gone there for help, they'd wanted to know everything about me. They even wanted to know when was the last time I had sex.

Employment I found much easier to take. When the rush hours were over, I had to leave the dining room and go back in the kitchen to wash dishes. Sometimes they'd be piled up over my head. They got so hot from the water in the dishwasher, and remain so until they would air-dry themselves.

As a bus girl, my job was to clean the tables and reset them with clean linens and dishes. We coloreds could work in the dining, but we couldn't eat there. We had to eat downstairs, in the hot basement of the hotel.

After working for awhile, I found an apartment. The rent was seven dollars and fifty cents a week. It had a bedroom, a bath, and a small kitchen. The bedroom was actually large enough for sitting and sleeping. I got the lady next door to take care of Lois for me while I worked.

Several times, I attempted to get Jennifer, but Albert continued to refuse to let me have her. I was never allowed to visit with her alone. Either Neal or he would supervise our visits.

Because this was my first time out on my own, I had a lot to learn about running a household. The expense of running one was quickly becoming a necessity for me to grasp. I'd had no previous idea what it cost to take care of a home and family. After the rent, lights, and gas, there was very little money left for food. More times than I'd cared to count. I didn't even have money for basic food. Charles hadn't sent a child support payment in years for Lois, and Mama certainly wasn't in the position to help. Mr. John and she were barely getting by as it was.

After working there for awhile, I began to notice that some of the women would come by the kitchen area and take a big pieces of chicken that been left on the customers plates, pretending they were taking it home to their pets, but I knew better. They were making themselves doggie bags all right, but they were feeding their families. I learned quickly to do the same thing for Lois and myself.

Vi, one of the women I met at work, and became friends with, taught me how to buy hamburger meat and prepare it in a variety of ways. Vi was a beautiful woman. Her skin was jet black and she had the most beautiful big brown eyes I'd ever seen. I can honestly say that Marilyn Monroe had nothing on this woman when it came to feminine figures. Vi had been more than amply endowed with a curvaceous body. There was nothing shameful or timid about her either. Regardless of her position at the hotel, she walked with her head held high, her presence exuding grace and style.

By this time I'd learned quite a bit from Mama, but not enough. Mama biggest concern was still that I continue my education. I couldn't be concerned with that at the moment. I was doing the best I could to make it for my daughter and myself. The time I'd spent with Neal, Albert's mother, certainly hadn't prepared me for anything. Vi, on the other hand, had four children and had been out on her own for years, surviving came instinctively to her by this time.

Some nights, after work, Vi and I would stop on our way home to have a drink, preferring the Cotton Club most of the time. I had learned to drink in moderation by then. People from all walks of life: teachers, doctors, waiters, and everyday people united at the Cotton Club, to see and be seen. Nevertheless, we went just to unwind from the hectic struggle of everyday life. Of course, the club being what it was, there were pimps hanging around, ready to recruit young women who happen to fall prey to their empty promises.

I could truly understand the allure of money and nice things. I found myself fighting to resist the temptation on more than one occasion, especially when you're as broke as I was. And pimps flashing rolls of hundred dollar bills in your face, it was hard. They were telling you how easy it would be to have one of your own. It was more than a little difficult to remember the reasons you continued to say no. I barely had enough to keep my lights and gas on.

Luckily, for me, I never said yes. I would rather have had my utilities cut off than to live that kind of life they were offering. I could live without the brutality they used to deal with the women in submission to them.

The more I got to know Vi, the more I found we had lots in common. Just like myself, she was single, trying to make it on her own, and struggling through without the help of the man who had fathered her children.

One night, a few of the waiters from the second floor joined us at the Cotton Club. I didn't know them, but Vi did. She informed me that they made over a hundred dollars a week, and that some of them worked as bellmen. All of them dressed nicely in white shirts and blacks slacks. Vi told me that many of them owned new cars, but they weren't able to drive them to work. When I asked why, she informed me that our employers wouldn't be able to accept the fact that coloreds owned new vehicles. In fact, she told me, they would go out of their way to make their lives a living hell, hoping they would quit and lose everything.

It was the early sixties and this was America and no matter how many times we heard them say, "ALL MEN ARE CREATED EQUAL," the reality was that it didn't apply if your skin happened to be black. I wanted to believe I had left that mentality behind me when I left the plantation. A few days later, the reality that prejudice was still very much alive hit me.

One night as I was working in the kitchen, the chef approached me and some of the other workers and informed us that we should address the white employees as "Sir" and "Ma'am." These were men and women about the same age as we were. I told him in no uncertain terms that I had no intention of doing it. The next day when I reported to work, I found that my time card had been removed. I had been fired.

I soon found another job working in a garment factory, making men's jeans and slacks. My job was to sew the side and end seams together. The machines we used were those big commercial brands that felt more like you were driving a car. The harder you pushed, the faster it would sew. As we worked, the supervisor timed us to make sure that we met our quota of pieces per minute. We were given only a few weeks to increase our speed in order to be paid our salary of fifty dollars a week. With an increase in salary, I was able to have enough money to obtain my divorce from Albert. My attorney advised me to get a larger house before trying to regain custody of Jennifer. I knew that the only way to make that happen was to get a second job, which I did. During the evenings, I worked for a lady, cleaning her house. I had to do what I had to do, in order to get custody of Jennifer, and that was a burning priority in my life.

12. Guy

"Hi, girl what you doing?" Vi asked calling me one night out of the blue. "I haven't seen you much lately. I'm having a birthday party Saturday night. Why don't you come?" she asked,

"Vi, I'm working two jobs now so I can get a bigger house," I told her. I had been too exhausted lately even to think about socializing with anyone.

"What you need a bigger house for?" she asked incredulously.

"When I take Albert and his mother to court, I'm hoping the judge will give me custody of Jennifer, if I can prove that I can provide for her." I informed her.

"Hell, I wouldn't bother going to no damn court, if it was my child. I would be kicking some ass," she said adamantly.

"Girl, you just don't know how crazy these people are. It's going to take the law to get my baby back, trust me." I assured her.

"Okay, but I'm still going to look for you, Saturday," she said, changing the subject. "You need to get out of that house. You need a break from all that shit you're going through."

By Saturday, I was ready for a break. I had someone I knew to watch Lois for me, and I got dressed for the party. I searched my closet and decided to wear a plain, black dress and a pair of flats. I looked fine, as far as I was concerned, it wasn't as if I was trying to impress anyone.

Vi lived a short distance from me, so I walked up the hill to her house, relieving some of the stress I'd been under. The walk had been just what I needed; I arrived there feeling refreshed and ready for a party.

After playing a few rounds of cards, I rushed for the food line. I noticed Vi standing in the corner talking to an extremely attractive man. I didn't recognize him, but I knew he wasn't her boyfriend, John. I'd met while him while playing cards and he was still playing.

"Bertha," Vi said, noticing me standing there. " Come here, I want you to meet John's friend, Guy," she announced with a smile.

"Pleased to meet you," I said extending my hand as I joined the two of them. "My name is Bertha," I said allowing my gaze to quickly assess him.

"Nice to meet you," he said with a warm smile.

"Same here. Have you eaten yet?" I asked politely.

"No, but everything sure looks delicious," he said looking over at the serving table assessing the menu spread before him.

When he turned to walk toward the food, I couldn't help noticing how his body had masculine grace and pride, and the way his clothes draped fluidly around over the tall length of his masculinity. When he returned to look at me, I noticed his face and his big, beautiful, brown eyes. Guy was a good-looking man, but I didn't seem to faze him a bit. I think I found that trait more intriguing than any of his other appealing traits.

"The food is as good as it looks," he said, taking a second bite as he rejoined me.

"It is that," I replied staring straight ahead.

"I love the food here. That's one of the reasons I enjoy coming home." He announced. "You just can't get food like this in California," he said with a boyish grin.

"Oh, you live in California?" I asked, intrigued by the man despite my objections of getting involved in another relationship until I had my baby back.

"Not anymore," he said with a charming grin. "I came back to live this time. I plan to work for my father."

"What type of business does your father own?" I asked.

"Landscaping," he answered, seemingly undisturbed by my questioning. We talked for hours and hours, and learned what we could about each other. Guy had children, a son and a daughter, whom he'd left behind in California. He and the children's mother had recently separated and he'd moved home after that. I revealed very little about myself.

"I see you're getting to know each other," Vi said grinning as she rejoined us later.

"Not really," I said, watching her surprised and disappointed reaction.

"I'd sure like to get to know her," Guy said staring at me, as if to read my innermost thoughts. With his words ringing in my ears, I walked thoughtfully back to the card table. Once there, I was able to forget the disturbing presence of the man. Although I thought he was a nice man, I wasn't interested in getting to know him better. I hadn't done much dating lately, and I wasn't interested in changing that. After working two jobs five days a week, I didn't have the time or desire to date.

I could feel Guy's eyes following me all night, finally ours eyes collided and I was left speechless, unable to break the contact.

"May I have this dance?" he asked softly standing close.

"Sure, why not?" I said following him to the dance floor.

As we danced to a slow tune, he held me close, the warmth of his body infusing mine. I was losing myself in his warmth. Recognizing the desire rising in me for what it was. I pushed him slightly away from me, reminding myself of all my reasons for not getting involved. There were too many things in my life more important than pursuing a relationship with a man. Before I could become involved with anyone, I needed to straighten out my own life.

The arguments I repeated over and over in my mind helped to free me from the strong attraction I felt for any man that night. "Thank God" I murmured to myself with relief. A few days later, Vi called again.

"Somebody's been asking about you," she informed me.

"Don't tell me, Vi." I warned her. "I don't care what you say, I am not getting involved."

"He just want your phone number, girl," she persisted.

"No way!" I shouted determined to hold onto my resolve.

"It won't hurt you to talk to the man." she argued, not ready to give up.

"You're getting on my nerves, Vi," I warned.

"Bertha, you might be missing out on something," she insinuated with an obvious smile in her tone. "Yeah, right. He could be fresh out of jail," I argued.

"I don't think so," she assured me. "Listen, I'll tell you what, I'll find out what I can about him from John, he knows every damn thing," she finished laughing. An hour later, she called back again.

"Girl the man just moved back from California. He and his girlfriend, he had out there, busted up. John told me that there's no way the man just got out of the cooler," she informed me, confirming what Guy had already told me.

"Okay, I'll talk to him," I agreed on a sigh. Vi seemed as determined that I give the man a chance as I was to avoid further contact with him — more, really, considering the fact that she'd finally worn me down. She must have called him as soon as we finished talking, because he called shortly after.

"Hi," he said cheerfully, "what you be doing since the last time I saw you?"

"Nothing but working," I informed him after the formalities of a greeting had been satisfied.

"Why don't you let me take you out sometime?" he asked after a few minutes of inconsequential chatter.

"Maybe," I replied evasively.

"I know you're a busy lady and all that, but you can take one night, at least, to enjoy yourself, can't you?" When I finally agreed, he said, "I'll see you Saturday night, okay?" before disconnecting.

Saturday night, Guy arrived around seven, dressed in a pair of navy blue pants and a beige shirt. Black shoes accented his attire. I'd almost forgotten how good the man looked, but seeing him again quickly reminded me.

Lois, who was playing with her toys in the middle of the floor when he arrived, only stared at the stranger in her midst. He seemed to enjoy playing with her as he waited for me to get dressed.

Guy's face seemed to light up as I walked into the room dressed in a black dress and black pumps. I had gotten my hair cut and pressed hard the day before, and I knew it was looking good. It seems that when my body decided to mature, it had done so in all the right places.

That night he took me to a new club that had just opened in town. Before we left, I took Lois next door to the neighbor, who babysat for me. Lois was five by that time.

The Colony Club was a nice club, with an unmistakable romantic ambiance. Soft lights and mellow jazz added to the mood. I liked the way Guy held me close as we danced. He seemed proud to have me at his side, and as we danced around the floor, all eyes followed our progression. As we sat alone in the corner table our eyes continuously found each other.

The more I looked into his eyes, the more handsome he became. It was the first time in years that anyone had made me feel romantic. Guy and I danced and held each other until the wee hours of the morning. When he kissed me goodnight at my door that night, I knew that it wouldn't be our last date.

Guy took me to meet his family on our second date. His family lived in middle-class neighborhood with well-manicured lawns. The exterior of their home was accented with beautiful stone bricks and the interior was decorated with some of the finest furniture I'd ever seen. Guy's father provided well for his wife, who was a homemaker.

From my observations, I assumed that Guy's family was financially stable. It wasn't hard to tell that he and his sister and brothers had never experienced a day of poverty in their entire lives.

Guy and I had a dated for about six months when he asked me to marry him. I didn't hesitate to answer him and there was only one answer I could give him. I knew without a doubt, that I was in love with him, and that was all that mattered. It never occurred to me that he hadn't said he loved me as well. I gave him a resounding, "yes." After that, thing began moving rapidly. We spent quite a bit of time together, but I was to find out later that I hadn't learned enough. I hadn't learned the truth about the man's honest and integrity. To be truthful, it wasn't something I thought about at the time.

Later, in December of that year, Guy came by and asked me to ride downtown, with him, but he refused to tell me why. When we got downtown, he parked in front of the courthouse, and grabbed my hand, holding it gently.

"Bertha, let's get married today," he said, his excitement contagious.

I was shocked by this unexpected turn of events. "I don't know what to say,' I sighed looking deep into his eyes, realizing that he was serious.

"We can get the license inside," he continued, dragging me behind him, not waiting on my consent.

His excitement was contagious and it wasn't long before I was running behind him as he raced up the stairwell, my legs were rubbery with nerves. When we came out of the office, we found a minister standing in the hallway.

"Hi," he said, greeting us with a smile. "you want to save money, I can marry you," he offered.

"What do you think about that, Bertha?" Guy asked, turning to face me with a wide grin.

"I'd do whatever you want to do," I sighed, unable to believe the man's timing.

"Just follow me." the minister said.

There were a few men standing around assembling Christmas decorations to put around the courthouse yard. The noise they were creating was so loud, I could barely hear myself think. We couldn't hear a word the minister said, both of us nodding where we thought it was appropriate. When we'd exchanged our vows, the minister called one of the men over to sign as a witness, and within seconds, I was Mrs. Guy.

A few weeks after we were married, we moved into a two-bedroom house. The house, though larger, was not in the best neighborhood, but it didn't matter. I was happy with my new husband and the family we shared with Lois. Also, I knew that because I had married, my chances of getting custody of Jennifer had suddenly increased.

Guy and I both put in an application at the ammunition plant just outside of Shreveport. Less than a week later, he was hired. It took almost a month before they notified me that I'd been hired as well.

Although we worked at the same place, Guy and I were unable to car pool. He was scheduled to work the day shift, and I was placed on the night shift. Actually, it worked out well, I didn't have to pay a baby sitter to sit Lois since one of us would be with her at all times.

13. Court Date

A COURT DATE WAS SCHEDULED LATER THAT YEAR. The months preceding it were pure torture. I wanted my baby back in the worst way, but I wasn't quite sure how the judge would eventually rule. The day of the trial, I was more nervous than at any other time in my memory. My palms were practically wet from the perspiration that covered my body. There was little I could do at this point, so I thanked God, my higher power, and asked for strength.

As I walked into the courtroom, I noticed Neal and Jennifer sitting a row over from where I would be seated, so I went over and spoke to them.

"Where is Albert?" I asked.

"He's in Kansas City," Neal snapped, refusing to say another word, determined to hold onto her anger and hatred.

I noticed as I was standing there that Jennifer wore an unfamiliar dress. I'd never seen it before, but I hated it. It was entirely too long, and inappropriate for a six year old to wear.

"Why is she not wearing one of the dresses I bought for her?" I asked Neal.

True to form, she said nothing, simply rolled her evil eyes up in her head and clamped her mouth shut.

"How are you doing, baby?" I asked Jennifer, ignoring Neal. My poor baby didn't know what to say she just shrugged her shoulders. Finally, after a few minutes of watching me, she seemed to garner the courage to say something. Her words broke my heart.

"Neal said you didn't want me," she said as tears rolled from her eyes, the pain and confusion she must have felt overflowing.

"That's not true, baby. Mama do want you," I tried to assure her.

Mr. Kennedy, my attorney finally arrived and I went over and expressed to him what my baby had said.

"Bertha, that is commonly done in these types of cases. Don't worry," he said reassuringly.

As the judge entered the courtroom, we all stood. There were two cases to be heard before mine, and then it came time for me to face the judge.

"Bertha Miller *versus* Neal Miller and Albert Miller for child custody," the bailiff announced in his detached voice. "Will you come forward, please? Where is Mr. Miller?" he asked when Albert didn't appear.

"He's in Kansas City," Neal answered.

"What is he doing in Kansas City?" the judge asked.

"Sir," Neal answered more humbly than I've ever heard her speak. "He went out there to get a job. I am keeping Jennifer for him," she finished.

"Why are you taking care of this child?" he asked.

"Sir," she said glancing at me out of the corner of her eye, "Bertha ran off and left Jennifer over three years ago," she blatantly lied.

"Sir, that's not true," Mr. Kennedy said in my defense. "Mrs. Miller came to me over three years ago and filed a judgment to have her child returned. The grandmother and father would not allow the child to leave with her mother when the father evicted her from the home at that time. She had to save money before she could bring the case to court, your honor," he explained.

"Mrs. Miller, is that so?" he asked me.

"Yes sir," I answered staring him directly in the eye. I had nothing to hide and I wanted him to know that.

"Were you living in the house with his mother at this time?" he asked.

"Yes sir. She complained that I was unsaved," I informed him.

"What do you mean, unsaved?" he asked then.

"I think she meant I was not going to heaven because I wore make-up, and was not a member of the church she attended," I answered crying.

"That don't make no sense to me," he snapped. "I never heard of such."

"Jennifer, listen to me," he said softly. "This here is your mother, honey. You are going to go home with her. I know your grandmother love you also, but that's how it has to be," he finished; trying to help the child understand the chaos the adults in her life seemed intent on creating.

"Mrs. Miller has a place for Jennifer to live?" he asked. "I am going to do what I think is best for the child. Mrs. Miller," he said addressing Neal. "Do you understand that you have no right to take a child from its mother, simply because you feel the mother is unsaved. You are trying to be God," he told her sternly.

"Bertha, this court is granting you custody of your child," he told me.

"Now, Mrs. Miller, this means that you can't visit, or take this child without the mother's consent. Do you understand?" he asked when Neal stood there saying nothing in response. "If you do not, allow me to say it again," he roared into the quiet of the courtroom. "Yes sir, I understand," Neal finally said.

I couldn't believe it. I would finally have both of my children at home. I couldn't have been happier. That evening when Guy arrived home, I met him at the door.

"She's here!" I shouted with excitement.

"Where?" Guy asked.

"She's in the other room with Lois," I told him, explaining what had happened in court that day. "The court granted me custody of her," I summarized.

"Bertha, you're a brave woman," he commented with pride.

The first few days after Jennifer came home were difficult for me. I now had two children with two totally different personalities. Jennifer longed to be hugged, she loved cuddling with me, and being her mother who had been forced to be without her for such a prolonged period, naturally, I accommodated her.

Lois, of course, noticed the attention I seemed to be showering on her sister, and gradually began pulling away from me. One day, as I was in the kitchen cooking dinner, Lois came in and sat at the table. "Mom, do you love Jennifer more than me?" she asked.

"No!" I answered, shocked that she even need ask such a question. "I love you both the same," I answered truthfully.

She didn't respond. Sadly, she turned and walked away without saying another word. I was still reeling from the fact that she'd asked such a question. Later, after I had thought about it, I realized I should have given her a hug.

Sometimes, as mothers, we hear what our children are saying, but we fail to listen at the words. When Guy came home, I asked him to help me reassure both of the children that we loved them.

As a child of a broken family, I longed for wholeness in my own family. I wanted my daughters to grow up in a nice home, each of them having their own bedroom. I was going to make sure they both had an education. I didn't want them to ever have to endure the life I'd lived.

Mama later moved to Texas. After my stepfather passed away, she wanted to live near my brothers and my sister Ella for a change. Therefore, I had no other close relatives living in Shreveport.

That same year, I received word that Charles had gotten killed in an auto accident. Lois was only eight years old at the time. I tried to help her through her grief the best I knew how, but I'm afraid I wasn't really equipped with the knowledge it took. Other than the loss of my grandfather, I hadn't really lost anyone close to me. Thank God, she'd had the opportunity to get to know him and spend time with him and his new wife. After his death, it seemed she began to slip even further into her shell.

Braiding in the Kitchen

After a hard day's work

14. Nightmares Come to Pass

Shortly, after I'd regained custody of Jennifer, Albert returned to town for the Fourth of July. He'd called and asked if Jennifer could spend the holiday with him. Understanding completely the pain of losing a child to an angry spouse, I refused to treat him the same. I willingly allowed Jennifer to spend time with him. He was her father, after all, and he loved her. I wanted her to know that beyond a shadow of a doubt. But that evening, just before dark, she hadn't returned home at our scheduled time.

"Neal, let me speak to Albert, please," I said calling there to check on things.

"Albert is gone," she snapped.

"Let me talk to Jennifer," I requested, refusing to be drawn in by her anger and bitterness.

"She's not here," she said in a low voice.

"Well, where is she?" I asked, becoming suspicious by her behavior.

"Albert took her back to Kansas City with him," she finally said.

My mouth fell open. Shock, pain, anger, fear, too many emotions to name assaulted me at once. The phone slipped through my numb fingers to the floor, and I soon followed it. My worse nightmare had just become reality. "Lord, I have lost my child again!" I moaned to myself, the pain consuming me.

Albert had taken my child back to Kansas City, and I had no idea where in Kansas City that he lived. She was just as lost to me now, as she'd been all the days when Neal had kept her from me.

The following day I went to see Mr. Kennedy, my attorney, and told him what had happened.

"Do you know where he lives in Kansas?" he asked solemnly.

"No, I don't," I answered.

"Bertha, they only gave you custody for the State of Louisiana," he informed me sadly, waiting patiently for me to absorb the full impact of his words.

"What do I need to do?" I asked then, my next breath held by the fear of what his next words would be. They weren't good, just as I'd expected.

"You will have to go through the state of Kansas to get her back," he informed me.

"I will do whatever I have to do to get my child back," I told him with steely determination.

The following week, when I returned to work, I requested a leave of absence from personnel. After that, I called my sister Annie and asked her about a classmate she'd had who'd lived in Kansas City. A few phone calls later, we got in touch with her and made arrangements to visit. I sent Lois to Mama's in Texas. I would need my undivided attention for what I was about to do, and I needed to be sure she was taken care of.

Guy's attitude did an about face. He was no longer pleased by my consuming desire to find Jennifer. He became moody, but he was a problem I would have to deal with when I returned.

Annie went with me. We caught the Greyhound from Shreveport to Dallas, then to Oklahoma, and on into Kansas. On the ride there, I didn't know what to expect. There was too much time to think about all of the things that could go wrong when we got there. I looked over at Annie as she slept; she was just as beautiful now as she'd always been. She was still young, in school, she had a year remaining before she finished college. Fortunately, her fate was far different from my own.

I remembered how I'd felt when she and I had been separated. Lois needed her sister and I wanted her to have her sister as she grew up, not later in life. Annie and I were sisters, but neither one of us really knew the other. We didn't know what the other's dreams were, or what we wanted for our lives when they were grown. That time had been taken from us, and I didn't want that for Lois.

I didn't understand it. Why was I having so many problems? "Was I being punished for being born?" I wondered silently. "Oh God, I'm just feeling guilty for allowing Jennifer to visit her father. Please, give me the strength to endure whatever I have to in Kansas," I prayed fervently.

We arrived around noon the following day and took a cab to Annie's friend, Donice's house. She lived on a street that had rows and rows of two-story homes. Almost every home we saw had two stories. We had dinner at her home and then discussed the matter of Albert and Jennifer.

Needless to say, I didn't sleep much that night. I spent most of the night wondering where in this huge city my little girl was being hidden. I so longed to see and tell her how much I loved her.

The next morning, I got up, ate a small breakfast and then began to scour the area phone directory for an attorney. They all told me the same thing, that it would take at least a year to even get a court date. But there was one who told me to call the DA's office and talk to him to see what my rights were.

When we arrived at the DA's office, I ran to the first person that I saw to tell my story. It was a short, white man with salt and pepper hair and a potbelly. It appeared that his only job there was to sit behind his desk and eat the day away.

"Where does he work?" he asked first of all.

"Sir, I don't know," I told him truthfully.

"Well, do you know his social security number?" he continued.

"No, sir. We are divorced."

"Do you live here, Ms?" he asked, sensing a reason to deny me any further assistance, I'm sure.

"No, sir. I live in Louisiana," I informed him, wondering what where I lived had to do with anything.

"Well, let me ask you this, do you have a court order for the state of Kansas?" he asked rubbing his head as he talked.

"I only have one for the state of Louisiana," I informed him.

"Well, Ms, I hate to tell you this, but it ain't much we can do to help you," he replied.

My heart seemed to splinter, right there, in the middle of his office, I broke down and cried. Perhaps he had children, for when he saw my reaction to his news, some of his coldness seemed to melt away.

"Now listen," he said finally. "I'm going to tell you how you might get her back. What grade is your daughter?" he asked. I told him and waited for his instructions.

"If you do as I tell you, you might be able to get her back. You've got to be ready to leave immediately, though. Make a list of all the schools she might likely attend. Since you're her mother, you have the right to visit the school. When you find out which one, simply stand outside and wait until she comes to you. When school is out, kidnap her."

"Kidnap my own child?" I thought to myself. As absurd as it sounded, if this was the only way I could have her back, I would do it. Leaving the DA's office, we immediately went to the bus station to get a ticket for her. Annie and I brought round trip tickets. We found out the bus left at five thirty that evening.

As soon as we returned back at the house, I got the phone book and looked under schools, making a list of all the elementary schools in the area. Making a list, we'd gone to about four schools before I finally got lucky.

Annie and Donice stayed outside in the car and waited for me, while I went inside to tell the principal that I had just arrived in town and couldn't wait to see my child. He sent someone to her classroom to get her. I remained as calm as possible, how I remained intact as I awaited her arrival, I do not know. It was the hardest thing I'd ever done in my life. When she finally appeared in the doorway, I couldn't wait, I ran to her, grabbing her up in my arms.

"Mommy, did you come to stay with my daddy?" she asked with excitement.

"We'll see, baby," I replied, feeling the principal's presence behind us.

I visited with her a little while and then let her return to her class. The principal told me that school let out at two forty-five. It was only eleven o'clock then. We still had plenty of time.

My heart was pounding with pure adrenaline as I ran back to the car. "I got to see her!" I exclaimed with excitement as I got in.

"You did?" they both asked in unison.

Donice lived in the neighborhood where the school was located, so I knew that that meant Albert lived not far away. We hurriedly returned to the house to make sure everything was packed and ready to go. At two forty-five, I was standing outside the school entrance when the bell rang. My heart was beating double-time by now. I kept imagining that Albert could come for her. "What would I do?" I wondered. I knew he would put up a fight. I didn't know how many children passed by, but after a few minutes when I still hadn't seen her, I became frantic with worry.

Then, as if a beacon in the night, there she was with her cousin Raymond, her aunt's son. Again, she was surprised to see me. I told Raymond I was taking Jennifer shopping and that his mother wanted him to come straight home. I took Jennifer by the hand and hurried to the car. I could see Raymond, still standing in the schoolyard, as we pulled away from the school.

We went straight to the bus station and had our bags checked in. I didn't know how long it would take Raymond to get home, but I was guessing, it wouldn't take long. I didn't know if Albert was off work or not, but I didn't want to risk him searching for us before we could get out of town.

"Annie, let's hide in the restroom," I suggested nervously. "We can stay there until the bus comes."

A few minutes later, when the dispatcher called out our bus, his voice was like that of a nightingale. "Annie, you go outside and scope the place to see if Albert is out there. If he's not, find out which line our bus is in?" I told her, keeping Jennifer's hand tucked securely in my own.

It seemed to take her forever to return. Jennifer occupied herself playing with the other children whose mother's were waiting also. It hadn't occurred to her what was about to happen. Finally, I saw Annie's face, beaming at the door. She beckoned for me to join her, and pointed to where we would board our bus.

"Come on, Bertha," Annie prompted.

"Somebody, God, help me," I said under my breath. Swiftly, I found my composure and ran for the bus. When I got to my seat my legs felt weak, limp, as if they were all muscle and tissue, no bone whatsoever. I fell into the seat and didn't move until the bus finally pulled into the

Oklahoma City station. I'd been too afraid to move before then, Albert might have seen me. I'd been too afraid to look out the window for the first hundred miles.

On the way into Dallas, Jennifer finally seemed to understand what we'd done. "Mom, where are we going?" she asked.

"We are going to Shreveport, baby," I replied calmly.

"But, Mom, I still have my books," she cried.

Although I felt bad, if her books were the only problem she found, we were doing okay. I began to congratulate myself. I explained to her that we had no other choice other than to take them with us for now.

"I want to go back to be with my daddy," she began crying again even harder than before.

"Honey, you mommy loves you and wants you with her," I told her.

"Mom, I don't want to go back there. I don't like Mr. Guy," she said.

Hmm, she didn't like Guy. That was something to think about, later. For now, I didn't ask her why she didn't like Guy, I was too tired to try. A few moments later, not much of anything could have gotten my attention, I fell off to sleep. Exhaustion finally claimed me as its victim.

When we arrived in Dallas, I called Guy and told him to pick us up at the bus station in Shreveport, giving him our arrival time. We arrived at midnight, and went straight to bed when we got home. Annie returned home early the next morning.

I got up to see Guy off to work, just as he'd been when we left, he was still acting strange. I had a few days off, so I figured we'd talk about everything and get things settled between us.

Sunday, Lois returned home and Monday, I put both girls back in school. Later Monday evening, I prepared a lovely dinner to celebrate the reunion of my family, hoping to surprise Guy with the gaiety when he came in from work. We were finally going to celebrate Jennifer's return.

Early painting of wagon going up Cooper Hill

15. Guy is Unfaithful

By eleven thirty that night, I was frantic. Guy, normally home by six-thirty, hadn't come home yet, and it was now almost midnight, six hours later than his usual.

I paced the floor anxiously waiting to hear news of what had happened to him. When the phone rang a few minutes later, I jumped to answer it. There was a woman's voice asking to speak to Guy. To tell you the truth, she sounded just as surprised to hear my voice, as I was to hear hers.

Thirty minutes later, when Guy finally arrived home, unhurt and unconcerned, I told him that a woman had called for him. He didn't bother to comment. Frustrated by his nonchalance, I told him that I'd been worried by his tardiness tonight and I'd appreciate an explanation. He calmly informed me that he'd stopped off for a drink with the boys, and without further explanation, he went to bed.

I was left there, frustrated, angry, and suspicious. All of these emotions were battling for supremacy, and I wanted somewhere to vent. The more I thought about the phone call, the more the voice sounded familiar, as if it were someone I knew, personally. But why would this woman be calling my husband?

Oh well, I was tired and didn't feel like questioning it any further. Everyone else had already gone to bed, I might as well join them. Stress and anger were fighting to keep me awake constantly these days, why should tonight be any different.

Mable, my next door neighbor, called around nine the next morning. "Hi, girl," she crowed. "I'm glad you're back okay. Were you able to get Jennifer back from that crazy ass fool?" she asked.

"Yeah, girl," I answered, wondering what she really wanted. I knew it wasn't to commiserate with me about Albert, she could have cared less unless it inconvenienced her in some way.

"Say, I need to borrow some sugar from you," she said. "Until I can get to the store," she added.

I should have known she'd want something, she always did. "No problem, come on over," I said.

"Girl, you sure do have this house looking good," she commented as she walked through to the kitchen, her shifty eyes going from one corner to the other, as she slid her stubby, brown body down in a chair at the kitchen table.

Mable was one of those people you knew you couldn't trust as soon as you met her. She was shifty, and could never look you in the eye, regardless of what she was telling you, which always made me feel as if she were lying. She smiled this sickening smile all of the time that made me sick to my stomach, she had entirely too many gold teeth in her mouth to smile that much. The only thing she really had going for her was her long hair. Her legs looked like two toothpicks stuck in a hamburger.

"Girl, let me tell you, that black, ass nigga' I got is talking about marriage," she said drawing my attention. "That shit is for the birds. I ain't going to mess up my welfare check to marry him!" she declared, as if she were talking about millions of dollars here. "If he keep that shit up, I'll put his ass out. He don't make that much money no way," she said as if she were in any position to turn her nose up at the man. At least he had a job. "Girl, you don't go anyplace do you?" she asked suddenly before I could comment on her last remark. "Damn if I'd be sitting around this house all the time. These men keep their asses in the streets. Hell, I take my ass out every Friday or Saturday night," she declared.

"I don't care about going out," I replied honestly. Generally, I was pretty happy with what I had at home. Sure, there were a few problems, but we'd get them worked out soon enough.

"Girl, give me a cup of that coffee," she demanded. "Shit, if I worked like you do, damn if I wouldn't go out sometimes," she continued on her tirade. "These damn niggas will take your ass for granted. That's one of the reasons I don't work," she declared. "Damn, work don't like me, and I don't like it," she said laughing at her own warped sense of right and wrong.

I couldn't figure out what was going on. Mable was talking more to me today than she had in the entire time that I'd known her. What she was doing today was totally out of character for her. It wasn't as if we were friends, far from it. Mable was one of those women it didn't pay to turn your back on.

I was just about to ask her to leave when she took care of it for me by volunteering to go. I'd really tried being neighborly to her, which was more than any of the other women in the neighborhood did. Most of them didn't even speak to her because she kept so much shit going. She was down on every woman around who was working and trying to accomplish something in life. It seemed as if she considered hard work one of the seven deadly sins.

After she'd gone, I was finally able to catch my breath and begin to think about what had happened the night before. Until then, I had been so puzzled over the fact that a woman had called Guy at that time of night that I hadn't really concentrated on the caller's identity. But I now knew with certainty who the late night caller had been.

That evening when the children came in from school, I questioned them about the woman caller. At first, they just looked first at each other, then at me saying nothing. Then, after a period of silence, confirmation came.

"Yes, Mom," they answered in unison.

I was furious. The nerve of the woman. How dare she call my home, to speak to my husband. I couldn't wait for Guy to get home. It was a good thing I had taken a few days off work, it looked like I was going to be needing them.

I was in Guy's face as soon as he walked through the door. I didn't give him time to get settled before I confronted him. "Why is Mable calling you?" I asked through clenched teeth.

"Hell woman, you can't give a nigga' time to get in the house before you start some shit," he shouted as he walked past me, slamming his lunch bucket on the table as he went.

"The word is out that she throws herself at every woman's husband," I screamed, unwilling to have him ignore me, and painfully aware that he had evaded my question. "I never dreamed you would be one of them," I screamed into his face, staring into his eyes unflinchingly.

"Bertha, go somewhere and get the hell out of my face, before I do some-thing to you I might be sorry for," he threatened between clenched teeth visibly trying to control his temper. "That damn woman ain't been calling me," he said his anger finally coming to the fore. Then, without another word, he walked out of the door, got into his car and sped away. He didn't return until around one o'clock the following morning.

A month later, he left home on a Saturday night with the excuse that he was going around the corner to have a drink with the boys. An hour after he had gone, I went out to sit on the front step. When I looked down the street, I noticed Mable, all dressed up in her red, sleazy dress walking toward the intersection of the street. She didn't notice me sitting there in the dark, and continued walking, almost to the intersection when a car pulled up and she got in — into *my* car with *my husband*.

I sat there in the darkness, fuming, humiliated, ready to murder either one of them, or both, and I do mean this literally.

"That lying dog!" I muttered through clenched teeth.

The bastard had lied to me. God knows, had there been another car at my disposal, I know I would have ridden around until I found them. I was determined to wait up for him. At four-thirty, I heard the car door slam. When he came in, I questioned him about where he'd been all night. He lied, of course. He told me that he'd had car trouble, and promptly rolled over and went sound to sleep.

Once again, I was left feeling angry and humiliated, each emotion battling for supremacy in my already stressed out mind. With no one to vent my troubles and emotions to, I finally gave up and went to bed.

I didn't confront the subject again until a weekend later. I wanted to wait until the girls were away because I didn't want them to hear us argue. But as soon as we were alone, I attacked. It was time we got a few things straight, namely what was going on between him and Mable.

"Guy, when I'm at work, are you here with the girls?" I began.

"What do you think, Bertha?" he asked nonchalantly.

"Well, Guy, I have to tell you I don't believe you are. I know for a fact that you're messing with Mable, I saw you pick her up," I finally exploded.

True to form, he didn't say a word, just picked up his comb from the dresser top, combed his hair and rushed out of the door. That was it, until two o'clock the following morning when pots hitting the floor awakened me. I rushed into the kitchen to find Guy, throwing pots from one end of the kitchen to the other.

"Get in here!" he shouted. What in the hell is this you cooked? This stuff looks like shit," he said with pure venom.

I was still trying to determine what, other than his tirade, was the problem. He had liver, gravy, rice and green beans from dinner all over the kitchen, both on the floor and walls. He continued ranting and raving as he stumbled over the pots he'd strewn all over the room toward me. For a brief second, I thought for sure he was going to strike me as he continued to stumble, ranting and raving louder as he drew closer to me, but instead he stumbled on into the bedroom, shoving me out of his way as he stumbled past me.

I stood there blatantly dumbfounded. This couldn't possibly be the man I married. "God, why is this happening to me? I can't get over one sore before another one pops up to replace it." I groaned. "When will it all end?" I wondered silently to myself.

Guy and I didn't speak for two weeks. A month later he came home from one of his late night outings. Once again I heard him slamming things in the kitchen, though this time I only heard the refrigerator door slamming. After a few minutes, I heard him come into the room.

"Wake up," he roared in his drunkenness.

I looked over at the bedside clock and saw that it was only two o'clock. "What is it?" I snapped, tired of his behavior of later.

"Bitch, get out of that damn bed and fix me some ice water!" he demanded.

"Why do I have to get up and fix you some damn ice water?" I asked him incredulously.

"Because I want your damn smart talking ass to do it," he screamed. Finally, he ran over to the bed and snatched the cover off of me and reached down pulling me up by my hair. It was then that I noticed his hand seemingly in slow motion as it descended toward my face. He held my hair so tight and hit me so hard, I felt as if the whole two hundred pounds of his body weight had been thrown up side my face and head. There was no use trying to fight him back, he was unreachable, anger consumed him and there was nothing sane about him, and I lay there screaming, terror overwhelming me.

The sounds of my screaming woke the girls, but that didn't stop him. My poor babies stood there watching this man beat me like a dog, yelling at the beast, "Leave my mommy alone."

Finally, he did stop, then slammed back out the door. I lay there between my daughters, my eye and lips swollen, blood and handfuls of my hair surrounding us.

The next day was Sunday, I stayed in bed all day long, to ashamed to face the kids, or anyone else. It seemed as though he didn't care if the children had seen him beating me. I don't think he really cared that his abuse had been witnessed.

I thought about leaving as I lay there wondering why this was happening to me. Then reality set in, I had no place to go. Mama had no room for the girls and me, we were stuck.

Late that evening, Guy returned home. His eyes were red and his breath smelled strongly of alcohol. I was terrified that he would begin beating me again, but instead, he looked at me and began sobbing and asking for forgive-ness.

"I was drunk, and angry because you accused me of having an affair with Mable," he said "I love you, Bertha," he swore tenderly.

Here was another side of him I'd never seen before. This convincing declaration of love was something I didn't know he was capable of. I believed him, everything he said I believed him.

That Monday, I wore sunglasses to work just as if nothing had happened.

One evening, Guy came into the kitchen and told me that Lois was giving him problems.

"She been playing with them little boys. I found her with one of them under the house," he said the epitome of fatherly concern.

I became seriously concerned. I couldn't let what happened to me happen to my child. I was so upset, I spanked her. She didn't say anything to me about it, but she stood there looking at me with pure unadulterated hatred in her eyes.

I realize now that I should have investigated the matter further, instead of simply reacting. Guy never complained about Jennifer, so I saw no reason to spank her.

More and more, as time went on, Jennifer and Lois began to fight. I couldn't determine the cause, regardless of how hard I tried. I'd thought I'd straightened things out, everything in my house, all relationships had been balanced, I thought, erroneously. I did everything I could to make sure my daughters knew that I loved them both.

"I hate you, Mama, and Guy," I overheard Lois saying to Jennifer.

What was that about? I understood why she hated Guy so much, but why Jennifer and myself? I can't begin to describe the pain I felt at her revelation, though she'd been talking to her sister when she'd said it.

I was working nights around this time. I knew I needed to be home with my daughters at night, but I didn't see where I had a choice in the matter. There was a possibility I could be transferred to days, but the waiting list was so long, I didn't see that happening anytime soon.

Although I knew that I wasn't the only woman whose husband had betrayed them with other women, I was still sorely depressed about what Guy had done. My friend Mary told me to stop blaming myself, pointing out that my working nights had nothing to do with Guy's infidelity.

"If he wants to see another woman, regardless of whether you work nights or not, he would do as he pleased, he'd find a way," she told me.

Sooner than I'd expected, I was offered a position on days. My prayers had finally been answered. I could be at home with my husband and children, just as it should be. I was so excited about my news, I wanted to surprise Guy with it. I waited until the following Monday.

I was so happy, I couldn't help starting the day with a smile. Without saying a word, I got out of bed and began dressing for work right along beside him.

"Where are you going?" he asked.

"To work," I replied my excitement bubbling over, my grin growing even wider.

He really didn't say much of anything to my announcement, disappointing me. I thought he'd be thrilled, but he wasn't. He walked out of the room to the front of the house, then came back into the bedroom, his smile no longer feigned, but absent. "Do you have a ride to work?" he asked glaring at me.

"Yeah, that car that's parked out front. You are going to work this morning, aren't you?" I asked not understanding the problem.

"Yeah, I'm going, but I have some more people riding with me," he said.

"You never told me you had riders," I said growing angrier by the minute.

This was not happening.

"Bertha, you are not riding to work with me this morning," he informed me. "You should have told me earlier," he snapped, walking out the door, leaving me standing in the middle of the floor speechless and hurt.

I didn't know anyone that I could call for a ride on the day shift. The only people I knew at work were those who worked nights. Nothing was happening as I'd hoped. Lois seemed to be growing farther and farther away from me, and nothing I said or did seemed to reach her.

And now my job had become a source of aggravation for Guy. I couldn't believe it, after three years of pleading with personnel for a position on the day shift, I would have to call in my first day.

We'd moved to a two-bedroom apartment on Pleasant Street by then. It was a much nicer place than the one we'd moved from. The grounds were beautiful with flowers all around. There was also more space, something that I was grateful for. The landlady, whom we all called Aunt Josie, lived next door. She was a very sweet woman and she was almost like a second mother to practically everyone in the neighborhood.

Leola, my next-door neighbor, had two children, a girl and a boy. She was a nurse who worked nights. We got to be good friends during that time. She had style and class. She was of medium build, about five feet seven, with the most beautiful brown skin. She was beautiful inside as well as outside. I loved her hair, it was black and thick. I used to love it when she had it done, it always had so much body to it. She was the happiest, jolliest person I'd ever met, and she kept me laughing about something all the time, regardless of how down I was. She and her husband had been divorced for several years, forcing her into the role of single parent.

Guy continued hanging out the old neighborhood, no longer caring who knew about his affair with Mable. Somehow, I convinced myself to accept things as they were.

Aunt Josie was good person to talk to, and I often found myself crying on her shoulder. I was convinced Guy would have been happier had I not gotten off the night shift. At least my children were happy that I was home with them. The evening of the day he'd refused to take me to work, he came home and took his bath, changed his clothes and left again, never saying a word to me, treating me as if I weren't there.

The next morning, we rode to work in tension filled silence. He listened to the radio, and I looked out of the window.

Downward Spiral

16. Downward Spiral

THINGS CONTINUED TO GET WORSE. *God, you know that I'm trying to be a good mother and wife,* I'd think on so many occasions. Every time I turned around, there seemed to be one disaster after another. Regardless of how hard I tried, I couldn't seem to get it together. I'd somehow, without realizing it, lost touch with the strong black woman that I'd become, the woman who'd once sworn that she would never allow anyone to drain her of power ever again. But that wasn't who I was anymore — the fight was now gone.

I lay in bed one night and listened as Guy came in late, something that had become the norm now. But that night was slightly different, instead of going into the kitchen, he slammed into the bedroom and flipped the light on. Then he turned, coming over to the bed and snatched the covers off of me. I thought, at first, that he was about to climb into bed beside me. I couldn't really see what he was doing because the bright light in the room was still shining in my eyes.

"Guy, turn that bright light off," I demanded. "Why did you pull the covers off me, anyway?" I asked growing angry by his abrupt behavior.

" I want your damn ass wide awake, bitch," he snapped, something that should have set the alarm bells going off inside. "Just wake up!" he continued. "I need to talk to you, bitch."

"Guy, what could you possibly have to talk about this time of night?" I asked through clenched teeth.

"You can play crazy, if you want to bitch," he shouted, as if I should know what he was yelling about instinctively. "Who the hell you been fucking?" he shouted. I was shocked before, I was now dumbfounded.

"What are you talking about?" I asked cautiously, the full impact of what his behavior could foretell finally hitting me.

"You nasty ass bitch!" he yelled as if he hadn't heard me. "You done gave me the clap!" he shouted out in his rage.

"I gave you what?" he asked, fear subsiding as horror took its place.

"I'm going to ask you one more time. Who you been fucking, bitch?" he asked again.

"I haven't been with anyone and you know it," I cried in my defense. The situation was rapidly getting out of control, and I knew that if I didn't change things soon, they would only worsen.

"Bitch, if you keep lying to me, I'm going to kick your damn ass," he roared, his body looming over me threateningly.

"Guy, I've told you the truth, I haven't been with anyone," I said calmly.

"Bitch, my damn dick been running for days," he said repeatedly as I attempted to go into the bathroom. He grabbed me suddenly and with determined force, slammed his fist into my nose.

The force of the blow sent me sailing across the bedroom floor. I lay there, blood running from my mouth and nose, and watch in sick fascination as he raised his foot and kicked me in my stomach.

The pain was instantly explosive, I could barely breathe, and a dark abyss seemed to loom just ahead, threatening to consume me. "Please, don't kick me anymore," I pleaded breathlessly.

"You get your nasty ass to that doctor Monday," he ordered. "I done made an appointment for you myself," he informed me then.

"I'll go," I swore barely above a whisper. Then suddenly I realized something, I neither knew what the clap was, or how I could have given it to him. I thought there must sure have been something wrong with me, so I pleaded with him to tell me how I gave it to him.

"You let the doctor tell your filthy ass," he sneered.

I tossed and turned all that night, holding my aching stomach and trying to make sense of the whole thing. I was so glad the children were gone for the weekend. I didn't want them to have to witness this beating, not like the last time, and I certainly didn't want them to know about this latest twist in our little drama.

Monday morning, confused and humiliated, I went to the doctor's office just as Guy had ordered. My body was so sore, I could hardly walk because of the beating I had endured over the weekend. I don't know why it didn't occur to me to have the doctor to check out my bruises, but it didn't. I was too embarrassed.

Humiliation had me almost tongue tied when I told them my name, and that my husband had sent me. The doctor asked about the bruises he could see, but I told him that I'd fallen down the steps. I refused to admit that Guy had done it. When he gave me the shots, I didn't even bother to ask what they were for, I just let him give them to me and left, as silent as I'd been when I came in, but relieved the ordeal was over.

Still confused about what the clap was, I called my brother, Odell, the next day and asked him.

"Have you been having sex with another man?" he asked openly.

"No!" I answered, shocked that he would even ask such a thing.

"Then you haven't given him a damn thing," he said vehemently. "You tell that bastard that I said so, too," he finished.

That was the first time that I'd told a member of my family anything about what was going on in my marriage to Guy. I was too afraid to tell Guy anything Odell had told me, I was afraid he'd beat me again and I didn't know what he'd do if he found out I'd called my brother. But I was even more confused now. Why would Guy want to beat me for something he had done himself? I should have known the answer: that was his way of ensuring that I went to the doctor.

I began drinking around that time. I needed something to ease the pain, and I had no one to turn to. I drank every day when I got home from work. I drank the most on weekends. There were times when I drank so muck I'd black out. Sometimes the kids would find me lying on the floor, or the couch in my own urine and vomit. The worst part was that I couldn't even remember how long I'd been there.

When I was sober, I'd tell myself that things would get better. I no longer had the confidence that I could make it on my own, so leaving wasn't an option. Guy's beatings became more brutal and more frequent, each attack worse than the last. But he paid the bill and made sure food was on the table and I didn't want to go back to the struggle I'd faced before we were married. So, I remained.

At the time, there were no support groups for battered women, no shelters for them to turn to when things became too dangerous in their homes. There was no support from church groups, either. The only therapy I received was talking to Mama, on those weekends I would drive to Dallas. But as much as I loved our time together, I never said a word about my problems.

I didn't know it then, but I was mentally and physically abused. The more abuse I suffered, the worse my drinking became, and the more I craved being alone. I was no longer there for my children, I was too busy trying to take care of me, just getting out of bed everyday was a struggle. I knew something wasn't quite right about that, but at the time, I couldn't think straight.

I spent quite a bit of my time and energy trying to make things run smoothly so that Guy wouldn't beat me. He no longer considered me as anything but an ignorant motherf--r which he called me so frequently. It became a common name for me. I no longer did anything right. Also he'd figured out by now that I was drinking far too much. Sometimes, he'd even drink with me. I'd sober up only to find him gone.

Women of the field

Old Man Cotton

17. Even More Pain and Confusion

Guy and I were invited to a retirement dinner later that year. One of our friends was honoring her mother and invited us to join them. I was leery about going, Guy's behavior had become too erratic, but being his usual overbearing self, he insisted we go. Actually, I was surprised he wanted to go with me, he ceased taking me out a long time ago.

When we arrived at the party, everything was going well enough. I even began to enjoy myself, it had been so long since I'd been out socially. Finally, deciding to make the best out of my situation, I began mingling with my old friends, meeting new people, and fully enjoying myself for the first time in a long time. I was even capable of giving the retiree my heartfelt congratulations on her achievement.

After about an hour had gone by, I began to relax even more. Everything was going far better than I'd dreamed they would, that is until I bumped into Mable. The night then took a decided turn for the worse.

There was no longer any pretense between the two of us. By now, she knew with certainty that I knew everything about her and Guy. I glanced across the room then and met Guy's eyes. I knew by the expression on his face that he was just as aware of her presence as I was. I could tell by his grin that he was daring me to make a scene.

Later on that night, as I stood alone at the bar, Ray, one of Guy's friends walked over and began talking to me. "Bertha, you're sure pretty," he complimented.

Smiling politely, I tried to brush him off. When that didn't work, I chatted about anything trivial, commenting needlessly about how nice the party was. Ray had had quite a bit to drink during the night, I knew, and as I glanced Guy heading our way, I knew there was going to be trouble. Guy made it over to where we were. Ray grabbed his arm and began to tell.

"Man, you sure do have a pretty wife," Ray said.

"Yeah, man," Guy snapped angrily. snatching his arms out of the other man's grasp.

"Man, how do you go out and leave this pretty lady at home, alone?" he continued foolishly taunting Guy. I prayed desperately for him to stop. I knew that someone was going to pay for his behavior, and that that someone was going to be me.

"What the hell's going on?" he asked pulling me aside. "As soon as a nigga' take your ignorant ass out, I find you hangin' all over another nigga," he said accusing me of instigating Ray's behavior. "Why can't you act like a lady?" he snapped, fury burning in the depths of his eyes.

I foolishly tired to explain to him that Ray came over on his own, that I'd had nothing to do with his behavior, but Guy didn't want to hear anything I had to say in my own defense. Rushing into the next room, he grabbed our coats. As we passed Ray on our way out of the door, Guy stopped. "You say she pretty, man?" he asked with an evil grin. "Well, the next time you see her, she won't be. Take a good look at her now," he shouted back as he threw me into the car.

As he pulled away from the curb, the car tires screeched, the engine sounded like that of a racecar. I could sense the unleashed fury in him rolling in waves to engulf me. "God, I don't believe this, he's going to kill me," I thought silently, fear eating away at my insides. Had we not been driving so fast, I would have jumped out.

Within a block of the house, he slammed on the brakes. The car screeched to a halt as he swerved to the side of the street.

"Bertha," he began yelling, "do you think you are pretty?" he asked not waiting for my response.

"I'll tell you what, Ms. Bitch, look at yourself in that mirror up there," he said, reaching up to pull the rearview mirror down toward my face. "Take a damn good look, cause when I get through with you, bitch, you'll be too ashamed to walk the streets," he shouted.

"Please, Guy, don't hit me," I pleaded.

"You better ask somebody about me, bitch. I don't take no shit," he said, spit flying in his venomous tirade. "I cut that damn bitch in California," he belatedly informed me. "I cut her fucking breast off. You done had it good," he shouted, grabbing my hair and pushing my face into the mirror. Finally, he snatched my head backward and forcing it down and securing it between the car's bucket seats, my face turned up. He hit me repeatedly, making certain that every last hate filled strike was on target.

After awhile, I could no longer see. Pleading with him to stop only seemed to cause the beating to worsen. When I realized that he had no intention of stopping by any of my pleas, I held my breath and pretended to be dead. I held my breath for so long, I must have passed out.

He finally realized I was no longer pleading with him to stop, and that I was, in fact, no longer breathing. With his hands raised, he paused, then I felt a gust of cold air hit my face as he threw the door open wide. I could hear him outside the car, but I didn't know what he was doing, I couldn't see him.

"Bertha," I heard a few minutes later as he came to the passenger's side of the car. "Bertha, if you don't stop acting a damn fool, I'm going to give you something to act a fool for," he promised.

I continued to feign unconsciousness. Finally, getting back into the car, he swiftly pulled back onto the street and drove home, still calling my name as we went along. I felt him carrying me into the house, lying me down across the bed. When I still didn't respond, he went back and forth into the bathroom wetting a towel, trying to revive me, as if he was so concerned about my welfare.

"Come on, Bertha," I heard him saying, pleading with me to respond to the man who'd done his best to beat me into a stupor. "Baby, look what you made me do," he cried, rubbing my head with the cool, wet cloth. The thought, *what I did?* filtered through the pain and chaos in my head.

By this time, my eyes were swollen shut and I couldn't have seen anything if I'd wanted to, the pounding in my head was reaching a new plateau by then. Finally, after he'd crooned and pleaded, I felt safe enough to move. The first thing I did was rush to a mirror to assess the damage he'd done.

"Bertha, I didn't mean to hurt you," he said hurriedly, fear apparent in his voice.

I didn't say anything to that, I just continued pulling myself up, trying to get into the bathroom. The pain was so intense, I felt as if I had two faces, each of them suffering their own torment. When I reached the bathroom, I used my fingers to pry my eyes open. My blood was everywhere, all over my blouse and pants, there wasn't an inch of me that wasn't covered.

"Oh, my God," I screamed in horror at the person I saw in the mirror looking back at me. Who was the poor, battered creature, I wondered, refusing to believe it could have been me. My nose and eyes seemed to meet together in the center of my face. I had two sets of lips; blood ran profusely from my mouth and nose.

Frightened for my life, I ran into the children's room and yelled for them to wake up and call the police. I could tell from the horrified looks on their faces they didn't yet recognize me, the recognition dawned.

"Mom, what happened to you?" they asked in unison.

The police were called, and when they arrived they came into the house and asked what was going on. They didn't bother talking to me. They took Guy outside and stood out there talking to him. Finally, one came back into the house and informed me that there was nothing he could do, since, after all, this was a domestic quarrel. Wordlessly, I followed him to the door. I couldn't believe that was it, they weren't going to help me.

"Can't you see he almost killed me," I finally shouted desperately. "Look at me, do something," I pleaded with the officer.

"You'll work things out," he assured me. Was he out of his mind!?

They hadn't been gone a good five minutes before Guy grabbed me and pushed me back into the house.

"This will teach you to call the law on me, bitch," he shouted raising his arm, a piece of wood that he'd torn from an old bar stool we had extending from his hand. The first blow connected with neck, just below my earlobe. I could hear the children screaming for him to stop.

"Daddy, don't hit my mommy," were the last words I heard before I sank into peaceful oblivion.

I must have been taken to the emergency room. As I slipped in and out of consciousness, I could hear the doctors and nurses around me, working diligently on me.

"What happened, ma'am?" I heard one of them asking me, as they shined a light into my eye causing my head to increase the pounding tempo that had begun as soon as conscious began returning. "What is your name? What day is it?" they continued.

I could feel them sticking needles into my arms, but I still had no idea how I'd gotten there or what had happened after I'd blacked out. I glimpsed Leola, my neighbor, standing over me as all of the chaos went on around us. Through the fog of my swollen eyelids, I could see Leola wore a look of disgust on her face.

I later learned that it had been Leola who had called the ambulance. She'd directed them to take me to the hospital where she worked.

"Do you want me to call your family?" she'd asked, concern and sympathy apparent in her voice.

"No!" I shouted abruptly. "I don't want them to see me like this," I tried to explain on a calmer note.

"But, Bertha, your family needs to know what this damn man has done to you!" she shouted furiously.

"I just don't know," I said, not wanting to discuss it further. "Where are my children?" I asked suddenly remembering the girls had been there to witness Guy's brutality.

"They're next door with Junior and Sheila," she informed me, calming at least one of my fears.

"Bertha, they can't give you anything right now. You've got to go to X-ray first," she explained with sympathy.

Finally, I was handed a cup of coffee by a nurse who ordered me to drink it.

"I don't like coffee," I informed her. "I'd really like something to stop my head and neck from hurting," I snapped.

"Ma'am, we don't want you to go to sleep until we check the X-rays for in-juries. Maybe after the doctor has checked them, we'll be able to give you something.

I finally made it to X-ray, then I was forced to wait again. Leola kept forcing coffee down me, insisting that she was only trying to keep me awake. When the doctor finally came into the room, he pulled Leola to the side. When she came back in, she told me that I was going to have to stay there for a few days.

"I can't stay here," I shouted. "I have to go home to my children," I insisted.

I was admitted, and nurses were in and out of my room all night, asking me the same questions over and over again. I would have gotten a lot more rest if they'd given me something for the pain and left me alone. My neck and head were killing me the next morning.

"Mrs. Harris, you have had a blow to your face and neck," a doctor informed me the following morning, as if I needed to be told. "Nothing was broken, you're just bruised real bad and have a concussion," he continued. I've instructed the nurses to give you ice bags to reduce the swelling some."

"I can hardly move it."

"Your husband hit you with something, I'm told, hit you with something," he said the anger in his voice surprising me.

It was then that I remembered that Guy had hit me with the wooden leg of the broken bar stool. "I'll prescribe something for the pain, that should help you relax," he assured me as he turned to go.

As soon as he left the room and the door closed, I began to cry. I ignored the pain to climb out of my bed and felt my way into the bathroom. I could only see my face vaguely, but what I saw made me turn the light back off, I didn't want to see anymore. When the nurse came in, I informed her that I didn't want any lights on, nor did I want to see anyone.

The next morning when the doctor returned, I told him the same thing. Later that day, when Leola came in she found all the lights off and the drapes closed, just as I'd requested. She pulled the drapes open and stood there looking at me. Wordlessly, I began to cry.

"Now, Bertha, it's going to be alright," she said reassuringly. I doubt if she believed what she was saying anymore than I did.

"I don't want to look at myself," I cried softly.

"But, Bertha, you've got to. Come on now, get up, you can't get well staying in that bed feeling sorry for yourself," she demanded, pulling me forward.

"I don't want to get up," I insisted. "Just close those drapes and leave me alone, please."

"No!" she stated adamantly. "I am not going to leave you alone. I called your mother and she will be here tomorrow," she snapped as if daring me to get angry, to feel anything but pity for myself.

"I've told you, I don't want to see her," I snapped.

Didn't she understand? I was too ashamed for Mama to see me in this shape. She thought the world of Guy. He'd convinced her he was a good man, acting charming and kind around her, going to church and singing in the choir, the perfect husband. Everyone thought we were the perfect family.

I covered my face the next day as soon as I heard mama and Leola at the door. "Is she asleep?" mama asked Leola softly.

"She might be," I heard Leola respond, as she pulled the drapes open.

I felt the bed give as Mama eased her body down beside me. Gently, she pulled the cover away from my face. "My poor baby," she cried when she saw the ravaged flesh she'd uncovered. "Why did he do this to her?" she sobbed.

Leola came over and comforted her. "She's going to be fine, Ms. Annie Bell," she assured her.

"Just look at her face," Mama said low trying not to wake me.

"Why don't we go get something to eat?" Leola suggested. "By the time we get back, she should be awake.

I lay there until I heard the door close, and then I jumped up and closed the drapes, going into the bathroom. I could see the swelling had gone down some, but my eye sight was returning to it's original clarity much more rapidly, although there was some talk that I would have to see an ophthalmologist for any possible residual damage to them. When the doctor came around later that evening, he told me that a specialist had already been consulted.

Finally, by the next day, I was feeling somewhat better. I stayed awake and visited with Mama most of the day, but I was still unable to look at her. She did her best to reassure me, telling me that she would take care of the children and me and that I shouldn't worry about Guy because he had moved out.

Mama had only been gone a few hours that same day when Guy paid me a visit. He came in with an arm full of flowers and a card, but he couldn't even look me in the eyes. The whole time he was there, he'd spent looking out of the window, sipping out of the bottle of alcohol he'd brought with him.

"Bertha," he began finally. "You know that I had to be drunk to have done this to you, he rationalized. "Plus, I'm jealous of you. You know that. I love you, Bertha,"

I was sick to death of his lies. I called the nurse and had them to put him out. I don't know how, but he always had the ability to make me feel that I was somehow responsible for his angry outbursts and the beatings he forced on me. I lay there trying to imagine how I would face people when I left the hospital.

The following day, Leola had had enough. She literally dragged me to the bathroom and made me look at myself in the mirror. "You see there, Bertha, the swelling is gone down, and it ain't nothing wrong with your eyes except they blood clotted. Now, though it might take sometime to clear up, you'll be fine."

Two days before Christmas I was still in the hospital, but I was ready to go home. When the doctor came around, I begged him to let me go home. He agreed, but only after making me promise to stay inside, and to come to his office for a visit the day after Christmas. Mama stayed and shared Christmas with us. I was more than certain that had Leola not told her about what had happened between Guy and myself, she would never have known. I know I wouldn't have told her, and I doubted very seriously if Guy would have volunteered the information.

Nevertheless, just having Mama with us that Christmas was worth more than any gift I could have been given. I loved the fact that she was there making sure that I was safe.

It wasn't until after she left that Guy began calling the house, and he called everyday. He talked so pitiful, I almost felt sorry for him. "I ain't never been away from my family for Christmas," he groaned in his pathetic whining voice. "Did you make any pecan pies?" he asked me, trying to sound cheerful.

"Bertha, I don't know what's wrong with me," he finally said, sounding emotionally distraught. All I can say is that I'm the biggest damn fool in town."

I didn't reply, just returned the phone to its cradle. I'd heard all of this before, I didn't want to hear any of it, not ever again.

"Bertha — why? Why would he do that to you?" my friend, Mary, asked one day when she came by to see me. Mary and I had become friends through my job, and when she came by that day and saw what Guy had done to me, she began to cry.

"I don't know why, Mary," I answered honestly. "I wish to God I knew why he beats me."

"Bertha, please, don't take him back. I'm afraid he is going to kill you one day. Your doctor told me that he almost killed you this time," she told me frantically. "I came to the hospital this time, you know, but when I looked into your room and saw what he had done to you, I couldn't stand to see you like that, so I just left," she informed me candidly.

A month later, I'd allowed Guy to charm me into allowing him to move back home. I knew I was making a mistake, but something inside of me couldn't, or wouldn't, let go. Deep down inside, I truly believed I wouldn't make it without him, and I was afraid to try. Then too, by then he'd convinced me that no one else wanted me, and that if I ever left him, my ignorant ass would go to the damn dogs. I believed every word of it. I'd convinced myself to accept my decision by reminding myself that Guy and I had already managed to save the money for a down payment on a house. And I really wanted my children to finish growing up in a real home of our own. Guy's mother had given us the land we needed to build on. We were set to go. Allowing him to come home was the only logical decision I could have made, I argued to myself.

Baptism near Cooper Hill

18. The Beast Hits Home

GUY HAD BEEN BACK HOME THREE WEEKS WHEN ONE MORNING AFTER WALKING THE GIRLS TO THE DOOR, MAKING SURE THEY GOT TO SCHOOL, I NOTICED A NOTE LYING ON THE BAR. It was addressed to me, in Lois's handwriting. Although I'd been told that my eyesight would heal, it hadn't completed its process yet, so I was having a hard time trying to read her handwriting. Frustrated with my failed efforts, I gave up and went next door to ask Leola to read the letter for me. She took the letter from me, and as she read it, I noticed that her hands began to tremble uncontrollably.

"Bertha, you'd better sit down," she said softly.

"What is it, Leola?" I asked.

"It's Guy, Bertha. According to this note, he's been molesting Lois," she shouted.

"What do you mean, Leola?" I asked; certain that I didn't want to hear the answer.

"He's been having sex with her," she said bluntly.

Leola was a nurse and knew the terminology that I didn't understand, but it did finally dawn on me what she was talking about. My legs became weak; they felt like liquid as they slid from beneath me, no longer able to bear my weight. My heart felt as if something was ripping it out, as only a wild beast could do. The physical abuse I had taken from Guy had been nothing compared to this emotional pain I was now dealing with. I felt emotionally depleted, as if I had nothing else to give. I was on empty.

"Why? Why, why would he want to do that to a child?" I kept asking myself.

"Bertha, what do you want me to do?" Leola asked.

I heard her, but I just couldn't answer her, I didn't have the words to say it. I was doing the best I knew how to comprehend what had happened, imagining Guy with my baby. I sat there staring off into space, praying that this was only a nightmare, that I would soon wake up and find that none of it was really true.

So this was the reason that Lois had been acting so strange. Why hadn't she come to me before now? It had never occurred to me that Guy would stoop that low. Mr. John might have been a loser in many ways, but he'd never even looked at me in a sexual way. How could I have let this happen to my child? I didn't want it to be true, I pleaded and bargained with God, but it was still there when I opened my eyes, still a reality. It clearly was the Beast.

I don't remember how I got back to the house that afternoon. I'd been in a daze since the moment Leola had read that letter. That evening when the kids got home from school, I stayed in my room until I thought I'd pulled myself together enough to talk them logically. It hurt so bad, I stood there struggling to find the right words to say. How do you talk to your child about something this horrid?

When I finally pulled myself together, I forced myself out of the room. I found them sitting at the kitchen table studying. Lois knew I had something on my mind, she continued working, avoiding making eye contact. She wouldn't even look up toward me.

"How long has it been going on?" I finally managed to ask.

"Mom, he's been touching me every since we lived in the other house," she cried.

"Every since we lived in the other house?" I cried breathlessly, my heart pounding against the walls of my ribs, trying to break the constriction. "I don't understand, Lois, where was I?" I asked, when I could again speak. "Jennifer, has he touched you, too?" I asked with dread.

"No, Mom," she answered. I thanked God and all the Saints. "He sometimes treats me mean, though. That's why I didn't want to come home," she added.

"Did you ever see him do that to Lois?" I asked, still unable to say the word "sex" out loud. "Lois, why didn't you tell me?" I pleaded patiently.

"Mom, he told me that if I told you, he would kill you. Every time he beat you, it was after I'd threatened to tell you," she cried. "He would come into our room at night after Jennifer had fallen off to sleep. Sometimes I would try to sleep with my arms around her, hoping maybe she would wake up, but she never did, and he wouldn't leave me alone."

"Lois, Guy told me that you were under the house with some boys one time, was that the truth?" I asked, thinking back to that time when I whipped her because of what he'd told me. I never gave her a chance to defend herself.

"No, mom, that wasn't true," she said, pain obvious in her voice.

"Jennifer, have you seen any boys around here?" I asked. I wanted so badly to believe that someone else had done this thing, anyone other than my husband.

"No ma'am," Jennifer replied steadily.

"He said you wouldn't believe me," Lois cried.

"It wasn't that at all, it's that I didn't know. I'm so confused right now," I told her honestly.

"He told me that you didn't love me, Mom," Lois said in a flat tone. "That's true, isn't it?" she shouted, her eyes accusing me.

"What else did he tell you?"

"He said he was the only person who loved me. 'Your Mom sure don't,' he would say, 'if she did, she wouldn't spank you all the time and not Jennifer.' Whenever I objected to what he was doing, he would threaten to tell you that I was being disobedient. Mom, I left you notes," she informed me then, leaving me cold. "I thought you found them. I know you found them and that's why I hate you!" she shouted at me.

"Lois, I haven't seen any other notes, not one before this morning," I told her truthfully, but I could tell she just didn't believe me. God, the man had actually brainwashed my child into believing the lies he'd told her. She actually believed that he'd been telling the truth when he'd told her that I didn't love her, just so that he could take advantage of her.

Guy had not only robbed my baby of her childhood, as if that wasn't bad enough, but he'd robbed her of her mother's love as well.

I could tell by the look in her eyes that day that there would be no way to repair the damage he had done. Guy had manipulated all of us into a program and only he had the agenda. As for the notes, Guy must have gotten rid of them before I could get home from work.

I thought back to all the times that he'd beaten me, never once trying to keep the noise down so the children couldn't hear. In fact, he'd orchestrated those beatings so that they *would* hear. He'd forced my baby into continuing to have sex with him by forcing her to listen and hear him carrying out his threats to hurt me. I have no doubt that the last beating he'd given me had been meant to kill me, but I still couldn't understand why?

Later, I paced the floor crying, trying to decide what to do. The only person I could talk to bout this was Leola. God, I sure couldn't tell Mama, it would kill her to know what Guy had done to Lois.

I couldn't talk to his family, they were too reserved, and I don't think they cared that much for me in the first place. They certainly never encouraged any closeness to develop between them and me. They were cold and as isolated from me as if they lived in an entirely different country. Their family business remained in their family, and they didn't consider me a part of them.

I waited that night for Guy to come home from work. If he'd known that I'd found out already, he most certainly wouldn't have come home, unless he'd come to kill me. I was more afraid of him now than ever before, but I was determined to confront him about what he'd done to my child. It was almost nine o'clock and I couldn't believe he hadn't made it home by that time.

Tired of waiting for him to come home, I picked up the phone and called the bar where he used to hang out. After awhile, he came to the phone.

"Who is this?" he asked sharply.

"It's me, Bertha," I replied.

"What the hell do you want?" he roared, obviously not interested in anything I had to say.

"Guy, I know the reason you've been beating me," I told him.

"What the f--k are you talking about?" he asked.

"You know as well as I do what I'm talking about, Guy. I can't believe you would actually have sex with a child," I screamed.

"Woman, have you lost your fucking mind?" he shouted, courageously bluffing his way through. "What child have I had sex with?"

"Lois told me what you did to her!" I informed him.

"See, there, I told you that damn girl's been hanging around them little boys," he shouted in his defense. "Y'all ain't putting that shit on me," he said, his voice trembling.

"Guy, I am going to call the police," I informed him.

"Call the mother f--kers if you want to bitch," he roared as he slammed the phone down.

I immediately called the police station. Whomever I talked to down there told me that I would have to come down there. I was afraid of going alone. I couldn't imagine what Guy would do if he caught me while I was on my way there. What if I went and they refused to pick him up again? He would surely kill me if he found out. With that thought in mind, I hung up without giving them any more information. I wasn't about to take that risk; I was still having nightmares from the last beating he'd given me.

How could I trust the police? They hadn't protected me before, but then, they were all men, what more could I expect? I lived in a society that treated spousal and child abuse with as much seriousness as a barroom brawl, and sometimes even less. Society, at that time, believed that I was his wife, therefore his property, therefore, I should forgive and forget.

That night, Guy didn't come home and the next morning I finally mustered the nerve to go to the police station, but before I left, I put his clothes outside.

"What can I help you with, Ms?" an officer asked.

I got as close to him as I could and whispered into his ear what Guy had done.

"We need to talk to your daughter," he informed me.

"Sir, can't you just take my word for it and go arrest him?" I asked, desperate for them to do something. "My child has been through enough."

"Ms, we can't take your word for it and just go arrest the man. How do you know she doesn't have a boyfriend?" he asked with a look of impatience.

"Sir, I don't believe my daughter would lie to me about something such as this," I said, furious that he would treat the matter so lightly. I stood there furious, yet impotent, at the point of hopelessness. I no longer had the strength to fight.

I didn't hear from Guy at all for the rest of that week, and that was enough to let me know that he was afraid of something. I knew Guy well, and if he hadn't been afraid of facing some serious jail time, I knew he would have come home, if only to beat me again.

The following week I returned to work, but my mind and spirit were elsewhere. I was still having vision problems and when I got to the main gate at the plant, I could clearly see only the words filling the big sign outside the gate that read: "WHAT YOU SEE HERE, HEAR HERE, LEAVE IT HERE."

The plant I worked for assembled classified products for distribution. I wore sunglasses and heavy make-up to conceal my black eyes. The doctor had forbidden me to return to work until my sight had completely returned, but it wasn't as if I had a choice in the matter. I was now my family's sole provider.

I called Tina, Guy's sister, later that week to talk things over with her. She told me that she didn't believe her brother would do anything like that. I shouldn't have called her, I was even more furious after talking to her.

Emotionally, I was strung out. I was so stressed; I couldn't function well on my job. At times my supervisor would come to my work site to find me staring off into space instead of working. I just couldn't concentrate, and I felt as if I were losing my mind. At break time, I usually sat alone, I didn't want to talk to anyone, it would simply have taken more energy than I possessed at that point.

At home, I was much better than I was at work. I spent most of my time walking around in a daze, if not that; I was either drinking beer, or sleeping. I couldn't bring myself to talk to the girls about the abuse; I hadn't dealt with it myself yet. All my life things like sex and incest had been taboo, it just wasn't discussed. How was I supposed to have it together enough to discuss it with my daughters? Perhaps incest had never been discussed because the abuser was usually a family member.

I found myself reflecting back to a time when a distant cousin had abused me. It had happened shortly after Annie had gone away. Mama had agreed to let me spend a summer with her with another one of her aunts. When I was alone, my older cousin had come into the room where I slept. He began by rubbing my face, then slid his hands down to touch my body under the quilt, massaging my breasts, then my thighs and my pubic area, thankfully he stopped there then left the room.

I lay there frightened and feeling helpless. I didn't quite understand what he'd just done, but I knew with certainty that it had been wrong. A few days later I told my aunt what had happened. Instead of defending me, she yelled at me as if it were my fault. I began to believe that it was my fault as well.

I felt so guilty after that; I didn't mention what had happened to Mama, or talk to anyone else about it. Mama and I visited her aunt after that, but every time we went there, I had some sort of emotional reaction. Over the years our visits became fewer and fewer.

I knew I wasn't doing well helping me through this. I believe she felt I was angry with her, but I wasn't, if anything I was ashamed by what had happened. My emotions were in a tailspin, and despite what I knew Guy had done, I was still in love with him. He was still my husband and I was finding it quite difficult to turn off my emotions toward him. Then, of course, there was the shame and the blame of dealing with what I had allowed to happen. As if we weren't already dealing with enough trauma, shortly after I found out Guy had been molesting Lois, I heard her telling her sister that she was late for her period.

"Lord, please, don't let it be what I'm thinking, don't let that child be pregnant," I prayed fervently. Well, there was no point in lying there, I thought as I pulled myself out of bed and headed towards their room to deal with this new issue.

"Lois, did I understand you to say that your period was late?" I asked on a sigh.

"Yes, Mom," she said. "I told Daddy a week before he beat you that I had missed my period," she sobbed.

That was why he'd tried to kill me. He'd suspected all along that Lois might have been pregnant and he knew he could no longer conceal what he'd been doing to her for all those years.

The following day I took her to see a doctor. I could tell by her facial expression that she was humiliated, as I had been, by the exam. The doctor performed the exam, not once questioning me about who the father might be. I guessed he assumed she had gotten pregnant by a boy her own age, and I was too embarrassed to tell him who the father was.

He informed me after the exam that she was only a few weeks along and that it wasn't too late for her to have an abortion. He told me that he didn't perform them, but that he knew of someone he would. As I left he gave me a piece of paper with a woman's name and number on it.

When we returned home, I went to my room and sat alone crying, trying to decide what to do about having the abortion done. If the pregnancy had been by anyone other than Guy I might have felt differently, but because the child was his, there was no question about what I would do. We had no alternative.

I called the number the following morning and made arrangements to have to procedure done. I never discussed it with Lois; I didn't see the need. There were no options to be discussed. It never occurred to me to consider her rights, I was doing what I thought was best, just as any other mother would have done for her child. Just as there were no legal abortion clinics available, there was no abortion counseling.

A tall, red headed black woman met us at the door of the big house with faded paint at the far end of a secluded street. Her facial expression was cool. She didn't bother with human emotion, never offering a word of sympathy or empathy, simply leading into the back room of the house and ordering Lois onto the examination table. She never told us what to expect, merely left the room and went into the bathroom and ran some water, then came back out with part of a wire hanger in her hand that had some type of rubber stem on it.

"Put your legs in the stirrups," she told Lois.

Lois and I were both horrified by her manner. When Lois didn't do as she'd been instructed, the woman harped, "you girls get yourselves in trouble and expect your Mamas to bail you out," she snapped with venom. "Be still!" she ordered as she pushed the hanger into Lois's vagina.

I stood silently by, not knowing what to do. I had no idea that this was how abortions were performed. The old woman had finished what she was going to do before I could even think to defend Lois. I'd wanted to, desperately, but I hadn't been able to.

Lois stayed home from school the rest of the week. She never said much about what had happened, just walked around the house like a zombie, saying nothing, still in a state of shock. I didn't really know if she'd understood what had taken place today — she was only a child of thirteen after all. I wished I could have had the nerve to stand up in her defense, but I hadn't, I was too ashamed of having to admit my husband was the father of the baby.

As time went on and things began returning to something similar to normalcy, I waited to see what would happen. Jennifer and I remained close, she would always hug me and be affectionate, but Lois continued to keep her distance from me. It was so painful to see my daughter turn away from me, because of what Guy had done to her, and now I was as bad as he'd been. I'd taken her child.

I had failed her in so many ways. Mothers were supposed to protect their children from that type of trauma and abuse, but I hadn't been able to do that for mine. I'd just never thought that Guy was capable of sexual abuse. Mr. John had never done it to me and it had never occurred to me that Guy would do it to my child. But then, Guy was different from Mr. John in another way too: I'd never seen him beat my mother, but Guy hadn't had a problem allowing my girls to see him abuse their mother.

Mary came by to see me a few times, trying to get me to go out, but I couldn't. I was too embarrassed to be around other people, so I remained isolated. I had to report to personnel about my work performance; it was beginning to suffer, as well as everything else in my life, and I'd called in sick too many days. I didn't make it; I was too drunk to go. Finally, they gave me a warning and told me that if I didn't get it together, I was out of there.

It was meant to be, I suppose. Three months later there was a lay-off in my department. I was one of the lucky ones; I was also one of the first to get laid off. Actually, it came as a blessing to me. If they hadn't laid me off, there is no doubt in my mind that I would have been fired.

However, I found that unemployment benefits were just enough to pay the rent and keep food on the table. The only money I had saved with Guy was for the down payment on our house. In order to get any of that back, I would have to deal with Guy, and the price was entirely too high.

I still wasn't able to talk to the girls about what had happened, even after all of this time had passed. Now that I wasn't working, I spent most of my days moping around the house feeling worthless and guilty.

Leola finally came over and advised me to stop drinking. She was sick of watching me destroy myself. "You need to see a doctor," she insisted.

I did follow her advice about seeing a doctor, but I didn't tell him what was really going on inside. I began to feel, after a while, that Jennifer would have been better off with her father, at least she could have avoided that environment that Lois had been forced to submit to.

I hadn't heard from Guy in months when he called seemingly out of the blue. He wanted to meet me for lunch, but I declined. I wasn't ready to get caught up with him again. He called again of course. The next time he used the house as an excuse, saying that we needed to discuss the plans.

"Bertha, we really need to talk," he insisted when I continued to refuse.

"Guy, I'm afraid to be around you," I told him truthfully.

"Bertha, I'm a changed man. I don't even drink anymore. I promise, I won't touch you, but we need to discuss what we're going to do about the money we saved, to have the house built."

I finally agreed and he picked me up the next day at noon. He looked old and tired, as if he hadn't slept in months. He had dark circles under his eyes, he'd lost weight, but he didn't appear to have been drinking — at least, I didn't smell any on his breath.

Neither of us had anything to say on the way, on our trip outside of the city limits in virtual silence. When we reached the site where the house was to be built, we discussed anything but what we'd come to discuss, trees, scenery, anything but what we were going to do with the money. We both seemed reluctant to get into that for some reason.

The site was truly beautiful. Tall trees of varying varieties, pines, oaks, weeping willows surrounded the property, and dogwood trees surrounded the lower end.

When we reached the actual site where we'd planned to build the house, Guy finally turned around to face me. "Bertha, we need to go on and get his house built," he cried.

"I can't do that, Guy. You know, I don't even think you realize how much pain you've caused my family. My child was pregnant, because of you and what you did to her. You're walking around here as if that it doesn't matter," I yelled. I told him everything that had gone on since his departure, including the fact that I'd had his baby aborted.

"Bertha, I don't know what made me do something so foolish," he confessed. "All that I can do is say I'm sorry for what I have done. All that drinking just messed up my mind."

"If you'd really loved me, Guy, I don't understand how you could have had sex with my child. She was young and innocent, and you took advantage of the fact that I had taught her to respect and love you as her father."

"Bertha, I need to see a doctor, and I'm willing to do that. I want my family back," he said, finally losing control of his emotions, crying into his hand.

"Guy, you're right, you do need to see a doctor," I agreed, refusing to let him off the hook because of his emotional outbursts. "Only a sick person would do what you did. Not to mention the fact, that on top of everything else you did, you were seeing Mable. That alone was enough to hurt me, but you didn't care. Why, Guy, why would you hurt us like that?" I cried, realizing even then that there were no answers, nothing he could say could erase the pain caused by what he had done, all the many betrayals of our family.

"Please, Bertha, I'm so sorry and I promise I'll never do anything else to hurt you," he pleaded, still crying.

After awhile, we walked back to the car and sat there talking for hours. The more he talked, the more convinced I was that he was truly remorseful for what he had done.

Finally, he kissed me and told me how much he loved me. My feelings for him were still in turmoil, but prominent among them was the war of hatred and love. I hated him for what he had done to us, but I still loved him. I finally told him I had to think about what he was saying. I wasn't quite ready to trust him again. I would let him know what I wanted to do about the house after I'd had time to think.

Guy and I began secretly dating after that, this went on for months. He'd take me to lunch, shower me with gifts and flowers, his romantic gestures easing the surface of the pain. The more time I spent with him, the more convinced I became that he was sincere. No one could have been more apologetic and remorseful.

Before long, I began thinking maybe the move would help heal the wounds of the past. What I didn't realize at the time and no one else seemed to know is that the battered woman syndrome was just like alcoholism or drug addiction. The only way to kick the habit was to remain out of the environment that fostered it.

At this time I was still battling the never-ending cycle of shame, blame, and guilt. Without realizing it, I had isolated myself from family and friends. I didn't want anyone to know what I had suffered.

Guy knew how vulnerable I was, and he preyed on the fact that I had no job or money. My self-image and self-confidence were nonexistent; they had long since shattered under the weight of the abuse. My sense of reality had become so warped that I no longer had the emotional equipment to fight.

Without thinking about it further, I said to Guy to go ahead and have our home built. I didn't tell Leola, my friend, what was going on. I knew she would lose her mind if she'd had any idea that Guy and I were going back together. I'm certain that she would have said I'd lost mine, and she would have been right. I'll be the first one to say that my mind must have been on vacation.

Those days I often thought about what I'd told my friend, Sue Mae, when we were children, about my dream house. God, I'd never dreamed I would be moving into it when I'd gone half way out of my mind. Though I would never have thought it possible, I found myself missing the comfort of the plantation. It had been the place where Mama so carefully safeguarded my child.

There were many delays in getting our house built, so Guy moved back into the old house with us. Leola found out and stopped coming over. She wouldn't speak to Guy, she couldn't stand him. I guess she finally concluded that I was a hopeless case and that there was nothing she could do to help me. Things in the old neighborhood were so uncomfortable that we ended up moving across town so that we could get away from everyone who knew us.

I never knew how Jennifer and Lois felt about Guy moving back in; I never bothered to ask them. I suppose I was afraid of what they would say.

At fifteen, Lois began dating a young man that lived within a few blocks of us and a few months later she became pregnant. I wouldn't discuss her pregnancy with her; all I would say was that the child she carried would not be aborted. There wasn't a lot more to say. I certainly couldn't lecture her, I still had Guy around, the same man who had abused her and manipulated her childhood thoughts and dreams.

A few months before the house was built, the baby was born. It was a boy and we named him Rodney. Shortly after he was born, I began taking care of him so that Lois could continue her education, in the hopes that she would have the tools to be able to make it on her own when she was older.

Hanging laundry

19. Our Home

IN 1971, WE MOVED TO THE COUNTRY, TAKING OUR DARK FAMILY SECRET WITH US, CLOSETED AWAY IN THE MINDS, HEARTS, AND SPIRITS OF US ALL, EATING AWAY AT THE CORE OF EVERYTHING THAT MADE A FAMILY POSSIBLE. The house was everything I ever wanted: three bedrooms and large enough for our family to move around in without stepping all over each other. The exterior was built of red brick. Just sitting there, as we drove up in the driveway, it dawned on me that this house was even more than I could have dreamed it would be.

The girl's school was within a few blocks of the house and I couldn't have been happier. Their education was my top priority.

I was distressed to find that moving into the house hadn't made things better in the family. The girls stayed as far away from Guy as possible. If he was home, they stayed on the other side of the house. Our home lacked the vital ingredients that were necessary to make it a home, love, respect and trust. The taste of victory became bitter indeed. For what had I won?

Guy and I had been back together a year and he had kept his word, he hadn't beaten me, but he never did go see a doctor. He seemed to adore Rodney, Lois's son. He brought him almost every new toy that came on the market.

I finally got another job and went back to work. This time I worked for the phone company, working on the assembly line, assembling phones. It was fast paced and I loved it, but after only three months there, I was transferred to the night shift.

Although my children were older, the thought of them being at home, alone all night with Guy sent me into panic. He still hadn't gone to a doctor about his problem. Every morning when I got home from work, I asked the girls if he had tried anything, but they denied it. I was quite sure, by now, that they knew to tell me if he touched them in anyway, but I wasn't willing to risk it.

On the weekends, the girls and I would take Rodney and go to the movies or a ball game. Lois was fairly active in school. She'd joined the ROTC and was a cheerleader. I couldn't believe how much she resembled me when I'd been her age. She was tall and as skinny as a beanpole, a dark brown complexion, and black coarse hair. She didn't smile much, though. She was often cool and rebellious, and she seemed to be angry with everyone and everybody. Regardless of how hard I tried, I could never seem to bond with her. Communicating with her had never been as easy as with Jennifer. I knew that most of her anger was directed toward me, and I understood. If anyone in our house had a reason to be angry, it was Lois. Of all of us, she'd been the most scarred by what Guy had done.

Jennifer, on the other hand, was outgoing with a jolly personality. She was short with shiny, black hair and big brown eyes, just like her father's, Albert. She kept those around her laughing about something all of the time. She also loved to talk on the phone with her friends.

Mama I remember

20. Mama

I continued to visit mama in Texas frequently. Regardless of how I felt when I went there, I always felt great after a visit with her. She never asked about Guy, and I didn't see any need to tell her about him.

Mama had gone into a new phase of her life where she talked about herself. Finally, after many years, she began talking about Cooper Hill and the family feuds that went on over Granpa Riley's land after my daddy's death. She never said it, but I sensed that that had been the reason for our hasty departure. As she'd fix dinner for us, we talked about her life and some of her regrets. Primarily, as far as I could tell, she regretted the fact that she had permitted her aunt to take Annie. She'd say that if she had it to do all over again, she would have kept all of us together.

She felt that Annie hadn't been old enough to understand why she'd had to go live with relatives. The other children had been older, they knew how mama had been struggling, but Annie hadn't. Mama had felt, at the time, that Annie would have a better life, and she had. Annie finished high school and had gone on to college. It was just the emotional factor that bothered Mama, I think.

"Bertha, you did right to get your daughter back," she said one day. "Whatever you do, keep both of your children together," she sighed, her eyes still in the past, remembering. I wanted so desperately to tell her that we weren't a happy family as she assumed we were, but I just couldn't tell her the truth and allowed her delusions.

Mama felt bad about the fact that relatives had raised some of her children, but I tried to make her see that she had done the best she could by us. When she'd gotten older, and we were grown with families of our own, she'd chosen to live alone instead of with her children. She hadn't wanted to be a burden on any of us.

Mama had had nine children. I was having a hard time raising two children; I couldn't imagine how hard it must have been for her to clothe and feed all of them alone. She'd been alone and struggling in the early forties, and that couldn't have been easy, especially when she had no source of income. There were no food stamps back then, they used ration stamps to buy sugar, gas, shoes, meat, and canned food. Very few people had the money to purchase these items at that time. It was during the depression and Franklin D. Roosevelt was President. It couldn't have been easy for mama.

Mama died of a heart attack in her Texas home a few months later. Oh, how I missed her. I missed the comfort of her bed, the heart-to-heart talks, and the many precious memories that had been forged over the years. For months after her death, I would find myself dialing her phone number, hoping to hear her voice on the other end, to make a mockery of the nightmare I couldn't seem to awaken from. Many times whenever I would visit my brothers in Texas, I would go by the place where she once lived, wishing that she were still alive. Each of my sisters and brothers, along with myself, dealt with Mama's death in our own way. I was finding it difficult. I found, three months after her death, that the things I'd been coping with before were no longer things I could cope with anymore.

Going to work was difficult and getting harder all the time. I worked only about three weeks out of a month. After awhile, I began to drink again. I never imagined that one day my mama would die, and dealing with the reality that she was gone was cruel beyond measure.

Bertha's hand-made dolls

21. Shut Down

Dealing with life's pressures was becoming almost impossible for me. I'd gotten to the place that I couldn't stand to look at Guy. Every morning, before going to work, I'd break out into a fit of crying. I'd gotten so depressed that I could barely move. At work, sitting at my workstation, I would watch my work going by on the assembly line and didn't have the motivation, or inclination to do what I was supposed to be doing. Frustrated with trying, I took a leave of absence.

I reached a point where I could no longer think straight. I would be cooking and forget, leaving the food on the stove to burn. My energy stores were completely nonexistent. I would force myself out of bed to see Guy and the children off and take Rodney to the babysitter, and then I would go back to bed and sleep all day. When I finally did get up, it was to drink my habitual three to four beers for the day. I wore the same old robe day after day, unbuttoned because I didn't have the energy to button it, I'd just tie a string around me if I wanted it closed.

I felt as if the only friend I had in this whole world was the spider that lived in the corner of my bedroom. I would lie there day after day and watch him coming and going. I was so far out there I welcomed the sight of him. He would be the only thing I would see all day until the children came home from school.

Guy never once questioned how I felt, or what was going on with me. He would merely look at me and continue on with his life.

Two weeks after I had been off work, a nurse called me to suggest that I might feel better if I came back to work.

"I don't have the energy to put my clothes on, ma'am," I told her.

"It sounds as if you're depressed, Bertha," she said. "I am going to give you the phone number for a psychiatrist. I strongly suggest you call him, maybe he can put you on some type of medication."

"Ma'am, I am not crazy," I informed her.

"You don't have to be crazy to see a psychiatrist," she informed me. "You might want to talk out your problems with someone, Bertha," she suggested.

I finished talking to her, saying what must have made her happy. When I'd hung up from speaking to her, I called Leola.

"Girl, this damn nurse at work suggested I see a psychiatrist," I told her, relieved beyond measure that she hadn't just hung up when she heard my voice, which is what I expected to happen. "I'm not crazy," I shouted into the receiver.

"Bertha, you know what kind of stress you've been under over the years," she began cautiously. I think you should go and talk it out with someone," she suggested.

After our phone conversation, I went into the kitchen and got a beer. "I'm just gonna forget this shit," I told myself as I gulped it down. "Black folks don't run to no psychiatrist," I continued talking to the empty house. "We are taught to pray and ask God to help us with our problems."

"Bertha, did you make an appointment?" Leola phoned later that afternoon to ask.

"No, I didn't!" I shouted, offended that she would even ask.

"Bertha, you need to get yourself together for the sake of those kids," she told me just before hanging up the phone.

I sat there for a moment, the phone still in my hand, contemplating what she had said. I knew that she was right, and I knew that my kids needed me. I'd been so wrapped up in myself that they spent a lot of their time with each other; I was always closed up in my room.

I replaced the receiver, and then decided to make the call.

The day of the appointment, it was as if my mind had completely shut down. I'd forgotten how to drive, or which way I was supposed to go. I was terrified of everything. I went back into the house and called the doctor's office to cancel my appointment until the next day.

By the time Guy got home from work, I had pulled myself together enough to tell him what had happened. I asked him if he would take tomorrow off to go with me. He agreed to do it, but I could tell he wasn't pleased about it.

The next day, we finally made it. My appointment was at nine. It wasn't until Guy saw his name on the door that he knew I was seeing a psychiatrist.

"What are you doing coming to this damn place?" he asked.

"Because I'm depressed. It might be a good idea for both of us to see him, Guy," I suggested. His response was typical Guy. He didn't say a word; he just stared at me as if I'd sprouted horns.

We sat in the waiting room for a long time before my name was called. The doctor stood in the doorway to greet me, holding my file in his hand. His name was Doctor Phillips, and initially he took a general background on me, and then talked to me in his calming manner, helping me to relax.

"Now, what brings you here?" he finally asked taking a seat behind his desk.

I wouldn't answer him. I just sat there, crying as the pain inside made it almost impossible to breathe. It was the first time I'd allowed myself to truly cry for me in years.

Dr. Phillips didn't say anything; he quietly went to the door and beckoned for Guy to join us. "Your wife is very depressed," he informed him. "I recommend mend that she be hospitalized as soon as possible. I'm on the staff at Brooksdale Hospital, and I can have her admitted there," he finished not really waiting for Guy to express his opinion.

Guy was silent on the ride home, looking straight ahead. After we pulled into the driveway, he finally turned to me, "Bertha, what the hell is people going to say? I guess you're supposed to be crazy now?" he asked slamming the door, leaving me in the car to cry my heart out.

When the girls came home, I tried to explain to them why I was going into the hospital. "But why do you have to go into the hospital," Jennifer asked after my first attempt, not really understanding. Lois didn't say much of anything; she just turned silently and went into her room. I believe all of them were embarrassed because I was being admitted to a mental hospital.

What they didn't understand, though, was that I had to go, I had no other choice. I was no good to anyone the way I was, least of all to myself.

The next day when Guy took me to the hospital, he went as far as the admitting office. I found the hospital looked more like a hotel than a hospital. It had multiple sitting rooms and bedrooms, and the patients walked around in their street clothes rather than their pajamas.

For the first two weeks I was too drugged up to remember much of anything. All the pain and disappointments that I'd suffered had left me lifeless. I had given Guy, the power to control in my life. And to abuse me, the abuse left me feeling barren. I couldn't remember the last time I'd been a mother to my children.

I was finally ready to talk to Dr. Phillips. I told him everything that had happened to me that brought pain into my life. I told him how ashamed I felt.

"You are blaming yourself, Bertha," he declared.

"But I should have known something wasn't right," I replied.

"How could you?" he asked simply. "You were being physically and mentally abused yourself. All of your energy was being used to cope with the fear and abuse you were forced to endure. You couldn't see the other problems around you. You were too busy trying to deal with the ones you had, and Guy knew that. He knew what he was doing," he assured me.

"I don't understand how he could do it," I cried bitterly. "I just don't understand how he could do what he did to a child."

"Bertha, most abusers are sick. Many of them have been abused themselves as children. Until Guy seeks help, he will never come to terms with what he's done."

I found people from all walks of life in the group sessions. I found that I had not been the only abused spouse; there were quite a few of them there. There were also women whose daughters had been molested and had gotten pregnant, by various family members.

Dr. Phillips wanted to talk to both Guy and myself. I called Guy to tell him, but he flatly refused.

"I knew you were going in there to tell that doctor a damn lie about me," he snapped.

"I haven't lied on you, Guy," I sighed.

"I am not crazy, and I don't need to see no damn doctor," he shouted with finality.

It was then that I realized that he was the same old Guy. He hadn't changed a bit. But I had, began making plans to get away from him. The girls had only a few months left before graduating, and I decided to leave right after that.

I knew I would have to be cautious and plan carefully. It was imperative that Guy not find out. Things had reached the point where I truly believed, that he would actually kill me before he let me go.

Grandma smoking a pipe

22. On My Way

Three weeks after I was discharged from the hospital, I returned to work. My outlook on life had improved immeasurably, and I could finally take care of myself. I felt like being around people, going out, I actually felt alive.

The girls and I began spending time together, going to games and such. Guy continued to go his way, never inviting me to join him. He no longer seemed to care for me. His pretense had long since ended.

In December, when my job had its annual Christmas party, I invited him to come along, not surprised by his refusal. When he saw the outfit I intended to wear, he told me he thought it looked cheap. He would have said anything to hurt me I knew that by then.

I didn't care about him not going, or what he had said about my clothes, I went to the party determined to have a good time. There was a live band, the food was delicious, and I danced all night, laughing and enjoying myself the whole time. Everyone complimented me on the way I was dressed and I enjoyed the fact that they found something about me to compliment. The time passed quickly and before I knew it, it was going on one-thirty.

Guy was standing outside on the carport when I got home, and he was furious. When I tried to open my car door, he jumped into the car, "Get over!" he ordered.

He jumped in on the driver's side and took the steering wheel. I knew he'd been drinking, I could smell the alcohol. He backed up to the end of the driveway and drove slowly down the road.

"Who you been with, bitch?" he asked.

"Guy, I went to a company party. I wasn't with anyone," I tried explaining.

"I thought you were supposed to be crazy," he snapped after a few seconds of silence. "If you are crazy, you'd better act like it. You can start by keeping your damn ass at home," he roared, swiftly accelerating.

I looked into his face and recognized the same look that had been on his face the night he'd tried to kill me a few years back. When he slowed the car, I reached for the door. There was no way I was going to let him hit me again, so I had every intention of running away. He must have recognized the fear, or have read my mind because before I could get out of the car, he grabbed me by the hair. "What do you think you are doing, bitch?" he asked, raising his foot and kicking me to the ground.

Before I could get up, he ran to the back of the car and pulled out a rifle. "I'm going to kill you this time, bitch," he threatened. "You being showing your ass off every since you went to see that damn doctor. I told you not to tell that damn doctor a fucking thing about me. What did you tell him, anyway?" he asked, his rage visibly building. "Did you tell him you that you got rid of a baby? You better say your prayers cause you are going to be a dead ass bitch tonight!"

I slowly pulled myself to my feet and turned to run. I stumbled and fell face down in the ditch, right beside our parked car.

"Please, Guy, don't shoot me," I pleaded as I lay there with my face hanging down. I could feel him standing over my head as he cocked the rifle handle and prepared to pull the trigger. Terror filled me as he placed the barrel of the rifle within inches of my head and fired. I don't recall how many times he fired, but I recall seeing sparks fly from the barrel, and the sound of the bullets, and the smell of gunpowder.

Certain that my time to die had come; I relaxed, my mind going over inconsequential matters. I thanked God that my children were not being threatened, and asked him to take care of them. I wasn't worried about them financially; I'd taken a life insurance policy out on myself sometime ago. Then I realized, that I was no longer afraid of dying.

I remember very little after that fact registered. When I again came to myself, Guy was standing over me with a slimy grin across his face, and bells were going off in the back of my head somewhere. I began to scream until he forced me back onto the bed.

"Shut your damn mouth and get your ass up and pull that thing off," he demanded. I looked down at myself and saw the mud and grass stains all over the front of it.

"Guy, please leave me alone," I cried holding my head, trying to ease the headache that was rapidly growing out of control.

"I told you to shut up," He yelled. "No damn wife of mine is going to be running around dressing like a damn whore. Get up!" he roared.

I finally managed to pull myself upright in an effort to pull off the jump suit. I guessed I wasn't moving fast enough because after only a few seconds, he reached over and snatched it off me, ripping it into shreds. When he had it in his hands, he threw it in the trashcan. I noticed that my knees and both of my arms had bruises on them that must have resulted from my fall.

I dragged myself to my feet and went into the bathroom and took a shower. The muscles in my body rebelled at the soreness that every move seemed to cause. I gathered from the look of my clothes and the condition of my skin that Guy must have dragged me back to the car and into the house.

When I came out of the bathroom, he'd removed his clothes and was sitting on the side of he bed with a strange look on his face. I knew he was going to do something stupid, but I wasn't quite sure what he would do. My knees weakened with the fear coursing through my body as I waited for his next move.

"Let me tell you this, bitch, if you tell another f--king soul about me, I'll kill you! Now get them damn drawers off, bitch," he brusquely ordered.

"Guy, I don't feel like having sex," I pleaded for his understanding, hoping that he had at least of grain of humanity within him. But I could have saved myself the trouble, he didn't.

"Woman, you better shut your damn mouth up and do what I tell you!" he roared, jumping up to grab both of my arms, holding me down to his will. He didn't bother trying to be gentle. I felt the pain slice through my body as he forced himself into me as I shuddered, hating every second, every touch of his hands on my body. "That's the way a whore gets f--ked," he said with a sneer when it was over.

The next day was Sunday. Guy went to church, but I couldn't get out of bed, where I remained most of the day. I was traumatized by everything he'd done to me the night before. I knew that my situation had grown more urgent. I had to find a way to escape this man and protect my family.

My recovery from depression of a few months ago was now no more than a memory. I hit emotional rock bottom after Guy's behavior the night before. I was an state that left me immobilized.

When I went to see him, tt took Dr. Phillips only a glance to know something was wrong.

"Bertha, have you stopped taking your medication?" he asked right away.

"No," I answered simply.

"Then what happened? You looks so washed out," he said bluntly.

"Guy threatened to kill me, then shot a rifle so close to my head, I could smell the gunpowder, and then he raped me," I told him sobbing my heart out.

"My God, Bertha, how long do you intend to stay around waiting on that man to kill you?" he asked with revulsion for Guy's behavior. His reaction was even greater than I expected.

But I tried to explain, "I can't leave right now, Dr. Phillips. My children have only a few more months before graduating high school."

"Bertha, how old are your children?" he asked thoughtfully.

"They are sixteen and seventeen," I told him.

"Has it ever occurred to you to leave them behind for now? Not forever," he hurriedly corrected, "just until you find a place to live."

"No, that's not possible. I can't leave my children behind, that's one thing black women don't do," I informed him. "Our culture teaches us to be strong and keep your children with us, no matter what else happens."

"Bertha, I usually don't tell my patients what to do, but this man is more than crazy. One of these days, he's is actually going to kill you. It may be accidental, or intentional, it won't matter really, either way you'll be dead. You're running out of options here. Either you learn to live in that mess, or you get up and leave," he suggested.

I didn't argue the facts with him, he'd been right. It was time for me to make the tough decision. It was one of the hardest decisions I'd ever had to make. The girls were old enough. Neither of them could be considered a child. They were both seniors in high school, and they both seemed to be functioning fairly well, under the circumstances. It was time for me to decide. I had to have a serious talk with them, which I did immediately. I told them what I was thinking about doing, and assured them that we would only be separated until they graduated from high school. Just as I'd expected, they were not happy at all about the idea of me leaving them behind.

They certainly had fears of their own, but they saw how battered I had become. I told them they had to stick together, protect each other and not back down.

Rodney was only three years old at the time. He didn't understand anything about the transition we were about to make. I felt in time it would make sense to him. Guy loved Rodney, but as for us leaving, I don't think he really cared one way or the other. We took care of Rodney as if he was our son, so Lois could attend school. Matter of fact, Guy was the only father Rodney knew and this was the only home he knew. We had a lady next door who cared for him while we worked, and I made sure she continued to taking care of him while Jennifer and Lois attended school.

Rodney was a happy, adventurous, inquisitive, and independent little boy. It wasn't nothing for him to slip out of the yard and go into the woods alone with his dog. We named his dog Lady, One day Rodney showed up holding Lady on to her collar. He was just skipping down a trail in the woods, not a sign of fear on his face. He was always such a brave child.

Although there was a lot of drama in our lives, Rodney always brought joy and laughter to us.

Talking with Lois and Jennifer was always very emotional. Jennifer had to know "why you can't just stay, Mom?" She would say, "We didn't want to stay down here alone with Daddy while you were in the hospital." She continued, "Some nights we could hear him hanging around our bedroom door making noise. Or he would yell and he'd tell us though the door that you were no damn good." That hurt me so bad that he would tell them things like that.

Lois didn't say too much. It seemed as though she was just angry and looked hateful. She snapped most of the time I tried talking to her, but I just couldn't reach her. She and Jennifer said ugly things to each other at times. I would know how it hurt to hear them during that time.

I stopped trying to talk — hoping when we would get moved I would have more time to just talk openly about the different things to mend our relationship.

When I went back to see Doctor Phillips, we talked about Lois's actions. He reminded me about her traumas, and that she was going to be angry. He would say, "Usually you think the pain and trauma is just going to be with you." But while I asked him to explain, he just said. "You are her mother, and in her mind you were expected to protect her. Also, in their mind you had a better choice. Guy made them think that he was the only one that really loved them."

Doctor Phillips said, "It might get better or it may not, only time will tell. Some children never get over it. After you get settled, I want you bring her in so I can see what help I can get for her." Doctor Phillips was always reassuring to me.

Immediately after I left Dr. Phillips, I visited my friend, Vi. She had recently added an extra room onto her house and she offered it to me. Quite a few of my friends and family thought that I was terrible for leaving my children behind. But they just didn't understand what living with Guy had been like for me. What\ they thought did hurt me, but all I knew was that I needed to get me and then my family out of there.

When I moved out, I hitchhiked back and forth to work with one of my co-workers always watching my back. I constantly prayed that Guy wouldn't come to my job looking for me. The thought that he might just show up frightened me to death. I was just working and laying low. For almost a year, Jennifer, Lois and Rodney came to see me every weekend. We went shopping or would go to the movies and walk in the mall. I was just happy for the time I could spend with them. We would always hug, and then we cried.

It was important that I had enough money to buy the things they needed as I searched for a place to live that would fit in our budget. I promised them that it wouldn't be long that we would have to be apart. We would be back together soon.

23. Moving

In April I met Jerry, and I felt like I might start anew. He was from Texas, but he worked in the area as a wallpaper hanger. He was doing a job at a hotel in Bossier when I met him. He asked me to come by and watch him one day. I was somewhat leery at first. I was, after all, still married to Guy. But the more I thought about it, I realized that we hadn't lived as man and wife for a very long time. I'd only been wearing his name for the last few years. So, one Friday after work, I went by Jerry's job.

Jerry was easy to be around. He was jovial and relaxed, and he made me laugh. It wasn't until I met him that I realized that I hadn't laughed in a long time. I liked watching him move. I could see his strength in the bulging of his biceps as his long, lean brown body moved fluidly around the room. He was so tall he could almost hang paper without a ladder. He had long black hair that hung in a ponytail down his back, and when he smiled, he had the prettiest white teeth.

That evening, when he got off work, he took me out to dinner where we sat and talked for hours. When he took me home later, he held my hands gently between his masculine ones. He pulled me slowly toward him. "Bertha, can I kiss you?" he asked.

"Yes," I murmured, enjoying the feel of his arms around me.

I can't say I was too surprised the next morning to find that it was Jerry calling me. "Bertha, how would you like to go to an air show with me on Sunday?" he asked. "There will be lots of airplanes performing stunts," he said.

"I would love to go," I told him happily. "But I don't know if I can," I said reluctantly. "My children and grandson will be up to visit me on the weekend and we usually spend that time together," I explained.

"Why don't you bring them along?" he asked.

"I'll let you know later," I said. I didn't want to rush things with him and the kids, not yet.

The kids thought it was a wonderful idea and Jerry picked us up at ten o'clock that Sunday morning. We had a wonderful time. The pilots twirled the planes through the sky, doing one acrobat stunt and then another. Rodney was so excited he couldn't take his eyes off of the planes as they dashed through the sky. He laughed, jumped up and down and pointed at them as they flew by. He had never been so excited in his life.

At the end of the day we were exhausted. Jerry bought take out for dinner and took us to his house to eat. It soon came time for the children to go home, and I hated to see them leave. Thank God, they only had a few weeks left before they could get out of that house.

Love

24. Death Strikes

Just when I thought I'd begun to heal, and things were going to be all right, the bottom fell out of my life. In May, of that year, the Friday before Mother's Day, I called the girls to discuss a menu for Sunday, Mother's Day. Lois was bathing, so Jennifer answered the phone.

"Mom, you know what I want?" Jennifer asked playfully.

"What?" I asked.

"I want some mustard greens cooked in neck bones," she said happily.

"All right, now go and knock on the bathroom door and ask Lois what she wants," I ordered with a smile, listening to the muffled sounds of their voices as they talked in the background.

"She said whatever," Jennifer said coming back to the phone.

"Okay, I'll see you tomorrow then," I said with a smile as I hung up the phone.

That Saturday morning, my brother Jimmy also came to visit. He went down in the country to visit Guy, who, for some reason he'd always been close to him. Later that day, Jimmy came back by with Lois and Rodney.

"Where is Jennifer?" I asked nervously.

"She hadn't finished her part of the house work yet when Uncle Jimmy got ready to come home, so she stayed to finish," Lois said.

"That's alright," I said. "By the time I finish shopping she should be ready, I'll get her then."

Later that evening I called Jerry and asked him to take me to pick up Jennifer. It was such a beautiful day, and the countryside was so colorful, we decided to take the long way around. By the time we got to the house, there were people standing all around the front yard, pouring onto the sides. I glanced around and noticed a Sheriff's car parked along beside the road with its lights flashing. As we pulled to a stop I noticed my friends Vi, and Mary running our way.

"Bertha, something done happened to Jennifer," they shouted in unison, trying to catch their breath.

"What do you mean something has happened to her?" I asked scared out of my mind as I threw the car door open in my haste to get out and reach them. I didn't wait to see what they had to say I ran for the house. The sheriff was at the door and stopped me.

"Are you the mother?" he asked.

"Yes," I answered, my heart pounding in my ears.

"I can't let you go in, but your daughter was found dead in the bathtub," he informed me solemnly.

"Please, let me see her," I screamed, trying frantically to get past him. Guy finally came over to me and I fell against him crying. "What happened to her?" I screamed.

"I don't know. When I came home the door was locked. I knocked and knocked, but no one answered. When she didn't answer, I went next door to get someone. We went in through the window and found her in the bathtub. We called out to her, but she didn't answer. We called the sheriff then."

"Where were you, ma'am?" the sheriff asked joining us.

"I don't live here anymore," I informed him. "My husband and I are separated. I came to pick her up for our weekend together.

"Who was the last person to see the young lady alive?" he asked looking around.

"My oldest daughter and my brother were with her this morning. She was fine when they left," I said thoughtfully.

"Where is your brother?"

"He went back to Texas, he was only visiting," I informed him.

He questioned Lois next. I watched as the pain, shock, and disbelief filtered across her expressive face. It was hard for her, but though the tears continued to flow, she answered their questions. When it was over, I held her close.

Still the sheriff wouldn't allow me in to see Jennifer, informing me that the body couldn't be released until the coroner had come. The coroner took forever getting there.

He finally did come, and told Guy and me that so far, there were no signs of foul play. He assured us that he would give us a call when the autopsy was over so that we could pick the body up and make funeral arrangements. He asked what funeral home I wanted to have the body released to, and with numbness, I gave them the information they requested.

Lois, Rodney, Mary, Vi, Jerry and I sat on the ground until the funeral home arrived. "Where is Jennifer?" Rodney asked, only three years old he was unable to understand what was going on.

As the funeral home wheeled the stretcher with the body of my lifeless baby on it, I lost control, running over to the stretcher, trying to pull the drape away from her body. I wanted them to let me see her before they took her away, but Jerry pulled me away.

I stood there watching the hearse drive away with my child and all kinds of terrible thoughts went through my mind. Maybe I shouldn't have gone to Kansas City, if I hadn't she might still be alive. Finally, Jerry pushed me gently toward the car, "Let's go, honey," he said steering me toward the car.

On the way back to the city, everyone remained in stunned silence.

"Curse if you want to," Jerry said finally as he pulled into the liquor store parking lot. I watched him go inside and come back with a bottle of beer.

"Here, take a sip," he encouraged.

I took a sip, but it didn't help. I was still in a daze when we reached Vi's house so Jerry decided to call Dr. Phillips. I sat there trying to convince myself that nothing had happened to my baby. It had all been a bad dream; it wasn't real.

After Jerry got off the phone, he tried to encourage me to shout out my emotions, to do anything except hold them in like I seemed to be doing. But I couldn't. I could only sit there and stare into space.

Finally, after not being able to reach me, he grabbed me by the hands and pulled me to my feet. "Come on, let's go outside," he said, pulling me behind him.

When we got outside, he walked over to his car and took out his hammer handing it to me.

"See that tree over there," he pointed out, "go over there and beat the hell out of it. Say anything you want to say, honey," he prodded, unwilling to give up. "Honey, Dr. Phillips told me to tell you to do it!" he yelled. "Just *do* it!"

He finally got through to me, and I did as he asked. I hit the tree. I cursed. I yelled until I was too exhausted to lift that hammer one more time. I finally cried, "Why? Why? Why?"

Vi called Neal, Jennifer's grandmother, to let her know what had happened. I was glad she did, I knew I couldn't handle Neal's bitter remarks. She did ask to speak to me, but I told Vi to tell her I would talk to her later.

So wrapped up in my own misery, Lois, once again, was left to fend for herself. I didn't know how to console her; I was too buried in my own misery. The phone calls began pouring in when word of Jennifer's death got out. I had Vi screening all calls. I kept my eyes on Lois, who still hadn't said a word to anyone, she just stared into the empty sky. My heart was broken for her.

Visitors and friends from work continued to drop by. Later that evening, Albert called. The first thing he wanted to know was the very words that had been haunting me since that morning, "You should have let her stay with me!" he yelled.

I couldn't take it. I began sobbing. Vi took the phone out of my hand and spoke to him. After listening to him rant and rave, I heard her say, "Albert, this is not the right time to bring that up, please!" she said, sounding frustrated.

The following Monday, Jerry took me to see Dr. Phillips.

"How are you, Bertha?" he asked as soon as I walked into his office.

"I really don't know how I feel," I told him truthfully. "It's a feeling I have never felt before. I guess I feel detached somehow. It's as if a part of me is some place else," I said trying to explain the feelings that were foreign to me before the death of my daughter. I was some place else, looking in.

"It's natural to feel that way," he assured me. "When you lose a child, you lose part of yourself. Jennifer was a very real part of you and she's gone. It stands to reason that you would feel that way. The grief you're feeling now is unlike any you've ever felt before, but you can survive it. How are you going to deal with this? It's for you to decide. You can choose to take what you have left of your life and go on, or you can choose to die completely, it's entirely up to you," he pointed out.

"I don't know if I can do it," I sighed, feeling drained from all the emotions of the past few days.

"You need to find a reason to live. You have Lois and your grandson still, what about them? Why not try living for them? You're a family and you're going to need each other now more than ever," he continued.

"I'm so angry," I told him.

"Who are you angry with?" he asked patiently.

"I don't know," I cried.

"Yes you do, you know who you're angry with, Bertha. Don't just say you're angry. Say you're angry at God. That's really who your anger is directed at," he said patiently.

"Yes, I'm angry with God, he took my child," I finally screamed, tears rolling down my cheeks.

"Bertha, there's nothing wrong with expressing your anger, or directing it toward who or what you are angry with," he said softly.

The following Tuesday, I had to go to the funeral home to make the arrangements for Jennifer's funeral. Through the fog of pain and tears, I chose a pink coffin and a white dress for her to wear. We'd scheduled funeral services for the next day and my family had already arrived from Texas. They all seemed to have questions about her death, but they wanted answers that I didn't have.

The night before the funeral, during the family hour, Guy and Albert had a confrontation. The word had gone out that Guy had had something to do with Jennifer's death, and Albert was furious. To tell the truth, I had questions about Guy's involvement as well. I intended to find out, as soon as the coroner's report was complete.

During the service, as I stood with my eyes on the soft pink coffin that held the remains of my baby, I overheard someone saying that I had run off and left my children alone with Guy. There were speculations about who I was married to at the present, some of them thought that Jerry was my husband, others were still guessing Guy.

Neal confronted Lois for leaving Jennifer alone. Lois was so upset I had to take her to see Dr. Phillips after the funeral. She was devastated that everyone seemed to blame her for her sister's untimely death. So distraught that she couldn't think, she kept wishing she had been the one who died instead of her sister.

After Dr. Phillips talked with her, he suggested that she be admitted to the hospital for observation. She didn't want to go in, but she needed to. I was afraid of what might happen to her. I wasn't capable of watching her. I was too distraught with my own agony, barely capable of holding myself together.

I had begun to feel the stress of the last few days wearing me down. The pressure had gotten so bad, I tried to avoid some people, especially those I knew who would say things deliberately meant to hurt me.

There were so many questions left unanswered, and I was left empty in a void that seemed determined to consume me. I'd forgotten that I had only three days off for the funeral, so I didn't return on the date they had me scheduled to return. The next thing I knew, I received a letter that informed me that I had been terminated because I hadn't called in to work.

When I went to the hospital to visit Lois, I found that she was pregnant again and was thrown into more turmoil. Lord, I didn't know what we were going to do. I had just gotten fired, and now I had another mouth to feed. I became depressed, got down on myself, and then there was Jerry. I began snapping at Jerry for no apparent reason.

Three weeks later, a woman called from the coroner's office. She informed me that the report was back. I rushed to the office, believing the questions were about to be answered. The report ruled Jennifer's death accidental, and used the fact that there were no signs of foul play as the reason they had drawn such a conclusion. "How could a healthy, seventeen year old accidentally drown in a bathtub?" I couldn't help wondering. I asked her the same thing. She confessed she didn't know herself.

When Vi came home from work that evening, I told her what I'd learned about the report. She just slid into a chair and slumped over, disbelief written all over her face.

I thought about the many times Jennifer had taken baths in water I considered too hot. Several times, I'd had to knock on the bathroom door to make sure she was okay. I remembered her telling me once that she'd passed out from the hot water when she'd gotten up too fast. I'd asked her to stop running her water that hot. Maybe she hadn't.

25. Regression

On my next visit to Dr. Phillips's I told him the results of the coroner's report. He didn't say anything, but he wore a strange look on his face.

"I lost my job, too," I informed him.

"Bertha, have you been back home?" he asked softly.

"No, I haven't," I said. "But I need to go and get the rest of Lois's and Rodney's and my things," I told him recognizing disapproval in his eyes.

"What about Jennifer's things?" he asked cautiously.

"What do you mean?" I asked wearily.

"Going through her things would help you say goodbye to her," he explained.

"I don't know if I can do that," I told him truthfully shuddering at the thought of going through her things so soon. I knew it would be too painful.

"Maybe it would help if you did a little each day," he suggested.

When Lois came home from the hospital, I told her we would be moving back home until I got something straightened out. As much as I detested the idea, I had no other choice. I no longer had a job and mentally I wasn't yet ready to return to the workforce.

When that was done, I called Guy and asked if we could come down. He agreed and picked us up. On the ride into the country we were all consumed by our own thoughts, relieving all of us of the need to make conversation. When we pulled into the driveway, Rodney jumped out of the car and ran to the door. "Jennifer, Jennifer," he began called excitedly.

I could feel myself losing ground as I listened to his playful chatter. My poor baby, he just didn't understand that Jennifer would never answer his calls again, that she was gone from us forever.

When we walked back into the house, feeling of familiarity overcame me. Though it had been four months since I'd last been inside the home, my heart still recognized it. I couldn't help feeling that at any moment Jennifer would come running out of her room. But, there was no sound, only silence and emptiness.

We sat at the kitchen table as a group and began to talk to each other. We talked, I suppose, to relieve the tension, and because no one was anymore ready to see the rest of the house than I was. I knew I wasn't ready to face any more reminders that my child was gone from me.

When we'd exhausted every subject, there was nothing left except silence, so inclusive that none of us could escape its existence. Finally, Guy broke the silence by playing with Rodney. Lois and I moved in unison, getting up out of our chairs, moving nervously toward the room where Jennifer slept.

Lois didn't say a word, but I sensed she was okay, for the moment, anyway. I continued to walk behind her because I knew I had to, but when we reached the door, I couldn't go inside. For a moment, it seemed that I could hear her voice. I couldn't shake the feeling that she should be here, with us.

I finally forced myself to look inside. Jennifer's posters still hung on the wall. Very little about the room had changed, but I noticed briefly that there were a few things missing, something was slightly different. "Why are some of them down?" I wondered, not realizing until Lois spoke that I had spoken aloud.

"I had a dream, Mom. Two days before Jennifer's death. When I told her about the dream, she told me that she was going to die," Lois said as if in a trance, moving swiftly through the room removing posters as she went. Then, just as suddenly, she stopped her frantic movements and turned to face me.

"Mom, I didn't know what to say. I didn't understand then, and I still don't," she cried.

I went back into the kitchen to talk to Guy. There was a bad taste in my mouth, something just didn't feel right. Guy and I avoided the subject of Jennifer's death for as long as we could, but I knew we couldn't continue on this way. Finally, I passed the coroner's report across the table to him.

"Good, she didn't commit suicide," he sighed, relief settling on his face. He must have thought there was some possibility that she would have.

When Guy went to work the next morning, Lois, Rodney and I all piled into the master bedroom and the kitchen where we remained until he returned. I still hadn't entered the bathroom where she'd been found. That night, Guy ran bath water for himself in there. He said it was to make sure the plumbing was okay. I supposed he hadn't been in there until we came back. I suppose he would want to avoid it, being here alone.

A few days later, I finally managed the courage to go into Jennifer's room. I began by removing the discarded posters that were strewn around on the floor. I gathered her books together and took them back to the school. I don't know how I accomplished it. Everything was so emotional. It was as if I was one large raw nerve. Returning to the school that she had loved and would have graduated from seemed to rub and blister me.

When I reached the principal's office, he held my hand with understanding and told me that Jennifer had had enough credits to graduate. I couldn't thank God enough that my dream for my children's high school education and graduation had been fulfilled. If only she could have been there to walk with her sister in that line to receive her diploma.

A few days after the graduation ceremony, Lois and I talked about her pregnancy. We decided that it would be best to stay in the country until the baby was born. Guy and I both realized that there was nothing left for us. Whatever we had shared was over now, and we could never rekindle the flames. Though I knew living there was best for the time being, I couldn't be happy and remembering Jennifer's death there didn't help at all.

Finally I forced myself to go back through Jennifer's clothes. It was the hardest thing I'd ever done in my life. I kept the things she'd loved the most and placed the rest in a bag to be given away. With tears rolling down my chin, I held each piece close to my heart before packing it away. I held each piece a moment because it was the only way I knew to finally say goodbye.

Christmas that year was hard. It was our first Christmas without Jennifer and I felt so lonely. Her absence was a stinging reminder that she'd been taken away from us. Trying to make things as normal as possible, I found myself baking the same four pecan pies I had made every year. It wasn't the same, though. Nothing would ever be the same again.

26. Goodbye to the Past

Just as we'd planned, Lois and I found a two-bedroom house in the city after her graduation. So that we'd have furniture, I took everything from the girls' side of the house and the second car that Guy had bought. He didn't appreciate the fact that I had taken the car and somehow he found out where we had moved and came by one night to hot-wire the car and take it back.

Lois and I had chosen a house next to a bus stop so that didn't matter. We were able to get food stamps for Lois and the children, but I wasn't eligible for assistance. Thank God the rent was affordable.

Two months later, things began to fall apart. All of the emotions I had suppressed during the hectic period right after Jennifer's death surfaced. It angered me to be around other people who hadn't experienced the loss of a child. I constantly found myself asking God why he hadn't taken one of their children instead of taking mine. I was so angry with God; I stopped going to church completely. I no longer wanted to serve a God who would allow such anguish and pain. I refused to listen to anything anyone had to say about Him.

I had been so wrapped up in my emotional tailspin that it wasn't until Lois and I began living together without someone else's interference that I finally realized the depths of her hatred for me. Guy had done his job well. She was so thoroughly brainwashed into believing I was the enemy that nothing I said to the contrary would alter her opinion of me.

Somehow she and I had never really bonded and that neglected tie had come to the surface in a big way. I had only myself to blame, I knew, but it wasn't from the lack of trying.

"Mom, I know you wish it had been me who died!" she'd screamed shortly after we'd moved into our new home.

"Lois why would you say something like that?" I asked shocked that she would believe such a thing. "I don't want you to die."

"Come on, Mom. Daddy and me heard you one day telling Jennifer that y'all had pretty round faces and I had a long, ugly face," she snapped, her voice ringing with accusation.

"Lois, I don't remember saying anything like that," I shouted in self-defense.

"I know you don't care about me. You had me put in that crazy hospital without asking me, too!" She yelled with venom, her eyes spewing hatred into those of my own as she continued her tirade. "Mom, you can't tell me that you didn't know about Daddy abusing me, I don't care what you say. If it had been Jennifer he had abused, you would have done everything differently," she continued, releasing all of her long contained anger and pain at what she considered my neglect of her. I just allowed her to talk, to vent it all. I knew she had years and years of emotion that she'd held back and there was nothing I could say in my own defense.

"Lois, I did what I felt was best," I said sadly after she seemed to have run out of venom. All of her anger was directed at me, and me alone. She wasn't angry with Guy, though he had been the one to abuse her. "I wanted to do something, Lois, but I didn't know where to turn for help. I tried the police, but they wanted to talk to you about everything. I thought you had already been through enough, I didn't want you to have to deal with them as well. I only wanted to protect you," I tried to explain.

"Please, Mom. You wouldn't even stand up for me when that old lady said all those mean, hateful things to me that day in her house," she cried, the pain and anger she felt toward me obvious.

"All I can say is I'm sorry, Lois. I can only ask for you forgiveness," I said realizing that she wouldn't forgive, not yet. These were wounds she'd only begun to drain the venom from. They were a long way from healing.

I knew that if she would trust him, Dr. Phillips could help her, but she was eighteen and I could no longer make that decision for her. It would have to be her choice, and she would have to live with it. She was old enough to file charges against Guy, if she chose to do so. It still wasn't too late. All I could do was tell her I loved her and try to prove it.

"Mom, I don't want you living with me and my children," she said sounding emotionally drained, her hatred for me written all over her face.

"Lois, I have no place else to go," I pointed out. "Let me stay with you, I can help you take care of the children," I pleaded.

"I don't want you around my children," she snapped.

Though I pleaded with her to change her mind, it was useless. Her mind was made up and she had no intention of changing it.

A month later, I gathered together the few things that I owned and moved out. I took a room in a boarding house located around the corner from where Lois and the children lived so that I could be close to them. I didn't have any money at the time, but the landlord allowed me to stay with her on my word that I would pay her what I owed as soon as I got a job.

There were five bedrooms that she rented out. All of us shared the same bathroom and kitchen. My room had a chair and a bed and rented for twenty dollars a week. Some of the men who lived there were drunks and occasionally would urinate all over the toilet seat and the floor, which meant that I had to go behind them and clean up any mess they made. The kitchen was just as bad. If I left any food in there, it was a certainty that one of them would eat it. I couldn't complain, though, I had nowhere else to go.

I stopped seeing Dr. Phillips and began hitting the streets, staying out all night, drinking and dancing, believing that it would ease the pain I was suffering. Sometimes I would get so drunk that when I woke the next morning, I couldn't even remember how I got home. I'd wake up to the smell of my own urine where I'd gone all over the bed. I'd feel like a dog until the next time I got drunk and forgot how I'd felt the last time. I was so out of it that one night I didn't even bother to close my door when I went to bed. I wake up and see it open and get frightened by what could have happened, but as soon as the fear was gone, I'd do the same thing again.

I mourned the loss of my family continuously. I felt that I no longer had a reason to live. No one in my family came around to check on me, and I was convinced that no one really cared about me. I did the best I could to survive on my own. I refused to call my family, or Guy's family for that matter, to ask for help.

I didn't blame Lois for hating me; she had every right to do so. She was right, I should have had Guy arrested for what he had done to her. Maybe God was punishing me for everything I had done wrong, for not protecting my child any better than I had.

Not long after Lois put me out, I met "Wash," an older man who lived the next street over from where I was living. Wash had retired from the gas company and hadn't really done much more with his life. He wasn't at all attractive with brown skin, but he had beady eyes that sunk into the back of his head. Whenever he smiled, his white, uneven teeth popped out through his lips. He did, however, dress well.

Wash drank liquor as if he were afraid there wouldn't be any left for him tomorrow and he made sure he kept plenty of it on hand. Wash also helped me to pay my rent.

Somehow, he found out what I was going through and offered me a chance to stay with him so that he could look out for me. I didn't hesitate to let him know that I wasn't about to lie up under no old man all night.

One Friday night, after I'd gotten dressed in my pretty red dress, I stood in the mirror congratulating myself on my appearance when he knocked on the door. He stood there saying nothing for a second, and then he ordered me to stay home. He was standing on the top of the steps, his gun waving around in his hand, as drunk as he could get.

"Where do you think you're going?" he asked, his beady eyes taking in his surroundings.

"I'm going out, and you'd better get the hell out of my way," I snapped, not about to cow down to another man.

"You'd better get back in that house," he demanded.

I'd had enough; looking around me I grabbed the flowerpot closest to me and knocked the hell out of him. Tossing the pot aside, I pushed past him. "Ain't no man going to run over me anymore," I said as I walked away.

He called the next day and demanded his money back for the rent he had paid. "If you don't get my money around here tomorrow, I'll come by and shoot you," he yelled over the lines.

I didn't know if he would follow up on his threat, but I wasn't taking any chances. When I got off the phone, I marched right down to the police station and had him placed under a peace bond.

I found a job at a convenience store later that year. I was required to take a polygraph before I could be hired. When the tester asked my age I told him I was thirty-eight, and then it dawned on me. Here I was thirty-eight years old, and I was starting my life over, again. That was enough to depress me all over.

Saturday nights were my nights to drink, but I was trying to work too. I would wake up in the mornings hungover. My eyes were sunken and there were dark circles around them. I looked so bad all of the time that I stopped looking in the mirror. I could no longer stand to look at myself.

I continued on this way for about a year before I found myself sick of being sick. I had lost weight and spent most of my time feeling ashamed of myself. I didn't want anyone to see me. It seemed that everything had gone from bad to worse without me realizing it. Finally, unable to stand myself any longer, I locked myself in my room and fell to my knees. With my whole heart, I cried out to God for forgiveness and asked Him to give me the courage to rise up out of the pit of hell that I was now living in. I promised that if he would only step in, I would stop trying to fix my life myself.

With that prayer, I found a strong sense of relief from my pain and anguish I had lived with for so many years. The anger that I had been harboring toward God was gone and in its place was a marvelous sense of peace.

What Dr. Phillips had said so long ago about my choices came back to me. I was certain the choices I had been making recently weren't the ones he'd intended. I longed for the days when Mama was still alive, how I missed her comforting presence in my life. She would have been so disappointed had she been alive to see what I was doing with my life. She was always reassuring that all we had to do was work harder and we would overcome our troubles. I knew too that Jennifer would have been hurt knowing the place I had allowed myself to be at this point in my life.

I can't remember how many days I stayed locked away in my room, but when I did come out, I felt like a different person. The first thing I did was to call an attorney so I could get a legal separation from Guy. I had faith that everything was finally going to work out when I went into his office that day.

A few weeks later we went to court and the judge granted my petition for a legal separation. Though he didn't want to, Guy was forced to pay me half of what the house was valued, plus alimony. It must have truly made him angry to have no other recourse than to do as the judge ordered.

Later that year I found a job working in a department store in Bossier as an alteration lady. My workstation was located in a small room adjacent to the men's department. I'd learned quite a bit about sewing, but I'd never dreamed I'd be doing it for a big department store. I found the work very challenging. My manager, Mrs. Miles, God bless her soul, had confidence that I could do the job. When she hired me she just knew I could do the work, and she'd been right. Six months later she were so impressed with my work that she promoted me to sales.

My big break came about one day when a man hurriedly rushed into the store looking for a shirt and a tie to match the suit he was wearing. I was the only person visible when he dashed in, so he rushed toward me.

"Miss, can you help me?" he asked frantically.

"I'm sorry, sir, but I'm not a sales person," I informed him.

"You work here, don't you?" he asked.

"Yes, sir."

"Then help me," he demanded. "I'm in a hurry!" he shouted.

Realizing that not helping him would only make things worse, I nervously began assisting him. I didn't have a clue about what I was doing, I'd never sold clothes a day in my life, but it must have come naturally. The first tie I grabbed went perfectly with the shirt he chose. He was thrilled. Later he came back to thank me. From that time on, whenever he came back in the store, he would ask for me by name.

One morning, as I was doing my routine job, Mrs. Miles came into the alteration room swinging her long, red hair. I was certain I'd done something wrong, she walked toward me with such purpose in her stride.

"Bertha, since you can't seem to stay off the sales floor, how would you like to become a salesperson?" she asked with a smile leaving me shocked to the core. Of all the things I'd been expecting her to say, that hadn't been one of them.

"You've got to be kidding," I said still in shock.

"No, I'm not," she said still smiling. "Come by my office tomorrow morning," she said turning to leave.

She'd made me an offer I couldn't refuse, and I was excited about it. But, I was also a little frightened. Everything seemed to be happened so fast now.

I fell in love with my job in the men's department, and I soon forgot about staying drunk every night. I had something to do that made me feel good about myself. The hope that Lois and I could mend our broken relationship still lingered in the back of my mind, but I knew that nothing would change over night. I didn't hesitate to help her out financially with the kids, though. I felt I had new purpose and I wanted to give back to Lois for my blessings.

27. Racial Healing

Mrs. Miles was an inspiration to me. She was a beautiful woman, not just on the outside, but on the inside as well. This is where beauty really mattered. I found out one day that she was married to a man in the Air Force, but I never really tried to get into her personal business, and she did the same for me.

As far as work went, she knew her job and did it well. She had quite a bit of retail background, I discovered. As a manager, she never failed to let her employees know when they were doing a good job. Unlike some, who approached you only when you'd done something wrong, she was quick to congratulate her employees on a job well done. But if you messed up, she would let you know it. It angered her more than anything, I believe, to see her employees standing around gossiping. She wouldn't hesitate to fire the guilty party.

She and I got along well, and within a year I was promoted again to department head in Misses' Sportswear. The subsequent raise I received allowed me to get my own apartment and move out of the rooming house. My new home was in walking distance of the store so I didn't have to worry over much about a ride into work.

Mrs. Rogers, a woman I'd worked with in the men's department, was nice enough to pick me up. She refused to hear of me walking to work. Every morning, she and her husband would pick me up, while listening to Dolly Parton on the radio.

Word soon spread around the store that I needed a car. There was a maintenance man who worked there who wanted to sell his car so that he could buy a new one for his wife. He sold me the car for little of nothing. I knew he was only doing it to be nice, he could have gotten much more than I paid him for the car.

God surrounded me with so many caring people. There were times I had to pinch myself to see if I was dreaming. Because I had so much time on my hands, I decided that it was time to go back for my GED. I went to school at night and soon earned it.

Though working all day and attending classes at night was difficult, I managed somehow to muddle through. Not once did it enter my mind to quit. I was finally going to accomplish the dream that my mama had held for me.

When I got my GED, I enrolled in a business school. I believe I was the oldest student enrolled at the time, and without realizing it, I'd motivated some of the younger students to keep working toward their degree.

When Mrs. Miles found out what I'd been doing, she came into my department, I assumed to congratulate me.

"Bertha, now that you're a high school and college graduate, what are you going to do with your education?" she asked sweetly one day.

"I don't know right now," I told her honestly. I'd just been so happy to have completed my goals, what I wanted to do hadn't occurred to me yet.

"The only other job you can get here is my job," she said with a grin. "I'm afraid I'm not ready to let you have that."

I suppose that in her own way she was encouraging me to spread my wings and fly away. I reached the top pinnacle as far as the store was concerned, there was nothing more to accomplish. The time had come to move on.

"This is all I have."

28. Yorkstone Insurance Company

IN SEPTEMBER 1983, I FOUND A NEW OPPORTUNITY. I began working for Yorkstone Insurance Company as a secretary and cashier. The work was challenging and I looked forward to every single day. I was responsible for handling customer payments, answering the phone, and doing monthly cash reports that were sent to the home office.

There were two staff managers in the office: a special agent who helped train the new agents, and Mr. Alexander, the District Manager. Mr. Elwood was the Regional Manager, and he worked out of the home office. Usually he would come up to visit our district once a month.

There were only blacks working in my district. Whites worked in the other two district offices that the company owned. They also had districts covering South Louisiana. I never did understand why a company as large as Yorkstone had segregated districts.

Mr. Howard, one of the men who worked in our district, once told me that some of them had once worked in the white offices, but had been transferred out. They'd been told at the time that it was because they weren't as productive as their white counterparts.

The company supposedly had generous benefits, such as profit sharing, health insurance, and bonus trips. However, I found out that no one out of the black district had ever qualified for one of the trips, only those in the white districts. I don't believe there were many employees in my office that knew about the bonuses. I'd only read about them in the Yorktown progress report. No one from the home office ever talked about them in our presence.

Mr. Alexander was supposedly tops in his field, but we couldn't see it. I can't remember a time when he tried to motivate the agents in our office to produce new business. In fact, he was always so tied up with personal business that he was rarely in the office. There were times we didn't see him for weeks. He would always tell me to tell anyone calling from the home office that he was in the field solving customer problems.

One day Mr. Elwood called. "Bertha, where is Alexander?"

"He is in the field," I answered.

"If he calls in, tell him, I said stay in the damn field." He shouted, with anger in his voice.

Mr. Elwood came up the next day and fired Mr. Alexander. Mr. Elwood stayed and filled in until he decided to hire someone else.

Mr. Elwood was a short man with a potbelly, red hair, and thick eyebrows, who wore a beard. He talked with a deep South-Louisiana accent. Some people called him a "coon ass" for some reason. He kept some chewing tobacco in his mouth. He loved western clothing and cowboy boots.

One day I was sitting at my desk doing some paper work. Mr. Elwood was sitting at his desk. I guess he was observing me.

"Bertha, you know this damn business, don't you?" he asked.

"Yes, I guess I do," I agreed, wondering where he was headed with this.

"If you had some agent and staff managerial experience, I sure as hell would make you district manager," he said in a sincere manner.

"I sure wouldn't mind. Mr. Alexander trained me how to do just about every aspect of the work a district manager does." I told him.

"The problem is that this damn company wants you to start from the ground and work your way up. How would you like to try being an agent?" he asked. "You'd make more money than you do now," he tempted unnecessarily.

"I'd love it," I told him with obvious excitement.

"You do good at that, maybe you can be made staff manager, and later you can ask to be promoted to district manager," he assured me.

After I'd helped Mr. Elwood find a replacement, I took a job as an agent at the company. Mr. Howard, our trainer, trained me well for my new position. I became one of the top agents in the office.

In August of that same year, Mr. Elwood introduced us to our new district manager. His name was Carter. He'd been sent from the home office as district manager. I'd never heard of him before, but there was something about him that made me very uncomfortable. I couldn't put my finger on what it was about him that I didn't like, but I knew he wasn't one to be trusted.

Mr. Carter wore arrogance like a second skin. He didn't simply walk around the office; he strutted like a peacock showing of his colors. He looked at the rest of us as if he was royalty and we were no more than his subjects. Every time he got near me, my flesh would crawl. The smell of stale cigars surrounded him as he walked around showing off his yellow teeth. Whenever he would leave our office, his stale smell lingered for hours.

Mr. Carter was fairly short, around five feet seven, and weighed about a hundred and seventy pounds. There was a deep, shuddering coldness in the depths of his blue eyes that left me feeling as if he'd read my secret thoughts. I was more than a little happy that he couldn't, though. I had no doubt that he wouldn't care for the unflattering thoughts that I continually had about him.

He was friendly enough, I suppose, and there was no doubt that he knew the insurance business. In fact, to be fair, he managed to get us benefits that no other manager had ever tried to get. He even tried to get us to relax around him by telling everyone to call him "Carter." Personally I had no intention of ever getting too close to him. I still didn't trust him.

Despite his arrogance, and my ambivalent feelings, I did try to work with the man. I kept reminding myself that with his guidance, my dream of becoming district manager could become reality. I worked as an agent first and Mr. Howard, the trainer, helped me learn the field side of everything. With his assistance, I soon made staff manager. My dream of district manager was drawing closer and closer.

Three months after Mr. Carter joined our team, I began feeling even more uncomfortable around him than I had in the beginning, and I hadn't thought that possible. I could feel him staring at me when he thought I wasn't aware of him. I avoided eye contact with him at all cost. I had the feeling that he was trying to say something to me with his eyes, and whatever it was, I didn't want to see it. I couldn't explain what it was about him, but I always felt as if my clothes were opened around him and that he could see me naked.

Not long after this, I began noticing that he made obscene comments to some of the women about their breasts. No one ever said anything, with the exception of Mr. Underwood, and he never really said that much, but you could see his anger written all over his face.

Mr. Underwood was someone who I really looked up to. He was one of those rare people who not only talked about injustices against the races and the sexes; he actually worked actively to bring about a change. He'd also been active in the civil rights movement and I admired him for that.

One day, after enduring one of Mr. Carter's degrading remarks, Mr. Underwood remarked, "This man obviously thinks he's operating a slave gallery!" It was the first time anyone had ever spoken out against Mr. Carter, but you can bet he wasn't allowed another opportunity to do it again. Not long after that, he was terminated.

With Mr. Underwood out of the picture, it didn't take long for Mr. Carter to show his true colors. After testing the waters by making obscene comments without any retaliation, he began to get vulgar with his remarks.

One morning he asked one of the secretaries for a cup of coffee. "Make it black," he said with a sick grin. "I like my coffee like I like my women, black and hot."

I couldn't believe he'd said that. I stood there staring at him, unable to do anything else. How in the world had someone with his mentality been allowed to rise as high as he had within the company, without someone recognizing him for the low life he was? He was probably in the black district because the white women wanted nothing to do with him, I realized later.

The excitement and enthusiasm I'd first felt for my job began to fade. I went to Mr. Howard and told him that I planned to resign if someone didn't do something to get Mr. Carter under control.

"He's just a dirty old man," Mr. Howard said in Mr. Carter's defense. "Just go on a do your job, forget about him," he suggested. Didn't he know that we couldn't simply forget the derogatory comments that nasty man was making to and about us?

A month later as I was closing out my books for the previous month, I noticed that there was a fifty-dollar outstanding balance that shouldn't have been there. I knew something wasn't right, I'd been doing this for a few months at the time and I'd never come up short. I decided to go talk to Mr. Carter, hoping he could tell me the problem.

"You must have used the money, or written new business on credit," he suggested.

I knew I hadn't done anything of the sort, and so did he, I finally realized. I leaned over his desk to point to an account on my books in an effort to clear up the error. His hand slid up my dress, his hand stroking me between my legs, before I realized what he was doing. His boldness and daring left me speechless. I'd known he was a lowlife, but I'd never imagined that he would go this far. When I realized he was trying to reach the top of my panties to pull them down, I jumped out of his reach.

I couldn't believe he would attempt something so stupid with an office full of people right outside the door. The humiliation and degradation I felt seared me to the spot. Why I didn't scream, or verbally protest his actions, I don't know, but I said nothing. My brain and body seemed to separate, but when I was once again safe, I became livid.

I ran blindly to my car, sitting there looking into space. I kept wondering what I was going to do. Regardless of how hard I tried not to, the image of my encounter with Mr. Carter kept rushing in to disturb my peace. The thought that he would do what he'd done to me again, made me sick to my stomach.

I ran to the bathroom as soon as I got home that evening. Though my sister was there at the time, I couldn't face her. I didn't want her to see how dirty I felt. I needed a nice, long bath to rid my body of the filth his touch left on me.

Later that night, after I'd gone to bed, I lay there in the dark, my mind reeling as I tried to decide what I was going to do. I'd worked too hard for my job to allow Carter to destroy everything I'd accomplished. I wouldn't give him the satisfaction of quitting. I would just have to find a way to deal with him; I had no other choice. There was no way I was resigning.

"Are you sick, Bertha?" I heard my sister asking from outside my closed door.

"Yeah, I just have a headache," I called back through the door, too exhausted and confused to discuss what was really disturbing me. I felt an awful, debilitating helplessness consuming me and I couldn't stand it. This feeling had been with me for most of my life, but for a while I'd escaped the weight of it. Because of Carter though, it had once again come back to consume me.

There was no sleeping for me that night. Every time I closed my eyes, I found myself reliving the nightmare of his touch. Even the memory of his acidic breath entered my delusions, making me sick in the stomach. I jumped out of bed and rushed to the bathroom. I made it there just in time. The calories I'd eaten that day would no longer present a problem.

My sister must have heard me in the bathroom because a few minutes later she was standing there. I could hear her outside the door, asking me if I was all right. "Yes," I said, too weak to be convincing. She offered to call my boyfriend for me, but the thought of telling him what Mr. Carter had done made me even sicker.

Weakly, I climbed back into bed, still smelling Carter on my flesh. Once again, I headed for the bathroom. After a while, I dressed and went into the kitchen. I thought perhaps a bolstering cup of coffee would be of some help, but it wouldn't stay down anymore than anything else had.

The next morning I got out of bed quickly, trying not to think about the fact that I would have to face Carter again. If I'd contemplated it overly long, I know I couldn't have gone in to work. There had to be some solution to this problem, but for the life of me, I didn't know what it was.

I felt trapped. I needed to talk to someone, but I was too afraid to tell anyone what he'd done. My job meant entirely too much to me. Besides, I couldn't afford to leave. I now had a mortgage and a car note, keeping my job was the only way I would be able to pay my bills. Not only that, Ella, my sister, had recently come to live with me because she was unable to work due to a disability. She was still waiting on her disability checks to be approved, which, once again, left me as sole provider of the household. With only a GED and a business college background behind me, I knew my options were limited.

Once I'd gotten to work, I couldn't bring myself to go inside. I sat there in my car, finally deciding to turn around and go back home for the day. When I got home, I called and left a message saying that I had several early morning collections to make, and if Carter didn't mind, I would be in later that day.

It wasn't actually a lie; I reasoned with myself, I did have a few collections to make. But the root of the problem was that I felt sick, barely able to function. I knew that what had happened hadn't been my fault, but I couldn't help feeling that I had encouraged Mr. Carter in some way.

For weeks I continued to have nightmares about my encounter with the man. I would wake up in the middle of the night with cold sweats. I felt as if a beast had suddenly awakened to take control of my life.

Finally, with no other choice, I went back into the office. It was time to make my deposits, so I had no other choice. I arrived determined to go in, do what I had to do and get out of there before Carter came into the office. But my plans were ruined when I found that Mr. Howard and some of the other agents from different offices had come in to the office.

I was so spaced out that when Mr. Howard began talking to me, I didn't hear a word he said. He finally realized that I was not myself and asked if I was sick.

"Yes," I lied. "I have a virus or something," I said fidgeting.

Carter came in about that time acting as if nothing out of the ordinary had happened between the two of us. My insides were churning, just looking at the man made me sick. I felt as if the room was spinning as I sat there. I knew I would have to make an escape. If I didn't get out of there soon, I wasn't going to make it.

That evening when I got home, Ella told me that Lewis, my boyfriend, had called while I was out. I knew that he'd been calling, but I wasn't ready to talk to him. I told her that if he called back that evening that she was to tell him that I wasn't home, regardless of where I was. I knew I was being unfair to him, but I couldn't help myself. He would be back in town Saturday, maybe by then I would be okay and he would never have to know what had happened.

Around five o' clock that evening a client wanted me to meet them, so that I could pick up a payment. I didn't want to, but I had no other choice. While I was out, I decided to visit a few other clients.

By the time I was finished, I realized it was seven and I could still make the prayer service at my church. I pulled into the parking lot where some of the members were still standing outside. I looked at them standing there, and couldn't get out. I tried, but I just couldn't force myself to get out, I was too ashamed to face any of them. I kept having this uncomfortable feeling that I had committed an unforgivable sin. It never occurred to me then that I had given Carter ultimate control over my life.

What he'd done to me was tearing me up inside. It was draining me of my life, and there was nothing I could do about it. There wasn't anyone really that I could talk to. Besides, even if there was, I was too afraid they would think that I had encouraged his attention in some way.

This thing began consuming me to the point that I continually put up emotional barriers, and I turned my anger on my boyfriend, Lewis. I remained in a constant state of frustration.

I knew my life was being consumed by a beast; I just didn't know its name. I found out later that the name of the beast eroding me from the inside out was Sexual Harassment. At that time, no one had ever heard of sexual harassment. Although I was certain that it went on quite frequently in the business world, I hadn't ever heard it mentioned. When the beast took greater control of my life, I decided it was time to move on. I resigned and told my co-workers that I was quitting to care for my disabled sister.

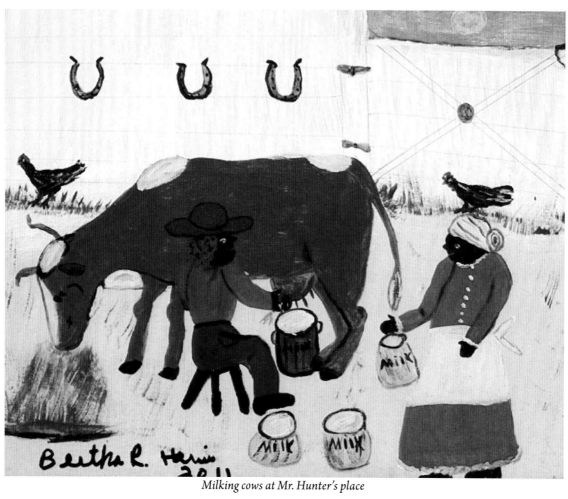

Milking cows at Mr. Hunter's place

29. Return to Yorkstone

After a few months of making minimum wage, I was forced to file bankruptcy. I was making nowhere near the money I'd made at Yorkstone, and the anger that I felt about the situation I'd allowed Carter to force me into was consuming me. He should have been the one forced to leave; he was the one who'd done something wrong. Because of him, I was in a nowhere job, barely able to make ends meet.

In October of 1987, Harry Burns, who worked for Yorkstone as staff manager, had been promoted to a district manager of a different location, indicating that there would be an opening for staff manager. He called me at home and asked if I would come work for him. The very idea of going back to Yorkstone made me more than a little uneasy. Working for Harry Burns didn't bother me, but the idea that I would have to come into contact with Carter made me sick.

I asked Mr. Burns to let me think about his offer and that I would get back to him soon. I couldn't help remembering how much I'd loved my job before Carter. I would no longer call him "Mister"; I didn't respect him enough for that.

I finally agreed to work for Mr. Burns, but I told him that I wouldn't work with Mr. Carter, not for any reason. After his assurance that I wouldn't have to do so, I filled out an application for the position. The company quickly approved me to start work.

Our district consisted of two staff managers and eight agents. My staff had two agents and I had to recruit three more to make a full staff. There were three women and one man under me. No one, not even I, doubted that I could handle my staff. I'd already proven my capability. The only thing I was lacking was the training required to be the staff manager, and Mr. Burns helped me to achieve that.

After three months on the job, my staff was up and running. We had one of the best sales and collections records within the company. My team and I got along well. I gave them respect, and in return, they respected me. I never asked them to do anything that I wouldn't have done myself. Just as they worked in inclement weather, so too did I.

In December of 1988, Mr. Burns broke the news to us that we were going to be transferred to Mr. Carter's district.

"You've got to be kidding," I said in reaction.

"No, Bertha, I'm afraid not," he assured me. The company complained that my district isn't making the quota we need to stay up and running," he said, disappointment obvious to me.

"Mr. Burns, I'm sorry, I just can't work under than man again," I told him sadly.

"Bertha, there's so many women working out of his office now that I doubt he'll even notice you," he said trying to make me feel better about the transfer. But I knew better.

Mr. Burns was aware of why I didn't want to work for Mr. Carter, I'd told him shortly after I returned.

Carter's district had moved from its original location into a larger one. He now had six managers, thirty agents, and two secretaries. Our two staffs would combine to make forty-five agents and eight staff managers. He would now have a team that was both black and white.

When I got home that night, I couldn't sleep. I kept thinking about the change that I was being forced to make. I came to the conclusion that with him supervising so many shifts, he couldn't possibly have the time to harass me. I knew for sure that I intended to avoid being alone in his company.

Bertha *and her agents at the insurance company award banquet*

30. The Transfer

THE FIRST DAY OF THE NEW ORGANIZATION BEGAN IN JANUARY OF 1989. I still felt nervous about returning to the office where I would be forced to work with Carter, but I was determined to see it through.

I walked into the office that first morning and knew he was "the same old Carter"; nothing about him had changed. When I walked in, he directed me to an area located right in the center of the office.

The new office was beautiful. The floors were covered with thick, expensive blue carpeting throughout. Carter had his own private office, and it had a beautiful view, nice chairs, a sofa, and all the trimmings that would make him comfortable. I latched onto the hope that there was some small chance that he had forgotten me, and what he had done to me.

I could see Carter come and go from where my desk was located. It seemed, for a while, that he had forgotten the incident that he'd created between the two of us. But I hadn't. Every time he came near me, I felt icy heat, the kind that only comes when you combine the two emotions of fear and anger, but I was finally able to convince myself that he had really forgotten.

I was sitting at my desk, going over an account with one of my agents when, at the end of March, I noticed a lady from one of the other divisions go into Carter's office. The look on her face reminded me of the day he'd disrespected me, and I couldn't help wondering if he'd just done the same thing to her. Later, I overheard her angrily saying to her manager that she wished he'd tell that old bad, breath bastard to keep his hands off of her.

I knew then that the loathsome bastard hadn't changed at all. He was still the same dirty old man he'd always been. I made sure I was never alone with him after that. I also warned some of the other women to be careful around him and told them how fresh he would try to be with them. In the end, I found myself being caretaker to many of the staff.

In August, my staff won the most increased staff award for that month within the company. The district was thriving. Therefore, I had to recruit new agents to share the load. I did what I could to recruit a few men, but none seemed to want to work there. If I could have hired a few men, my job would have been much less stressful, and Carter would have been less likely to continue his blatant harassment. Alma, my new agent, was a single mother with two children. She was very attractive and very intelligent. As soon as Carter saw her, he dove in like a vulture diving for fresh meat.

Alma worked extremely hard and really seemed to be enjoying her work for about three months, before her attitude changed completely. I later learned that Carter had tried to touch her breasts and had openly asked her to sleep with him.

When I found out what he had done, I went into his office to confront him. "Carter, Alma complained to me that you touched her breasts. It is beginning to affect her work," I said calmly, trying to reason with him. "How do you expect me to manage the women on my staff if you are doing things like this, and trying to get them to sleep with you?" I asked.

If looks could kill, I'd be a dead woman. Without saying a word, Carter turned toward me and stared me down, holding his cigar in his hand. I kept waiting on him to say something, but he didn't, letting his eyes speak for him.

"When are you going to let me have some of your nookie?" he asked me, as if the previous conversation hadn't just taken place. It was my turn not to respond, and I didn't. I turned around and walked out of his office. How I hated the fact that I couldn't fight him and keep my job.

Women all over the office began complaining about Carter and what he was doing and saying to them. They were afraid to be in the office alone with him, and I couldn't blame them. I refused to be in his office alone myself.

Ruth, his mistress, had been promoted to a district manager's position and everyday she would visit our district. She was bold, not even trying to hide their relationship. "Me and Carter are going to the motel and make some babies," she would say on many occasions, acting as if she was his wife. As a matter of fact, many of the newer employees thought they were man and wife. Every affair that our company sponsored, she was there. We had gotten so sick and tired of her that we sometimes called Jan, Carter's wife, and asked her to join us. That made Ruth sit at the other end of the table, flashing her baby blues in his direction.

Some of the employees there owed Carter thousands of dollars, I learned later. One Monday morning at a sales meeting, he stood and shouted, "Some of you people owe me money. You need to get off your asses and go to work," he yelled.

This happened in the late eighties and I couldn't believe people would allow themselves to get in such a position. Nearly a century ago, W. E. Dubois warned of this very same thing when he wrote *The Soul of Black Folks*.

It was all part of the system back then to keep colored people indebted to whites. We would always be at their mercy.

Carter had managed to get whites as well as blacks indebted to him. Back in the fifties, when Mama and my stepfather and the other workers on the plantation owed money to the plantation owners, it was because they couldn't do any better. These people were supposedly educated men and women, yet they had allowed this man to make them no better than slaves.

Carter kept a black book in his office that he used to keep records of the loans he made to the people in the office. Whenever they got a loan, they were forced to sign over their possessions as collateral. He didn't care that he might take everything that person owned, and he didn't care who saw the book either. I was just glad my name wasn't listed in there. The word was out among the office staff, "Don't get your name in that book."

In 1989, after working closely with my agents, our staff rose to second place with almost seven thousand dollars record in premium increase over the year. This catapulted us in line for the President's Club, and an all expense paid trip to a convention in Florida.

It was wonderful; everything was first class. We were treated like kings and queens. The convention was held at the Disney World Resort in Florida, and the company had a special table set up for the top managers and agents. Dear God, I was more than a little proud to be among the elite.

We found the time to tour the Magic Kingdom and Sea World. Seeing Shamu the Killer Whale and the laser fire alone were worth the trip. The time we shared was like greeting old friends and meeting new ones. Carter was presented the gold cup for being the number one district manager for the year, which qualified him to bring his entire family. Mary Randle of South Louisiana was the number one staff manager that year with an almost eight thousand dollar premium increase, and I rated the number two staff manager. She and I were the first black women to receive gold cups in the history of the company.

The money that Mary and I earned, the other managers only dreamed of. The district that I worked out of was the highest producing district the company had. When you worked out of there, you were considered to be somebody within the company.

I just wished we didn't have to work in such a hostile environment. There wasn't a day that went by that I didn't believe someone high up in the company knew what was going on.

Bertha receiving insurance company award for Top Staff Manager

31. The Godfather

THE FOLLOWING YEAR, WE WERE AGAIN NUMBER ONE WITHIN THE COMPANY FOR OVER A MILLION DOLLARS IN PREMIUM INCREASES. Though I was proud of our accomplishments, I was very much aware that our success increased Carter's power within the company.

I guess it must have gone straight to his head, because several times I heard him actually cursing his boss, Richard Sterling, out over the phone, telling him to tell his boss to kiss his ass.

Carter ran his district like he wanted to. No one out of the home office could tell him what to do. Some of the agents and managers referred to him as "the Godfather of the insurance business." Others likened him to God, and his boss to Jesus. Carter obviously possessed enough knowledge about the insurance business that he could share, but if you were a woman, there was a price to pay, and it was entirely too high for most of us to even try.

When we went to manager's training school, I tried to learn as much as I could. I'd quiz my roommates from other districts about the accounting end of he business or whatever their specialties were. The more I learned from other managers, the less I needed to meet with Carter.

I felt sorry for the managers who didn't know how to do their own accounting. If they needed his help, Carter would control their staffs. Then the staff members became forced into seclusion with him in his office. It meant the door closed with him to get help closing out their accounts. Thank God, my agents didn't have to go to his office on account day. I had a few agents who didn't heed my warning about Carter; unfortunately, they were forced to learn the hard way.

After Carter lured them into some level of flirtatious or consensual relationship, he dropped them as he did others before them. He expected everyone to act as though nothing was going on. Some of the women seemed to anticipate such privileges. Some went so far as to become possessive of him; other slacked off on their production. At that point I or whichever managers, their behavior affected, was forced to deal with the problems that followed this change in attitude. Reprimands included anything from lecturing to termination.

In June 1991, Ron Blackstone, a new staff manager from our district, and I qualified for a sales convention that was held in Toronto, Canada. Ron finished second place that year and I finished third.

This time we were put up at the Four Seasons Hotel. This trip was only for the upper elite and it was considered a royal trip. Our suites were the best, and here too we were treated like royalty. Our suites were equipped with a full bar, and many of us took advantage of them. Of course, when we got the bill, we wished we hadn't. A coke alone cost two dollars. You can imagine what a beer or a small bottle of liquor cost.

Those of us who smoked had to pay six dollars for a pack of cigarettes. I just thanked God I didn't have to pay for anything more than a few items, which included souvenirs. I'd taken my grandson, Rodney, with me to celebrate his graduation. This was his first real vacation, and he had a blast. He had grown up so fast. I wanted him to spend some quality time with me. It was important to me that we redevelop some sort of bond.

Because of the quantity and quality of films made in Toronto, it had been nicknamed "Hollywood North." The first night we were there, our tour guides took us to the Opus to eat. It had halogen lighting and was furnished with an eye for style and comfort. The service was excellent, and they had the most sophisticated dishes imaginable. I had fish layered with fresh basil and tomato sauce with a glass of wine.

Our second night there was our networking night in the ballroom. It had a breathtaking view of the city of Toronto. Because this was my second year out, I was proud to be showing off my handsome grandson to some of my old and new friends. Managers from all over surrounded me to congratulate me on my success. It was hard to believe that I was the same little nappy-headed girl from Homer, Louisiana, born and reared in poverty. I'd come a long way from the battered wife I'd once been, who suffered so terribly. I couldn't believe that I was now standing here rubbing elbows with millionaires and other everyday people with a smile on my face, and having a good time without fear of retribution when it was over.

On day three, I, along with the rest of the group, took a ninety-minute drive from Toronto to Niagara Falls in Ontario, Canada. We first viewed the falls from the Skylon Tower, which was more than seven hundred feet above the falls. It was a breathtaking view. We went under the Maid of Mist by sail boat and sailed right to the foot of the falls, thankful for the yellow rain coats that had been provided for our comfort, when the mist began spraying all over us. It was truly a trip of a lifetime for me as we sailed through one of the greatest wonders of the world.

That night was award night. The banquet room was elegant; the tables were adorned with beautiful white linen tablecloths and napkins with beautiful china place settings. The food was superb, and champagne bubbled from one end of the table to the other. As my grandson would say, Grandson and Grandma had it going on!

We were homeward bound on day four. When I left Toronto, I was fired up with dedication and determination. I knew that it would take both to qualify for the 1992 sales convention, and I was determined to be in Las Vegas with everyone else.

I hired Grant Mason about three months before going to the convention and I it didn't take long for me to realize his potential. Carter hadn't been very happy when I'd informed him that I was hiring Grant. He questioned me thoroughly about my decision, as if he would be able to find some flaw that would prevent me from hiring him.

Carter didn't like men very much, especially if they were handsome and had brains. "Don't mess with my women," he'd always say in a joking manner, but we all knew he meant it.

Grant became one of my best agents. Although I'd trained him to manage his accounts, sell and collect, and keep his records, he remained confident, inquisitive, and highly motivated. He was also community conscious and very aware of what went on. It didn't take him long to express interest in professional advancement, and I knew that it wouldn't be long before he was ready for management. So, once again, I had to put on my recruiting shoes and find agents to replace him.

Carter had also told the other staff members and me that a new district would be opening soon in our area. Bennie Jones, one of the other staff managers in our district, had been promoted to district manager. She had been with the company long before I went to work for Yorkstone Insurance Company.

32. Carter Loses Control

WITH THE CHANGES THAT WERE TAKING PLACE WITHIN THE COMPANY AND THE FACT THAT I WAS MEETING AND EXCEEDING THE REQUIREMENTS FOR MY POSITION, I HAD HIGH HOPES OF BEING MADE DISTRICT MANAGER. Richard Sterling, our regional manager, had mentioned to me a few times that I was being considered for something else other than what I was doing at the time. He hadn't said specifically what that was, but I'd assumed it would be a district manager.

During this time I hired Randa, a young nurse who worked at a nursing home and had three children, to work with us part time as an agent. I'm sure she found the extra money she was making there helpful. Randa did a good job with collections and sales in her assigned area and I had high hopes for her. She worked mostly evenings and weekends, which meant I didn't get to see her that often.

On the evenings I was unable to work with her, I asked that she leave her reports on my desk. For about three months everything went well. One night she called me at home. As I talked to her I detected the terror in her voice. This was unusual for Randa was usually happy and excited whenever she called.

"Bertha," she cried, "Mr. Carter was in the office this evening when I turned in my report," she said receiving my undivided attention. "He asked me to come into his office for a few minutes, he said he needed to talk to me about something," she said taking a deep breath.

I remained silent. I knew what she would say, I already knew the scenario, but still I remained silent, waiting on her to tell only what she felt comfortable retelling.

"After I got in there, he sat behind his desk and told me he could make my job easier, if I would let him have some nookie. Bertha, I was shocked," she said, her voice rising. "Then he told me to come over to his desk, that he had something to show me in a book lying on his desk. As I got closer, he pushed his chair away from his desk. I couldn't believe, he actually had his penis in his hand moving it up and down, masturbating. What is wrong with that man, Bertha? He doesn't know me that well, and I know I didn't do anything to make him do it," she said terror residing as anger began to replace it.

"Calm down, Randa," I said. "I will talk to him in the morning," I assured her. I was so angry I couldn't sleep that whole night.

The next morning, when I got to the work, I went straight into his office. I was so angry, there was no chance I would be intimidated this time. "Carter, what you did to Randa last night is a damn shame," I said as soon as I reached his office.

"I don't know what you're talking about," he snapped.

"Yes you do," I snapped. "There is nothing you can say that would convince me that woman made up the things she told me. I am tired of hiring agents only to have you run them off," I yelled into his face, not giving him time to say anything before I turned to walk out of his office.

Around nine-thirty, after the other employees had arrived, Carter came out of his office still grinning, walked to the center of the office and stood there. "Guess what y'all?" he said with a dramatic pause, waiting to make certain he had everyone's undivided attention. "Bertha accused me of trying to get some nookie from that fat agent of hers. Ain't that something?" he said sounding as if that were the most ridiculous suggestion he'd ever heard.

A brief silence, interrupted only with embarrassed laughter filled the office. Though some laughed, I don't think anyone found his announcement humorous. But, he'd made his point. He was still in control.

That evening Randa came by my house to turn in her debit book and forms. She told me then that she couldn't work there anymore. I could see the pain in her face and hear the terror in her voice. I understood what she was feeling. I'd been there. I told her how much I regretted what had happened, as I sat there trying to fight my own memories of my experience as lead in that play. I understood her pain, but I was at a loss as to how I could help her resolve her problem. And it was also my problem.

Talking to Richard Sterling was an option, but it wouldn't have done any good. Carter would remain in control of that office. The only thing I could do was to complain, just like the other females in the office.

I began suffering headaches and the old nightmares that I'd thought were long gone. However they had returned with a vengeance. Carter began pressuring me to hire another agent, and I was determined not to hire another woman, but a man this time. Eventually, though, when I realized finding a man was close to impossible, I hired Nicole.

Nicole was twenty-two, married and the mother of three children. She had a passion for the insurance business, so I was more than glad to have her. But I couldn't help wondering how long it would be before Carter ran her away.

After she'd been on the job a few months, Nicole bought a new car. She and her husband began making plans to do all the things they'd dreamed of doing since their marriage. I did what I could to keep her in the field, so that she could avoid Carter and his disgusting lust. It was my best hope for all of our successes.

By the time Nicole was fully trained, I had to leave her to work independently for a while. I could no longer protect her. I had to begin concentrating on some of the other agents and their needs.

33. Carter Tries to Rape Me

Tammy, one of my agents who had been with me since 1990, had to go into the office to pick up some forms as well as take a break from the heat. Carter, unfortunately, was in the office at that time.

When he heard fresh women's voices in the outer office, he came out to investigate. "How's y'all?" he greeted them, walking slowly forward. He continued walking around for a few minutes, holding his hand and pretending to read the production boards. He was like a hawk swooping over the field. When he finally strolled over to where we were standing he started in on Tammy.

He began slowly, complimenting her on her pretty blouse. The blouse she was wearing was a little low cut, but not overly revealing. I'd be willing to bet, though, after Carter's beady eyes made their way over every inch of her body, she felt naked.

Carter, never to employ tact in any situation, sat down next to Tammy where he could easily look down her blouse. I saw that Tammy was quickly becoming uncomfortable, and I was sure Carter knew it as well. He eventually placed his hand on her shoulder, letting it slide down toward her breasts.

Tammy, however, was unlike any of his previous victims. Before he could reach his goal, she'd moved his hands away from her body. She made a well-calculated turn and faced him eye-to-eye. Without hesitation she clearly snapped, "If you touch me again, I'll knock the hell out of you!" The fire burned in the depths of her eyes, adding indisputable conviction to her words.

Carter was frozen in time and space. He didn't say a word. He just got up to leave, stopping to pick up a penny off the floor, throwing it into her blouse. We were both so disgusted by his act and everything about Carter; we left without saying another word. I felt guilty about what had happened. I was, after all, Tammy's supervisor. Yet I couldn't protect her.

"I am so sick of that man asking me to sleep with him," Tammy finally said heatedly. "I've been fighting him off and cursing him out for the longest. But I have had enough. I can't take it any more."

My concern for her welfare was real, and I knew with three children, she couldn't afford to lose her job. I understood how she was feeling. No one should be forced to endure Carter's unwanted attention.

I went back into the office around two o'clock. The office was almost empty, the other agents having gone into the field, leaving only the secretaries. I was determined to try to have one more talk with Carter about his behavior.

When I walked into his office, he was bent over some paperwork that he had spread out on his desk. In a low, calm tone I asked if I could speak to him for a second, only walking fully into his office when I received an affirmative answer.

"Carter, it's getting harder and harder to manage Tammy," I began. "She is not producing sales, and her collections are down. What are we going to do about it?" I asked, despising him. "You seem to be the problem," I pointed out quickly. "Why don't you leave her alone?"

"Tammy complained to me that you were not giving her the help she needed," he said evading everything else I'd said, his eye shifting swiftly around the office, the ever-present cigar hanging from his mouth.

"Well, she complained to me that she was tired of you trying to sleep with her," I said bluntly, watching as his face turned as red as fire. "Furthermore," I continued, "I don't believe she has any respect for me as her supervisor, because of your lack of respect towards me."

He leaned back into his chair looking at me making me feel as if he could see through me. As I waited for his inevitable response, I sat there growing angrier and angrier. Finally, he rose up out of his chair and began walking forward. I assumed he was walking out, but instead he closed he door and locked it. Throwing his cigar into a nearby ashtray, he came toward me, looking like a mad man.

"What the hell is this damn man going to do?" I asked myself. I had no further time to think because it was then he threw himself at me, throwing me down and pinning me to the sofa, trying to pry my legs open and unzip his pants at the same time.

"Bertha, I got to have this nookie today!" he said in a voice that I didn't recognize. He looked down at the couch then, as if he were having trouble locating his penis. I reached over and picked up the debit book that was lying on the sofa next to my ruse and knocked the hell out of him. The blow landed on the side of his head. He rolled off the sofa onto the floor, and I grabbed my things, stepping over him to reach the door. As I made my escape, I looked back to find him sitting on the floor, his breaths coming out in loud, ragged sighs.

I don't know if the secretaries noticed me as I ran through the office, and I didn't really care. By the time I reached my car, I was trembling uncontrollably. When I got home, I sat out front, still in the car, trying to make sense out of what had just happened. I was as angry as hell.

What Carter had tried to do was reprehensible. I couldn't believe he'd had the nerve to actually try raping me. I didn't know what I would do, but I knew that something had to be done. He could no longer be allowed to run free without a leash. He was like a wild animal, totally out of control. Nothing I had said or done had any effect on him.

I had heard from one of the older agents that Carter had pinched her on the neck. A few days later, he'd come into the office area wearing a rubber glove, saying that he wanted to examine someone. One of the older agents got on the table and told him to go ahead. Afterward, she'd said that she'd finally gotten him off her back.

That shouldn't have been necessary. None of us should have to deal with the man who acted like he had. We received more respect from our clients than we did from Carter. This was a white man in a sea of black women and I knew that if I reported his behavior, I'd be the one catching hell. I was sure this was still a case where they would believe the white boss over all the black women.

I knew there was a chance that some of them would believe that I would have done anything to increase my chances of advancement. Approaching Carter for resolution was hopeless, I knew where that would lead. I'd even gone so far as to remind him that he had a wife, "she would have to have the best p---y in town for me not to get it elsewhere, and that she don't have," he'd remarked with his usual crass attitude.

I even tried reminding him of his mistress, but his only comment was that he could get that anytime. The man was impossible; he had his answer for everything. So, I began wearing loose fitting clothes, hoping that I would no longer attract his attention.

I refused to allow him to force me to resign. My income had reached forty thousand dollars a year and I just couldn't walk away from that. I truly believe that if a car had hit Carter, it wouldn't have mattered enough to me to shed a single tear.

A man like Carter had no business in the business world. His greatest thrill was strutting around the office, terrorizing the women who were forced to work under him. The fact that they were black only made him feel more superior.

I noticed when I returned to work that Carter wore a Band-Aid over his head to cover the area where I'd hit him. I had to admit I received a small sense of satisfaction from that. It was one shining star I found in the gloom. My future was looking mighty bleak that morning, and seeing Carter's injury was just a small solace.

Carter requested that all managers come to his office for a meeting. I slowly rose to my feet. I was getting sick just looking at him and smelling that cigar. That was the last thing I wanted to do, was to be closed in room with him. During the meeting he informed us that the company was going to form a new district.

"When the company is ready to interview managers." I will let Ya'll know." he said. Not looking at me.

"Dance, children! Dance!"

34. Searching for an Out

News that the company had begun its search for new District Managers was the best news I could have heard. It would mean that I would finally be free of Carter's supervision. There was some concern, though. It seemed that the company made their decision based on Carter's recommendation.

There was no question that I was the most qualified for the job. My staff continually had over twenty thousand dollars in premiums. No other staff manager there could make that boast. Once again, my staff was going to the sales convention, this time it would be held in Vegas. This was our third time qualifying, and we set unprecedented records within the company.

As excited as I was about the prospect of my job and the trip, my frustration about Carter continued to grow. Trying to pretend that life was normal was stressing me out more and more. So when I spotted Dr. Islam's ad in a local newspaper, I felt as if he was he answer to my prayer. I hoped that he could help me with the headaches, dizziness, sweating, chest pains, and faintness I'd been experiencing. I really needed to consult a professional.

Dr. Islam diagnosed my symptoms as panic attacks and post-traumatic stress syndrome. I hadn't told Carter that I was seeing Dr. Islam. He was a psychiatrist, and I had already had first hand experience in what people thought of anyone who had to see a shrink.

As part of my treatment, Dr. Islam prescribed anti-depressants and tranquilizers, which helped me to function, at least well enough to attend our four-day convention in Vegas. As a treat, I invited my daughter, Lois, to go with me.

We arrived in Vegas, the city that never sleeps. Our accommodations at the Bally Hotel were superb. The trip was as glorious as those preceding it, but not my spirit. On the night we received our awards, I couldn't enjoy myself because I couldn't help feeling that my future was hanging by a very thin thread, one that could break at anytime

That year Carter's district finished the year in second place with the company. I finished fourth place, Bill Brent a new staff manager in our district finished third, and Ron Blackstone finished first place with the company.

I knew that unless something was done soon to keep Carter from harassing the women in the office, I would no longer be able to continue my façade.

On the fourth day we returned home. As nice I'd found Vegas to be, I found that it was much easier to be miserable at home.

We'd only been back a few weeks when word began spreading that Ron Blackstone had been hired as manager for the new district. Carter had told us he would let us know when the company was ready to interview, but he'd lied.

The following day, I confronted him in his office. "When are they going to interview for the new district?" I asked as if I knew nothing about the rumors that were circulating like wild fire.

"That district position has already been filled," he said sheepishly, unable to look at me.

"It's been filled?" I asked dully.

"Yes," he replied growing more and more restless, still unable to face me. "They hired Ron for the position," he said after a few minutes.

"Why Ron?" I asked.

"Because of his record," he said quietly, more subdued than I'd ever seen him.

"I have a record too, and I want to be interviewed for the position," I demanded heatedly.

"I guess me and you gonna need to go to the motel and talk about this," he said pushing back in his chair to put his crossed legs on top of the desk. "You can let me have some nookie while we're at it. Cuz you're long overdue, Bertha," he said, his tone and arrogance infuriating me.

"Did you take Ruth, Bennie, and Ron to the motel?" I blurted out.

"You don't get something for nothing around here," he snapped finally losing his composure.

I stood there looking in to his cruel eyes, fuming at his attitude towards women. "I sure as hell was not going to sleep with you to get a position," I said allowing my distaste at the very idea to infuse my words. Even if I had been foolish enough to go to bed with the damn man, I knew in my heart that I would have killed him for seeing that I didn't get the position after all.

A week Carter came out of his office and announced, "If any of y'all managers want to interview for that district, y'all better get your résumés in with a cover letter,"

Gary Randall, the agents' director came up the next week and went through the formalities. Richard Sterling, the regional manager, called me a week after Gary left. "Bertha, I am sorry to inform you that we chose Ron Blackstone for the position. If it makes you feel any better," he continued, "I can tell you that you were the second choice." I'm sure he meant well, but I'd already known what they were going to do. There was no way they were going to remove Ron.

I didn't understand why they would hire a man who had been with the company for less than a year. I knew he was Ruth's son-in-law, but that didn't necessarily qualify him for the job. So that was what Ruth had hoped to gain by sleeping with Carter.

35. No Enthusiasm

I was finally beginning to understand that it was impossible to escape Carter's control. The incident with Ron left me less than enthusiastic about the company. I began to feel that if I couldn't go up, there was nowhere for me to go but down. All of my hard work had been in vain. If Mr. Elwood had still been regional manager, this would never have happened.

Things continued to spiral downward and in September of that year, Nicole's books came up three hundred dollars short. She'd let a few clients remain on her book without receiving any money; that what cause the shortages. I tried to stay on top of things because Carter was becoming more and more unpredictable. Because of the discrepancy, Carter held her check and ordered me to do an audit of her books. That made her furious and she resigned.

I felt so bad about what had happened, I didn't know what to do. When she called me at home, I told her I was sorry about what had happened, but there was nothing I could do.

A few days later, Carter asked me to call Nicole and have her come in so that he could talk to her about her check. I assumed that he would pay her then. But, a few days later, she came back in again. This time, she brought Carter a surprise. Instead of coming alone, she brought an older woman with her. The pair went straight into Carter's office. After a while, I could hear their voices raised in a heated argument. The longer I listened, the louder the voices became.

"If you want to pull your pants down right now, you son-of-a-bitch. I'll shoot your nuts off," the older woman was saying, drawing stunned glances from everyone in the office.

Keeping my eyes and ears trained on the door, I rose from my desk, walking even closer to see if I could grasp what exactly was going on. I could see Carter sitting at his desk. Instead of wearing his typical smug grin, he wore a look of fear. The woman had not only threatened Carter, she was actually standing over him with a gun in his face. It was priceless. I don't think Carter doubted for a minute that she meant business.

"Ma'am," I said coming quietly into the office. "You don't want to do this and get yourself in trouble, please."

"This old bastard pulled his pants down when Nicole came in here a few days ago and tried to get her to have oral sex with him," she said furiously. "I want him to pull them down today. I'll shoot his damn balls off."

"I didn't do no such thing!" Carter shouted in his defense, still shaking in his boots from the very real threat this woman posed.

"Yes, you did," Nicole shouted emphatically. "You told me if I wanted my check that I would have to give you some head, or go to jail," she swore furiously.

"Where did this damn man come from?" the older woman asked, "He has no business running no office. I want you to give her check, right now," she ordered, facing Carter without restraint.

Correctly guessing that the woman had no intention of backing down, before she shot him, Carter leaned toward his desk and pulled Nicole's check out of stack and gladly passed it into her waiting hands.

"Something needs to be done with your damn ass," the woman said between clenched teeth. You done messed with the wrong person this time. I'll kill you about my niece," she said clarifying her relationship to Nicole. "I reared her from a child and nobody ain't going to run over her as long as I live," she snapped, her fury obvious.

I followed them outside when they left the office. "Nicole, I assumed he'd given you your check that first day you came in," I told her feeling bad that things had gotten this out of control. "I'm sorry this had to happen."

"How do y'all work around that man?" Mrs. Green, Nicole's aunt, asked me.

"It's not easy," I told her truthfully. "I have no other choice right now. I'm the sole provider of for my home and family."

"Auntie, my husband and I are separated," Nicole informed her aunt, though why she chose then to have this conversation, I didn't know.

"Done broke up, why?"

"He thinks I've been seeing another man. I can't stand him touching me since that damn Carter started in a few months ago," she cried.

"I thought something was wrong with you, you haven't been yourself lately," Mrs. Green said with compassion and understanding.

"I just feel so dirty. That's why I've been wearing these loose fitting clothes to work," Nicole explained.

"We're going to go home, and I don't ever want you back here, Nicole," Mrs. Green said adamantly.

I'd stood there watching them turn to leave after a hasty goodbye. It wasn't that I cared whether she'd shot and murdered Carter, I couldn't have cared less. But I didn't want her to spend one single day in jail because of Carter; he wasn't worth it. Carter was the one who should be in jail.

He must have seen them leave for a minute hadn't passed before he was out of the door, to his car and sped away. I have to admit, I enjoyed seeing him this way. Too bad he wouldn't stay that way.

Finding a replacement for Nicole wasn't easy. I searched and prayed over and over again. Finally, I hired Sean Kelly. Sean was a well educated, and zealous young man who had the potential to reach the top level within the company. We experienced tremendous growth during this time, and consequently the managers were required to work on Sundays to complete all of the required paperwork.

Morale was at an all time low, and how we grew under the conditions we were forced to work in could only have been called a miracle.

Whenever I thought about being around Carter, I would have a panic attack. For a while I thought I was going to have to go in the hospital. Because Grant Mason had worked on my staff prior to being promoted, I had talked to him about Carter. I asked him to call me when he arrived at the office. So I wouldn't be alone with Carter. Having him in the office worked out well, it certainly helped keep Carter at a distance.

One Sunday, to my surprise, Carter found me alone. I was standing at the black board, balancing my production when he surprised me from behind. "Bertha, I need to f--k," he said, the stench of his breath and body odor reeking. He stepped back then, looking at his crotch. I would have thought he'd gotten enough after that incident with Nicole's aunt, I know I wouldn't have forgotten a gun pointed at me.

36. Carter's Behavior Worsens

A FEW MONTHS LATER, BILL BRENT HIRED AN AGENT ON HIS STAFF BY THE NAME OF PANDORA. She was a beautiful woman with fair skin. She too was a wife and mother of five. After she'd been on the job for about three months, I began noticing that Carter was coming out of his office much more frequently, and on those occasions he would grab her by the arm and pull her into his office. He didn't care that the whole office was looking at his wretched display.

I sat there praying that he wouldn't run Pandora away as he'd done the other agents with his lewd, disgusting behavior. Pandora was writing a lot of new business, but I didn't know for certain whether she'd been getting the money on it. Although I had heard Carter telling some of the agents that he would prepare their accounts himself, I was positive that he would capitalize on their inexperience.

As time went on, Carter continued to monopolize Pandora's time in the office. On several occasions, she complained to Bill, requesting that he keep that bastard away from her. Everyone in the office was aware that the situation would soon reach its peak, so they entertained themselves by speculating on what would happen next.

"It's my business who I go to bed with," Carter announced one Monday at our district meeting, subtly trying to tell us he was tired of the gossip. "If some of you weren't so damn fat, I might take on some of you."

Same old Carter, he firmly believed that he could do what he wanted to do, and no one should have a word to say about it, regardless of who was victimized.

Speculation about the inevitable run in between Carter and Pandora continued to mount. It happened in 1993. One morning Pandora came into the office, her hair clipped, looking very sassy. When everyone asked her why her hair had been cut so short, she informed them that one of her children had cut it while she slept. A week later, she stopped coming to work.

We didn't get to attend the sales convention that year. I missed it by a few dollars. I was at the point by then that I just didn't care. My heart was no longer in it. In September of the same year, one of my older agents informed me that she planned to retire early in the next year, forcing me to hire another agent.

This time, I hired Gail and trained her to fill the empty spot. Gail was fairly attractive, and looked quite a bit like an Indian. She was married and the mother of three. When Carter noticed her, he began prowling through the office again.

"Bertha, can I talk to your new agent?" he asked one day.

"Carter, please, don't do that," I pleaded with him as Sarah, one of the secretaries looked on.

"Sarah, tell Bertha to let me talk to her new agent," he said.

I did what I could to keep her somewhat distanced from him, but it wasn't enough; it never was. A month later, she began to complain about his advances. One day as we were standing around in the office talking before going into the field, Carter came over and greeted us, doing his best to catch a glimpse of Gail's breasts.

"Looks like your breasts have grown," he commented, the vulgar smirk on his face sickening. Poor Gail could only stand there with her mouth open.

In October, the company acquired another failing insurance company, including their agents in the deal. The new staff consisted mostly of well-educated, young, black men. They knew the business well and were not opposed to confrontation or controversy. Carter disliked them right away.

If there was one thing Carter disliked above all others, it was working with someone who knew the insurance business as well as he did. He didn't mind blacks that he could manipulate like damn monkeys, and these brothers did not fall into that category. When Carter found out that their staff manager earned almost as much as he did, it almost drove him over the top, and to tell you the truth, I enjoyed every minute of his discomfort.

Looking back now, I realize that one of the reasons that Carter had been able to manipulate those of us in his office for years was because we knew that he controlled our prolonged economic status. Responsibilities to our family's home and personal needs superseded our pride. Financially, we were living high, but our self-confidence was bankrupt.

In November, I lost another agent, this time to surgery. Because she would be out for three months, I was forced to hire someone to handle her debits. Denise was a young newlywed who I hired to fill that responsibility. Having three new agents was more than a little stressful. I couldn't keep up with everyone, making protecting them all impossible.

Carter was becoming bolder with Denise and Gail. Every time I walked into the office, he had one or the other of them in his office. He was having the time of his life. Carter's lewd behavior had escalated to a dangerous level, yet it seemed that those around him had become virtually indifferent to his antics.

"Carter cornered me in his office, rubbing up against me and told me he liked his coffee like he liked his women, black and hot," Gail told me one day. It seems that Carter had told her that if she weren't going to give him some nookie, she'd pay for it. "He caught me off guard and fondled my breasts and buttocks once," she continued. "He even asked if he could see my nookie once," she said fury building. "I can't take it any longer, something needs to be done about that man," she finished. And she was right.

Carter was out of control at a new level, even Denise had begun complaining about his behavior, telling me that Carter had crept behind her one day while she was talking on the phone and grabbed her breasts. She'd been too embarrassed to say anything. On another occasion, he'd invited her to accompany him to a motel.

Whenever Denise asked Carter questions about business, he'd automatically steer it around to sex. Something had to be done, and soon. We were coming apart quickly.

37. The Turning Point

Just as had happened with female agents before, Denise and Gail had had enough of Carter, and they were ready to do something about it. When they came to me, they were thinking about seeking legal advice and quitting. Both of their husbands were threatening to come to the office and meet Carter, physically. It was becoming more and more impossible for me to run the office and keep the peace at the same time.

I was furious that such a disgusting man was permitted to sabotage the moral fiber of every woman he encountered. I couldn't imagine what motivated him to act that way. What was his rational for trying to force women into submission? There were so many questions, yet I was finding that the answers weren't quite so simple.

I'd been making excuses for the man for six years and I was fed up. I refused to tolerate it anymore. Grabbing the nearest phone book, I turned to the yellow pages. There had to be an attorney somewhere in this town that I could speak to about my options.

Before going ahead with my plans, I spoke to Gail and Denise. After speaking to them, I called some of the other women who'd left because of Carter's reign of terror, to see if they would like to file a suit against Carter as well. Only Nicole wanted to join my battle. I didn't really understand their reluctance; I knew I had more to lose than any of them.

The only recourse Carter had left open to us was through the legal system. I needed my job, and I knew it was impossible to fight Carter alone. Nicole and I spoke to Nelson Cameron, an attorney who specialized in such cases. Bonnie, his secretary, was a very sincere and sweet person whose smile made me feel comfortable. She directed us to the conference room, where we waited.

Mr. Cameron was friendly, but professional. After taking our statements, he informed us that he would have to first file our complaint with Equal Employment Commission, and then they would send a letter to the company within four weeks, notifying them of our complaint. Unfortunately, we'd have to wait six weeks while EEOC finished their investigation. If nothing were resolved in six months, we would then have the right to issue a letter of intent to sue.

He was curious to know if there were other victims, I assured him there were, but I doubted if they weren't willing to come forward. Most of them won't talk because they owed Carter money, I informed him. When he asked why I'd waited so long, I told him the truth that I didn't know who to talk to. Carter was my supervisor and he had the power to hire and fire. We worked with people who considered Carter some kind of God. The company had given him quite a bit of power because his office was consistently one of the highest producing districts within the company.

I must have talked to Mr. Cameron for hours. It was the first time I'd ever told anyone the details of what Carter had done, and once I began, the words tumbled forward until there were none left. When I'd finished, Gail, Nicole, and Denise were crying as hard as I was.

That night, when I got home, I still couldn't stop crying. I felt as if I had turned on a member of my family. As a matter of fact, Yorkstone Insurance Company *was* my family in so many ways. I'd spent more time with my co-workers than I had with my own family. It was difficult for me to realize who all stood to be hurt by this investigation. No one in my family was aware of what had been going on, but I was afraid that before this was over, everyone would know.

Gail and Denise returned to work after our interview with Mr. Cameron, but I just couldn't go back. My daughter found me crying and took me to the hospital. My head ached so bad that I barely remember arriving. My daughter told me later that I was screaming, "I should have killed him! I should have killed him!"

My head ached for days. I was forced to hold my head to one side, trying to ease the pain. Whatever they were giving me for the pain didn't seem to be working.

My doctor tried to get me to talk about the case, but I couldn't do it. He might have been sensitive to sexual harassment, but I wasn't willing to risk it. My roommate, a young, white woman, was struggling with sexual abuse committed by her father. Because she was finding it difficult to have normal marital relations with her husband, he assumed that she was having an affair.

"Bertha, how can I tell my husband that it was my own father?" she asked one day.

I was sickened by her story. Why would a man want to have sex with his own daughter? There were plenty of women out there that would sleep with them, why didn't they just go find one of them?

Once my doctor realized that I wasn't able to discuss my problem with him, he assigned a female social worker to me. She was very sensitive to my problem and seemed truly angered by the horror of my story. Once I began talking, I cried for days. I expressed my concern for Carter's wife, Jan, and told my social worker I didn't want to see her hurt.

I truly liked Jan. I had met her on several occasions, and I knew she couldn't be held responsible for the man her husband had turned out to be. My social worker suggested that I write her a letter, which I did, appealing to her for her understanding.

When I'd finished the letter, I placed it on my nightstand. Whenever I began to feel guilty, I would take it out and read it. I grew stronger and stronger as time went on and was finally able to talk about the harassment to my group as well as to my daughter and grandson.

I was released on the seventeenth of February in 1994. I knew that whatever took place from this point on wouldn't be easy. Every flower that blooms had a hard time coming through the dirt. I had had some hard times in my life before I gained the courage to fight the beast, but I was no longer afraid and I would fight him.

On March 1, 1994, when I returned, the company had still not received their letter from EEOC. My attorney suggested that I keep a daily log of everything Carter did.

One day not long after my return, Carter called me into his office and talked to me about my staff. He wanted to know if I was capable of handling my duties. I assured him I could. He went on to tell me that production was down.

On March 3, 1994, Carter received a copy of the letter from EEOC. I assume the original had been sent to corporate headquarters. Carter jumped all over me.

"Over seventy percent of the people in this office told me you were trying to set me up," he roared. "Is that right?" he screamed.

I just remained calm.

"I'd been protecting you. Richard Sterling told me to fire you. Nicole quit after all these years and it's your fault. Your staff has gone to shit!"

"You still don't get it, do you?" I asked incredulously. "Those women didn't quit because of me, they quit because of you," I snapped.

He ignored that, but continued on. "You got this whole office in a damn uproar," he said pointing his finger. "I loaned your agents my money and fixed some of their accounts so they wouldn't get fired," he said as if it was my fault he'd made the loans in the first place.

"Whose account on my staff did you fix, other than Sean's?" I asked suspiciously, not believing him for a minute. Carter knew I didn't approve of his loaning my staff money. It made them harder to manage. "That's why he's out of control," I pointed Sean out as a perfect example.

Finally sick of him and the entire matter, I told him to stop loaning my staff money behind my back. It made him furious to see that I was actually standing up to him.

On March 9, 1994, Carter asked Gail, Denise, and me to join him in the office the next morning at nine o'clock. "The home office attorney wants to talk to y'all," he said as if we should be frightened.

"Bertha, telephone," Carter called out to me the next morning, handing me the receiver with a smug look. Someone from the other line began screaming into my ear, "What the hell is going on up there?" he shouted. "I need to know so that I can get to the bottom of it," he snapped.

"Sir," I said remaining calm. "You will need to speak to my attorney, I'm sure he'll be glad to clear things up for you."

"Do the other ladies have an attorney?" he asked, his anger still palpable.

"Yes they do," I assured him.

"Thank you," he snapped, throwing the receiver back into its cradle.

On March 11, I began getting feedback from the other employees about the impending case. People that I had known for years walked away from me, ignoring me. Even Richard Sterling, our regional manager, avoided contact with me. They treated me as if I had been the one to create the problem. It was even going on within the office. People actually made up excuses so they wouldn't have to sit with me.

"If you don't keep your mouth shut, you might come up missing," Bill whispered to me one day. I refused to be frightened by his threat. I had already made up my mind that I didn't mind dying for my right to be treated with respect.

By the twelfth, word had gotten around the office that Denise owed Carter nine hundred and fifty dollars, and that that was the reason she had reported him. They also stated that Gail was furious because he wouldn't lend her any, and that I was still angry about not getting the district manager's position. These rumors made it look as if the three of us had a vendetta against Carter, and I couldn't believe how many people seemed to believe it.

I caught hell all of March and into April. By the eleventh of April, I was exhausted and drained. The home office had still not sent anyone to investigate the charges, just continued on acting as if they didn't give a damn, and they probably didn't.

On the eighteenth of April, I saw Jan for the first time since I'd filed charges against her husband. Like so many others, she too walked by me as if she didn't see me. I understood that she was a woman standing by her man, but I can't deny how much her dismissal hurt.

Pandora returned to work in May, her hair having grown out some, but still shorter than before. She went back to work on Bill's staff. Carter was more than a little happy to see her, obviously not taking the actions filed against him seriously, but he was being less public about his innuendoes.

One of our ex-employees, Linda, called in June. She called to tell me that if I needed a witness, she would be more than happy to accommodate, God bless her. What Carter had done to her still angered her and she wanted to let everyone know how disgusting he really was.

One day, as I sat in the office with one of the secretaries, a client came in to see Carter, leaving suddenly as if something awful had taken place. "Why didn't you son-of-bitches tell me that my pants were wet," Carter said running out of his office. I wondered why he thought that we were responsible for policing his pants. We weren't getting paid to monitor him and I didn't hesitate to tell him so.

Linda told me that one day he lured her and another secretary over to his house. He assured them that his wife would be there when they arrived, and would prepare lunch for them. When they got there, Jan was nowhere to be found.

Carter went in and ran some water in his hot tub, trying to get them to get naked, so the three of them could f-ck. Linda told him to cut it out and take them back to the office. He reached over towards her and grabbed both of her breasts, pinching her nipples so hard they were bruised. She hit him so hard then, she knocked his glasses off, but that only seemed to turn him on more.

They finally ran to the nearest phone booth and called Linda's father.

"Bertha, I'm so glad someone turned him in. He fired me because he couldn't control me. Later, when I went to see him about a job reference, he tried to come on to me. He closed the office door, locked it then grabbed my hair and twisted around his hand and tried to force me to have oral sex with him. I bit the hell out of him; then he let go of my hair so I could run. I had moved back to Texas before I could get another job. That bastard ruined it for me.

"Someone from the office called my father and told him you had filed a complaint. My daddy is so upset and angry, he wanted to know why the man is still working here. I didn't understand either. How can he do what he's done to so many women and still get away with it?" Linda said, beginning to cry then, wanting to know if she could get him put in jail for what he had done.

"Let me discuss it with the other ladies involved," I told her. I was hoping that because Linda was a white woman, we would be able to put Carter in jail.

The more I heard the cries of the women who Carter had harassed, and thought of the other battered women in the world, the more angry I became. I was more determined to win than ever. I wouldn't allow the system to tell me again that things would get better. This time I was going to fight. I would fight hard enough and long enough to make up for all the years I allowed Guy to abuse me. This time, someone would have to listen to my cries for help.

Unable to find a crisis group for sexually harassed victims, we attended a support group at the YWCA's rape crisis center for a month. We endured much of the same pain as those of women who had been raped. Both groups were forced to endure flashbacks, nightmares, fear, self-blame, depression, anxiety, and insomnia.

During one of our groups, we met a woman who was a screenwriter. She'd been raped before coming here. We told her that the company had known about our complaint since February of that year and still hadn't investigated it.

"The only way y'all are going to get that company to listen is to put that bastard in jail," she told us. "I put my rapist's picture out all over the damn TV," she concluded.

I thought about what she had said; it made a lot of sense. Linda had said something about she and her father wanting to press charges. I wasn't sure if that was the right thing to do, but I was certainly going to discuss it with Mr. Cameron.

Linda returned to town in July. She called me to find out where things stood with Carter. Things were moving so quickly that it was sometimes hard to keep up with them. She was still determined to file charges against Carter. On the twentieth of July, we all met at Linda's father's house for strategy planning. We also called the screenwriter from the Y to sit in on the meeting. She became so involved with our problem; she suggested we write a screenplay about what had happened and drop it off at each of the television networks in town.

Someone noticed. Sandra, a news reporter for one of the largest stations here, wanted to do the story. After talking to my attorney, he agreed; he wanted to go on television himself.

Linda, Gail, Denise, and I were the only ones willing to go on television the next morning. We met there with our attorney and videotaped our stories. Linda's father joined us. From there we went to the Shreveport police station to insist that Carter be arrested. We were directed to a Sergeant Spencer in the sex offenders division, who told us that we would be hearing from someone as soon as the necessary papers were processed and sent to the DA's office. Then they would send someone over to pick him up. At that time, he would be charged with six counts of sexual battery.

Three weeks went by and still I heard nothing from the DA's office. Growing anxious and more frustrated with each passing day, I finally called to see what was causing the delay. I was told that because they were running behind, the paper work hadn't been processed.

Another week passed, and still nothing. The following week, Carter went on vacation. I called Sergeant Spencer again. "When will Carter be arrested?" I asked again angrily. "I'm continuing to be forced to work with this man. I want him arrested," I demanded.

"If you keep this up, you might not have a job for long," he snapped. I couldn't believe it. This man was supposed to be responsible for protecting us, and here he was threatening me because I insisted he do his job.

By August, we were furious enough to go back downtown, this time we visited the DA's office. I was so angry, I could swear smoke was pouring out of my eyes and ears. The receptionist in the office took one glance at us and knew without a doubt that we were six angry women; our demeanor said it all. Immediately we demanded to know why Carter hadn't been arrested, when we'd filed charges against him a month ago.

"If he'd been a black man with these charges, y'all would have gone out the same day the complaint was filed. You would have thrown him down on the ground and shackled him so fast it would have made his head swim. Now, we want this damn man arrested today, or we're going to announce it all over the world the injustice," I leaned over threatening her with exposure if something wasn't done today.

"Wait, wait, let me go back and ask somebody what the delay is," she said, coming back to promise us that Carter would be arrested that day.

Glad to hear it, I rushed right home and crawled in front of the television. The sergeant called to tell me that he had turned himself in that afternoon. Maybe I was being irrational, but hearing that he'd been allowed to turn himself in instead of arrested in front of everyone at the office really made me angry. I wanted him to be humiliated.

I called the newsroom to talk to the reporter to whom we had given the interview, and she got right on the case. Even though Carter hadn't been humiliated as I'd hoped, I was still glad that he'd been arrested. He posted bail shortly after that, but he had finally been arrested and the story made the headlines. It read simply that sexual harassment charges had landed a local businessman in jail. Included in the news report was our interview.

That night, the phone rang off the hook, as other women were eager to tell me that Carter had also sexually harassed them. All except one of them wanted to remain anonymous. Patsy, the one person who didn't care, told me how she'd gotten fired because her staff manager had taken two thousand dollars of her money, and Carter tried to use the lie that she'd stolen the money to force her into having sex with him. "He's a sick old man," she said. "He needed to stay in jail. If you need me to, I'll be glad to testify against his ass."

When I returned to work the next day, Carter was standing around with that nasty cigar sticking out of his mouth. He didn't say a word to us, but his posture said it all. I was called a nigger bitch, troublemaker, crazy bitch, and every other derogatory name under the sun. I was even threatened. Some of the employees crashed things, saying that that would be me if I continued to pursue my claim against Carter.

I found out that Carter had known a week before his vacation that he was about to be arrested. Someone from the DA's office turned out to be one of his golf buddies.

One of the managers whose desk was next to mine walked by my desk one day and deliberately farted. Whites and blacks alike turned on me. Their retaliation got so out of control, that I was almost forced to fight back. I called my attorney when things had really gotten to me. But he insisted that I say and do nothing except hang in there. "If one of them actually carries out his threat and hits you, we'll own the company," he said giving me the strength to go on.

I couldn't believe that my black sisters would turn on me as well, instead of standing up for me. I couldn't understand the mentality behind that behavior. This was 1994, not 1894. I suppose their actions could have been more financially based though, we all needed our jobs.

In August, six months later, after we got the company's attention, someone from the home office finally came to investigate the claim. They spoke to everyone except the three of us. I knew they somehow had gotten the ones who hadn't talked to lie, in a misguided effort to save Carter. After the company interviews, they formed a group of their own and left us to fight alone. Even those who had been on my staff for years no longer wanted to have lunch with me. The home office spoke also to Carter, but they still ignored the three of us.

In September, I noticed a poster and newsletter had been posted with information regarding sexual harassment. I had gone in and out of that room for years and had never before seen anything about the subject. I guess they could say, "At least we made some small change."

In November, charges of sexual battery were dismissed against Carter. We were told they dropped the charges because of lack of evidence. I knew they were lying. They hadn't looked for evidence, there was too much of it facing them. We waited a while hoping the DA would call to question us, but he never did.

Mr. Cameron called the DA's office and was told we could come in, after we made formal depositions, then they would see if they had enough evidence to charge him with a crime. There was no longer any doubt left in my mind that this system of justice cared little about right and wrong, true justice and injustice. Men were permitted to do whatever they wished to women.

A week later, Pandora called to tell me that she had applied for a staff manager's position, but because she wouldn't sleep with him, Carter had given the position to a man. She wanted to talk to Mr. Cameron, and wanted me to go with her.

When we arrived in Mr. Cameron's office, Bonnie, his secretary asked us to wait in the conference room. Pandora sat with her back to the door and when Mr. Cameron slammed the door behind her, I thought she was going to jump through the window.

"Please don't close the door," she pleaded. "I can't help it, it makes me uneasy," she screamed with unfeigned hysteria.

Mr. Cameron wore an expression that asked what the hell was wrong with the woman, but he said nothing just opening the door before he took a seat. I couldn't help wondering exactly what had really happened to Pandora to make her act that way.

With the door opened and Pandora calmed down, Mr. Cameron sat and asked Pandora to relate to him what had happened between herself and Mr. Carter. I sat there carefully listening to her tell the full story of the degradation and humiliation Carter had subjected her to in the company.

Pandora started, "When I came back to work my manager Bill promised he would keep Carter away from me. That didn't happen, Carter told him to train me to be a staff manager. Because they were going to be minus one soon, he was referring to Bertha's staff. I didn't want to see Bertha fired. But I did want to be a manager."

Pandora then went to the beginning, "The first time Carter asked me about sex was in 1992. I told him I was married and I didn't cut out on my husband. And he said, 'what's marriage got to do with it?' he asked. It was late in the evening. I was sitting at my workstation filling out some applications. When I finished and attempted to leave, he grabbed my arm and pulled me into his office. No one was in the office but the two of us. I was so shocked I couldn't yell out. He closed and locked it, then he open his desk drawer and place some accounts on the desk with my name on them."

"Look at all this money you owe the company, and I've been protecting you. I need to get some pay," he said grabbing my hair and twisted it around his hand and pull my head down on his penis and he fell to the sofa. I turn my face back and forth trying not to touch it. But he was able to run it again my face. After that happen I felt dirty. When I got home I took a shower and still felt dirty. I couldn't stand for my hair to touch my skin. I took a pair of scissors and cut it off as short as I could, telling my husband that it was hot on my head. When I came to the office I told everyone that my child cut it while I was sleeping," she cried.

As I sat there listening at those lurid details of her story, I was forced to relive my own nightmares brought on by the man. Bonnie noticed the tears flowing and came over to comfort me.

In December the isolation and retaliation had become almost unbearable. I didn't have any more agents working with me so I demoted myself to an agent. Gail and Denise had already resigned, they simply couldn't take anymore.

After Pandora filed her complaint, she didn't return. I tried to keep working, hoping they would do something with Carter before he killed me, or I killed him. The tension between us was so thick you could cut it with a knife. He did whatever he could to make my life a living hell. Once he called an audit saying that he needed to go over my books to make sure the money was there. I'd gotten to the point that looking at him turned my stomach.

I knew that he hated me for exposing him. One night, I waited alone for him to come into the office. Thank God he didn't show up, if he had I believe I would have been able to commit murder, I'd planned to shoot him dead.

There was no longer any way to continue working there. Just the thought that this man could push me to the point of murder warned me that things had indeed gone to far. I made my resignation official at the end of December.

***Jimmy**, **James** (barely visible in front of doorway),*
***Odell**, **Eddie**,*
Bertha**, **Ella**, and **Annie

38. History Repeats Itself

I GOT A JOB WORKING IN A CONVENIENCE STORY IN JANUARY. Twenty years later, I was back in the same place, not knowing what the future held for me. My salary had dropped from forty-five thousand a year to four dollars and twenty-five cents an hour, which left me feeling hostile, angry, and less than human most of the time.

Was this what I got for trying to make my workplace peaceful, and less hostile? I'd never asked Yorkstone for anything more than an opportunity, and in return they'd shown their appreciation by allowing an uncomfortable position to escalate into an impossible one.

I now found myself wondering how I would be able to pay my mortgage, and utilities. I'd gotten my home renovated in 1992, which had exhausted the savings. I finally went to the food stamps office and filled out an application. They were not sympathetic to my plight at all.

The system had passed welfare reform, complaining that women were having more and more children to collect welfare and food stamps. Now, I'm a firm believer that all able bodied women should get off assistance and hold down a job just like the rest of us. But I find myself wondering, will the system enforce the law against discrimination and sexual harassment so that these women will be protected when they lose their benefits and have to go out of the work place because of some man, or will they be treated as we were? I can only believe that this despicable behavior will continue unless lawmakers not only pass the laws, but also see that they are enforced.

I went to work for another insurance company in February of 1995, hoping I could motivate myself. The retaliation and sexual harassment had taken its toll on me and I'm afraid I lacked significant motivational work skills. I couldn't shake the fear that I would fail again. I could no longer tolerate being in a group, and I felt uncomfortable around white and black men, so I avoided them at all cost. Eventually, I was fired for the first time in my life due to my poor performance.

In March of 1995, I was forced to file bankruptcy again. I no longer had any money coming, which forced me to forfeit my home, the very home I'd fought so hard to hold on to all these years. History was indeed repeating itself, I was in this same position when I'd quit Yorkstone in 1986, but then I'd been able to hold onto my home.

So many memories were tied up in that home, holiday dinners and the times spent with my daughter and grandchildren. My grandsons had roots on that street. Because they'd lived only a block away, everyone on my street knew them by name. I realized that with the income I'd been earning I didn't have to live in Allendale. Allendale was located in North Shreveport, reputed to be called the "Ghetto" or the "Hood" That neighborhood had been good to us and I didn't want to leave it. Allendale was a drug-infested neighborhood where only three out of ten families included more than one parent, and being a high school dropout was more than a statistic — it was a reality, but my grandsons had beat the odds and not become one more statistic. They are all, I'm happy to say, doing fine. Rodney, the oldest, graduated high school in 1991. Rodrick graduated in 1994, then joined the military. The youngest, Jonathan, graduated in 1998 and had played varsity football.

I hated the fact that they were often stereotyped because of where they lived. My daughter and I made a point of enforcing success in their hearts and minds. We wanted them to know that if they worked hard, stayed out of trouble, and got an education, they could live the American dream. I didn't know how I would explain to them what I was going through now, yet I didn't want to lie to them. God help me, I was so confused. I knew that they were hurt by me losing my job. But Carter had been sexually harassing their grandmother, and they understood. They wanted to beat Carter, which was one of the reasons I hadn't told them what was going on at first.

I sat around for days looking out of the window. I tried working again, to no avail. I simply could not cope.

Mary, a long time friend of mine, invited me to stay with her until I got back on my feet, but my pride wouldn't allow it. I called Kerry Kemphill, a counselor in a homeless shelter, and talked to him about moving in. I'd met Kerry when I worked for an office supply store.

"Bertha, you're welcome to come here, but I know you are a fighter and you are not ready for this, not yet," he said softly. "Think it over a little longer then call me back and let me know what you decide."

Kerry was right, I was a fighter — a fighter who had been knocked down, but not out. All I needed was the courage to get up, brush the dirt off, and come out fighting again.

My daughter asked me to move in with them. I readily agreed. The move was a special blessing. For years I'd spent very little time with my grandsons, and now I was finally given the opportunity to get know them, especially my youngest, Jonathan.

Jonathan is one of the most supportive and caring young men I have ever known. During my stay with them, my daughter and I renewed our relationship. She even told me that she was glad I was living with them.

I asked God to transform me so I could have the strength to be able to show my grandsons that we hadn't lied to them, they were still able to achieve their goals. I would have to impart to them the message that freedom isn't really free. To have true freedom, we must pay with sacrifices and suffering at times.

39. The Depositions

In April of 1995, we received a letter informing us that our depositions would be taken on about September 28 of that year. Over fifty men and women were sworn in to tell what they knew about the sexual harassment charges against Carter. Some of them told the truth, others didn't. Witnesses were both black and white. The varied statements they made were too numerous to put in a book.

Here is the list of charges that were made against Carter:
1. Kissing them against their wishes
2. Pinching someone's breast, on several occasions.
3. Yelling dirty expletives and jokes, propositioning inappropriately.
4. Massaging his penis in public.
5. Exposing his penis to women on several occasions.
6. Inappropriate fondling.
7. Inappropriate sexual relationships with subordinates.

Attorneys for Yorkstone and those representing Carter questioned us harshly, seemingly trying to make us seem like whores. They took Denise's deposition first, questioning her for eight hours in front of a video camera. They made it appear that she was the sex offender instead of Carter. They forced her to stand on her feet and demonstrate to them how Carter touched her. Through tears of humiliation, she did exactly what they asked of her.

My deposition followed second. They also questioned me for ten hours in front of a video camera. I had to give chronological dates from my past, from the time I'd entered the world from my mother's womb, until 1995. I was treated like someone who was only out to get money. As Mr. Cameron saw the effect the questioning was having on me, he objected to their tactics.

Pandora was questioned for over ten hours as well, also in front of a video camera. They asked her to demonstrate how Carter held her hand on his penis. She was asked what color it was, and if it had any spots on it. "Looked like he had age spots to me," she commented.

Gail, was questioned over eight hours, her deposition was on video as well. She was asked what she thought should be done to Carter as a punishment. "He should be made to pay for counseling for all the women he has sexually harassed," she said.

Nicole was also questioned in front of a video camera for hours. They asked her too what she thought should be done to Carter, "I wish they would publicly hang him up by his balls and his penis pulled off, so that he will not be able to show it to another woman," she cried.

Somehow, throughout all the hours of interrogation, we maintained our dignity and integrity.

Mr. Cameron said that Carter was one of the vilest, most disgusting harassers that he had ever seen. He used his money and power to attempt to manipulate each woman that had the misfortune to work under him into sexual acts and establish control over them by promising promotions or more favorable terms of employment. He wielded considerable power and influence in the company. As a whole, almost every person promoted to district manager in North Louisiana came out of Carter's district. Carter's authority had been magnified because many of the employees in North Louisiana came to him to voice their grievances in their district, rather than going to the regional manager, Richard Sterling.

Carter had engaged in a blatant and habitual pattern of sexual aggression against individuals over whose possessions, future, and even lives he controlled. There were many female employees who were sexually harassed, even after the initial complaints were filed with EEOC.

Carter gave his deposition after ours were finished. He sat there for four hours and lied through his teeth. "I didn't touch any of them women and that is the truth!" he cried incredulously.

"Mr. Carter, if you are telling the truth, how is it that all of these women, some who have never met each other, have testified that you harassed them in the same way?" Mr. Cameron asked.

Finally, Carter broke down and admitted he probably told dirty jokes to the women, and perhaps touched them in places that were inappropriate. He admitted making comments about liking his coffee hot and black just as he liked his women, he also admitted saying that a tee shot in a game of golf is like black p---y, it may not look good, but the lay can be great until you get caught, from a personal standpoint.

After Carter's deposition, we were told that the company director flew to Shreveport to terminate him the next day. The home office faxed our attorney letters offering us our jobs back, with one month's guaranteed salary, to be calculated by the average of the best three months of production during our employment with the company. They also offered me a District providing I take all the women who were going through the lawsuit on my staff.

It sounded to me that they were trying to offer me that forty acres and a mule they've been offering blacks during slavery. Personally, I wasn't a forty acres and a mule type woman. I demonstrated that to them, by getting with the women involved and forming a picket line. We marched in front of each office they had in North Louisiana. That got their attention like nothing else could have. When they called Mr. Cameron again, they called to offer a settlement. When you consider the mental stress we endured, and the fact that the company didn't care how we'd been treated as women, I knew I would never be able to trust them again.

I didn't want a job with the company any longer; it was time to move on. Ray Alford had been hired as the new district manager. He was one of the new black men that had transferred over from another company.

I still believe that Carter should have been sent to prison, rather than being fired. Men like him feel that they are above the law, and they will continue to sexually molest women, but we didn't force the issue. We were too emotionally stressed out to fight to have him tried for sexual battery.

In December of that year, Yorkstone settled out of court, but they never accepted responsibility for Carter's abuse of so many. In March of 1996, Carter settled. The monetary settlements would never erase the emotional nightmares each of us still experience.

This thing we now call sexual harassment and sexual abuse numbs your soul, spirit, pride, and dignity. Some of us will never be the same again. We have been so scarred that we find ourselves too often running from our responsibilities like frightened chickens, running from job to job, relationship to relationship, and husband to husband, never finding the solace we so desperately sought. We were physically and emotionally abused.

Milk time on Cooper Hill

Bertha & Alce Harris

40. P.S. Loved & Cherished

I met Alce Harris, my husband since 2001, when I was working as an outside salesperson and service tech for Time Warner Cable Company. He happened to be on my disconnect list.

When I arrived at his home he was sitting on his porch drinking coffee in the middle of the day, to my surprise it was about 100°F outside, I wondered why was he drinking that hot coffee? I felted as if I was about to burn up. I had on a shirt and a pair of knee shorts. A cold drink of water would have done me justice. Anyway, that wasn't my business. I was there to cut his cable off.

"Hey, are you Mr. Harris?" I asked.

"Yes, that's me," he answered.

"My name is Bertha. And I am with Time Warner Cable Mr. Harris. You are on my disconnect list, I need to get a payment from you today or I will need to cut it off."

He rose up out of his seat right quick when he heard that. "Hey," he said, "I don't get paid till Friday. Can you come back then?"

"I can't do that Mr. Harris," I said, turning to fetch my ladder from the truck so I could climb up the pole and disconnect the cable wires.

He stood there with a surprised look on his face like he wasn't believing what he heard me say. He shouted, "Hey miss, could you please leave it on till next Friday. My wife passed a few months ago and this is the only thing I have to keep me company. Come around 4 pm. I'll make sure I pay it."

"Ok, this time," I answered.

Standing still looking surprised, he finally asked, "Hey, do you really climb up them poles?"

"Yes, I do," I answered.

"Women doing all kind of jobs now. I can't see you climbing up poles," he said.

"If you don't have the money when I come back next Friday, you will find out if I can climb up there," I said jokingly.

He just didn't know. When it came to working I would try most anything. It was odd to see a woman my age climbing poles, but I was very fit from working out every day, and that helped.

As I walked away I could feel his eyes checking me out. I had kind of checked him out also. He was a tall and handsome older man. He had on a T-shirt and a pair of jeans with holes in the knees. It looked kind of sexy. Later on in our relationship, I teased him about how he was checking me out. He told me in a flirtatious way he was admiring my pretty short legs.

The next Friday rolled around and I remembered I needed to go by and collect the money from Mr. Harris. When I arrived, he stood up from his seat.

"Hey, do I need to get my ladder down?" I asked.

"No, no," he said. Grinning as he opened his wallet and pulled some bills out.

I gave him a receipt, thanked him and turned to leave.

"Hey, would you care to have a cold drink or water or a coke?"

"Yes, I believe I'll take a coke," I said. He went inside to get it. I sat on his step and drank it.

"Hey, what is your name again?" he asked.

"Bertha," I told him.

"My name is Alce. You don't have to call me Mr. Harris."

"That is a nice name. Never met anyone name Alce before."

"Well, Bertha, how long you been doing this type of work?"

"Almost two years," I answered.

"What type of work do you do?" I asked.

"I do construction work for Locke property. We build homes all over town," he went on and on.

"That sound like interesting job, Alce," I said.

"I got to get back to work before I won't have one," I said jokingly.

"You be careful out here in some of these neighborhoods. Do you let your husband ride with you sometimes? I would if I was your husband." I knew that was just a way of him to find out if I was married or not.

"The company don't allow that," I explained. "And by the way I am not married."

"Well if that the case, could I call you sometimes?" he asked.

We talked on the phone for a few weeks before he asked me out to have dinner with him.

We had dinner the following Friday. I picked Piccadilly in Mall St. Vincent. He asked if I had children. He told me he had eight grown children living in Texas and California and an 8-year-old grandson that lives with him. He and his late wife had raised his grandson Joshua from a baby. He spoke so highly of his family. I was so pleased to hear that.

After dinner we went and sat on a bench in the mall and talked for hours. I found out he and his late wife had been married for thirty-two years. Also, he had worked as a long distance truck driver for Enron Oil Company for years, before they went under.

I told him I had worked for an insurance company before Time Warner, but didn't tell him why I had resigned. That was not something I talked about much anyway, nor my past married life.

The more we talk the more I liked him. He took me home around midnight. He kissed me goodnight at the door and said good night.

He called around noon on Saturday. "Want to ride with me out on my job site?" he asked.

"Yes!"

"I'll be there in about twenty minutes. Ok?"

We didn't talk very much on the ride out. He had to check all of the homes they had finished to make sure the doors were locked. "Some items had been stolen from one or two a while back," he said.

"Why don't we go by my house to eat dinner?" he asked. He had cooked a rice casserole with turkey wings, and green beans and green salad for the side dish. Everything tasted good and I told him so.

"I bet you didn't think I would cook," he said.

"I sure didn't. Who taught you how to cook?" I asked.

"My grandmother taught me," he said proudly. He invited me to have a seat in the living room, which was very comfortable and clean.

"Where do you attend church?" I asked.

"I am a member of White Temple," he responded. "And you?"

"I am a member of Praise Temple Full Gospel Baptist."

"Why don't you go to church with me tomorrow? I will go with you next Sunday." From then on we did the same rotation for three months. Finally he told me he liked my church and Pastor Brandon, and he was thinking seriously about joining.

"That is up to you, but I would like it very much," I told him. After dating for about five months I could tell this was getting beyond liking each other. We had fallen in love with each other. I liked being with him. Alce was fun and he made me laugh. He brought out feelings in me I thought were gone forever. Most of all, he was a gentleman. He was a good man; he had a good heart. And he loved his children and grandchildren. If he had lots of woes, I couldn't tell. He did mention that he once had an alcohol addiction problem years ago, but that that was under control.

He also cared about the children in the neighborhood. You could always find a yard full when you went to his home. My daughter and my grans liked him a lot. For my daughter to like him he must have been special.

After church one Sunday Alce asked me to have a seat in the back of the church and wait for him while he went over and talked to Pastor Brandon about something. I couldn't hear what was being said, but whatever it was they were just hugging and laughing. When they finally settled down, Pastor held his hand and prayed. When Alce came back to where I was waiting, he still had a grin on his face.

"What was that all about?" I asked.

"I'll tell you later," he said. "How about we go and have some dinner." We went to Pete Harris's to eat. We were half though eating when he reached over the table and grabbed my hand with affection. He looked me in the face and asked me to marry him.

"Don't you think it's a little too soon after your late wife's death?" I asked. "You know how people talk. They will think you must have been seeing me before she passed away, if we get married too soon."

"I told Pastor Brandon how I felted about you. And I believed you were the woman that God wanted me to marry. I'm not thinking about what people say. God knows the truth and that's good enough. Pastor Brandon was so happy for me. So will you make me happy by saying yes?"

"I need to seek God about this," I replied. Boy, I had to get my thoughts together. I know I loved him but I didn't think marriage would come up this soon. I had talked to him a few weeks before and expressed my beliefs to him about sex before marriage. To my surprise he respected that. That's what made him so special from the rest of the guys I dated before him. Most of their conversation was all about sex. That left a bitter taste in my mouth. Ladies, if you meet someone and that is all he has to talk about is sex, **run!** Nine times out of ten he has children all over town, and other women saying, "That's my baby's daddy." I know you have heard that song before, so don't become a victim.

When I got through my forgiveness process, I made a promise to God that I would present my body as a living sacrifice for him. I wouldn't have premarital sex any more, because that was a big reason why my past life was in such a mess in the first place. Premarital sex can lead you down a road of shame and destruction and babies out of wedlock, if we are not careful. You are open to all kinds of sexually transmitted diseases. And we don't want to go there! If you just can't hold out, please use protection. I recommend that you just don't have sex before marriage. It saves you from a lot of heartaches and sorrow. As the Bible says, sex is designed for a husband and wife.

So much for that! A few weeks after seeking God, I went and talked to Pastor Brandon to see what he thought about us getting married so soon. He prayed before giving me the answer like he always does.

"Mother," he began, as he so affectionately called the older women in the church (as a matter of fact he was young enough to be my son, but I respected him as my leader and adviser in Christ).

Pastor Brandon reminded me that both of us were grown, he believed we both loved each other and shouldn't worry about what others might say.

He went on to say, "Mother, Mr. Harris was with his wife for thirty-some years before she passed, he's not used to being alone and he's not going to stay single for long." That was the confirmation I needed to hear. I said yes to Alce.

A few weeks before Christmas he wanted me to meet his family. They were all coming into town for the holidays. To my surprise, he told me that they were not his biological children, but he loved them as if they were his own. He married their mother when the children were small and his two biological children lived in California. They were by his first wife he married when they were very young and it didn't work out.

I met his family, two girls and four young men and the grandson Josh. They were friendly, and I was so impressed with how they respected Alce. They all had good jobs, which told me somebody in the Harris home did a good job raising them.

I told Alce to wait a while before telling them that we had planned to marry. We waited almost three months before getting married. Matter of fact, we went for a ride over to Texas and he pulled up to the courthouse. We sat there for a few minutes before saying a single word. Finally, he asked, "Can we get married today?"

"Why today?" I asked.

"Because its time," he answered. "I don't want to spend another night by myself. We can go in that courthouse and get the license today."

"I thought we were going have a small wedding," I said, disappointed.

"Well, if that is what you want to do, we can." he said.

I didn't know what to say. I got out the car and stood under a shade tree near the courthouse steps so I could get my thoughts together. I knew marriage was and is a total lifetime commitment. And it is a bonding together. When we get married we become one. Two personalities are going to be merged, blended, and glued together. If I write another book, I know I will get more in depth on the marriage subject.

Alce got out the car and walked over to where I was. "Bertha." he said, "you don't have to worry, I going to treat you good and take care you."

I never felt he wouldn't do that. Alce was a kind and honest person. And I liked that he was a family man. And I really believed that he was the man that God intended for me to marry. With that thought in mind I agreed to get married. We found out later that we had to wait 24 hours even after we got the license before we could get married. That was the law in most states. That next day we stood before a judge and repeated our vows.

This time around, I wanted to be sure that this was the right thing to do. In my past marriage I had experienced hurt, bitterness and strife. Now, when God touched my life, it seemed as if those things never happened. I was not taking a lot of past baggage into my current marriage. I try to live by this scripture: Philippians 3:1 says, "forgetting those things which are behind." It is only in this "forgetting" that we can reach forth unto those things which are before. This man I had married was nothing like my past husband and I wasn't going to make him suffer for something my ex did.

We got through that part, so we had to make the living arrangements. We decided he would let his children have his home and he would move into my home. I felt that was the right thing to do.

Some people thought the marriage was too quick. And Alce must have been seeing me before his wife passed. We let them talk, because the first time I had met Alce was the day I went to cut his cable off. Non-believers would think that way.

I have no regrets at all of eleven years we have been married and we haven't been apart over a week. I enjoy being around my husband. We built our marriage on trust, faith, and thus says the Lord. My husband is the head, king, and priest of our home, and I respect that. Being the head doesn't mean he should dog his wife out. Wives stay in your lane and let your husband drive. If there is something he is not strong in, help him with love, not condemnation. Don't try to show up his weakness by talking down to him around others. Tell God about it. Only tell others the good things about your husband. He will love and respect you for that.

In 2003, Alce began to have leg cramps and pain in his lower legs. After seeking medical help, the doctor informed us that he was suffering from poor blood circulation. After the diagnosis he started getting all kinds of treatment, but there still was very little release. The pain became so unbearable and the pills they gave him for the pain just kept him about out of his head. I called the doctor and told him how bad it was, so he told me to bring Alce in and get him admitted to the hospital for observation. Alce had a very hard night. The following morning a team of doctors came in to check his legs and he was sent to x-ray. The x-rays showed that he had blood clots in each of his legs and no blood was getting to his feet. Both his feet and legs would need to be amputated. The doctors informed us that some of the problem stemmed from my husband having been a smoker.

Alce and I hugged and cried. Alce told me just go home and don't come back. He didn't want to be a burden on me. "I am not going anywhere," I told him.

That night I slept in his hospital bed with him. I told him we are going to get through all of this together. I only went home to change clothes and check on the house. I called his children to inform them about all that was happening and asked his daughter Rose to come talk to the doctor to find out if there was anything that might could be done to save his legs. Rose worked in a large medical center as a cardiology tech and she knew exactly which questions needed to be asked. Plus, I felt it was the right thing to have his children help make the decisions.

The next day after we had our family discussions and knew a little more about what was happening, we all knew and understood what needed to be done. We found out that the amputation was necessary to save Alce's life. It may have needed to be done, but I was just devastated. That was my tall handsome husband who would no longer be standing and would need to be confined to a wheel chair. We grieved together.

This was a test of the vow I make to God. I vowed that I would love and care for my husband through sickness and health, for richer or poorer. The transition was not easy. Alce went though sadness, anger, and depression. He was not able to return to work and I had to resign from Time Warner.

So I was going to have to take up the slack. I was going to need to get some extra income to support our family. We needed to move into a house that was handicap equipped. All that took money. While I was taking care of him, I was not able to work for almost a year and neither was Alce. We had just about used up our little saving.

I did seek some of the services that had been available for the handicapped and that helped us some. We just weren't used to getting handouts. We were working people. I was constantly seeking God help to see us though this. I sought God's help, knowing I needed a job I could work from home such as a craft or art I could sell at shows or anything that could help us keep together and be productive.

I had a little experience with crafts and had made things like handbags for a few shows before, but that didn't work out so well. All the other vendors were selling them and had more experience than I did. I asked God, to help me see and appreciate my unique skill that only I had.

One day, while I was sitting at my kitchen table adding up bills and doodling around on some paper, trying to figure out how was I going take care of all these bills with no money and no job, I looked down and realized I had penciled a drawing of this little man that reminded me of my grandpa. A light went on in my head. A voice said so loud to me that I thought Alce was talking. It just kept saying to me that my family history and my story needed to be told. And I was the one who needed to start telling it. I had always been able to listen and understand the deep history we had, and now I needed to tell it.

I told Alce that I was going to be the one to tell the story through my eyes and hands. I just had to believe in myself and do it in the same way others did before me. Like Clementine Hunter, I could use paint and other elements to relate the story of our history in northwest Louisiana. From Homer to Bossier and Shreveport and all the associations we had, our family and everyone we touched had a history that needed to be told.

God showed me that I could paint my family history, so I went to the local Walmart and bought all kinds of paint and brushes. I got some pieces of cardboard and drew my family picking cotton like it really happened.

Most people today don't realize that until as recent as fifty years ago, families were still picking cotton by hand around here just to put a little food on the table. This and so much more really happened and it's all stories people can understand through art I could create.

The rest of the story is history. I hope I can continue telling this story to others for a long time.

I truly believe, if we do the right thing, God will bring so many blessing to our lives. My husband Alce is doing fine. He has me and many friends and family around him who love him. With our hard work and our faith we are at peace.

He still chases me around the house just like he did when we first got married. God is good!

Claiborne Jubilee to Feature Parish Native

When the Claiborne Jubilee opens on May 19, 2008, visitors will be treated to the works of the artist being hailed as the next Clementine Hunter. Bertha Cooper Harris was born and raised in the St. John's Community of Claiborne Parish and has brought her memories of those years to life in her paintings which she only began a year ago. Mrs. Harris now lives in Blanchard but for years has wanted to give back to her home parish and share some of the richness of those early years with today's residents.

Mrs. Harris is a completely self taught Southern folk artist who has worked in fabric art for the past ten years, but who has only recently begun painting. She likes to recycle old objects into useful items such as purses and fabric wall art incorporating colorful fabrics. Her paintings depict scenes and experiences from growing up at Cooper Hill and on Beene Plantation. "I use my art to express the dreams and visions I have experienced throughout my life." Often she paints on scrap cardboard from grocery boxes as well as on canvas and wood.

She has exhibited her work at Melrose Plantation, Shop Till You Drop, Shreveport Regional Art Council's ArtSpace, the Shanty Folk Art Gallery, the Peddler Shows as well as in shows throughout Texas. Her family consists of her husband, one daughter, three grandsons and eight great-grandchildren, as well as an extended family throughout the area.

For more information on the Claiborne Jubilee contact Cathy Emerson at 548-1272 or Cynthia Steele at 927-2566.

BERTHA HARRIS

Claiborne Jubilee draws large crowd

Artist Bertha Harris a big hit

The Guardian-Journal photo/ K.H. Hightower

Bertha Harris shows off her artwork with this painting of the White Lightning Feud 2. Harris and her work were the main attraction for the show this year. During the Jubilee, a quilt show was held and citizens got to choose their favorite for "Best of Show." Others set up booths around The Square to show off their talents and wares. Everything from woodwork to quilting was on display for everyone to enjoy. Also, the Ford Museum was open for tours during the Jubilee.

Painting from the Heart and Soul

*By Su Stella- *Smiley**

You can almost smell the greens cooking and hear the songs from the field when you see Bertha Renter Harris' artwork. Bertha is self-taught in the southern folk art style with inspiration from her childhood experiences growing up at the Cooper Hill and Beene Plantations. During her childhood people worked the fields doing back bending labor in the heat; only in modern times did automated farm equipment become the norm. Washer women, outhouses, and memories fill her colorful and imaginative work.

For the past decade Bertha painted functional items like purses. Her passion grew and she began painting on found and recycled objects like cardboard, canvas, and wood. These new techniques began opening doors for her that functional art didn't and she's been told on many occasions that she is "the next Clementine Hunter". Both women have art portraying a simple time that tells a story of lives now past. With this in mind, you may want to start collecting her work now as it will probably increase in value as her fame and recognition grows.

Bertha and I have known each other for about a year as working artists in venues throughout the Ark-La-Tex area. Her beautiful displays only enhance the style of her work. Her work is displayed at The Little Shanty Folk Art Gallery on 7102 Line Avenue in Shreveport (318-861-3308). On most Saturdays starting October 18 thru November 22, Bertha can be found at the Shreveport Farmers Market at Festival Plaza from 8:30 until noon. November 11 finds her at the Henderson Heritage Festival in Henderson TX, and on December 5 and 6 at the Dixie Cotton Gin in Dixie, LA. From mid-November, visit the Deck the Halls Art Show at ArtSpace located at 710 Texas Avenue in Shreveport. You can email Bertha with opportunities and commissions at lacebre2@bellsouth.net. To contact Smiley, email her at NotMyPlanet@live.com.

Bertha Cooper Harris *at work*

Conclusion

I CAN TRULY SAY THAT I'VE LEARNED SOME VERY VALUABLE LESSONS THROUGH THESE EXPERIENCES. Women, we must fight to strengthen our laws so that they will be an unbending deterrent for this type of behavior. Monetary settlements, small or large, aren't enough. I believe it is imperative that the offenders face prison terms and that constant psychiatric counseling should be mandatory.

In 1998, there were still large numbers of men who hadn't gotten the message that sexual harassment was against the law. Women all over the world were complaining about it everyday.

Because of the physical and emotional abuse, a battered woman will suffer and act in ways that confuse those who wish to help her. Because people generally don't understand why battered women do what they do, their friends or people who want to help often call the victim crazy, unstable, lazy or shiftless because the woman can't keep a man or husband.

Sometimes due to loneliness, we find ourselves abusing drugs and alcohol and repeating the same old cycle, until we get professional help. In order to help you understand why battered or sexually abused women and sexually abused children do what they do, you should try to understand the information below that has been so helpful for me:

According to the *Domestic Violence Sourcebook*, the battered woman can suffer from what is called "battered women syndrome." The concept of battered woman syndrome typically refers only to women, for these reasons:

A battered woman is a woman who has experienced at least two battering cycles as described in dating and domestic violence.

A battered woman will stay in these dangerous relationships for a variety of reasons, including:
- Economic dependence upon the batterer.
- A false belief that they can keep the peace.
- Fear of danger if she were to leave
- Threats made by the batterer to hurt her or her children if she left.
- Loss of self-esteem.
- Depression or loss of psychological control.

There are four general characteristics of the syndrome:
1. The woman believes that the violence was or is her fault
2. The woman has an inability to place responsibility for violence elsewhere
3. The woman has an irrational belief that her abuser is omnipresent and omniscient.
4. Most recently, battered woman syndrome has also been associated with post-traumatic stress disorder in the that domestic violence involves exposure to severe trauma and so the reactions of a battered woman may be due to flashbacks or other intrusive experiences from previous traumatic events so that the women believes that she is in danger, even if she is not.

Sexual Abuse

www.mamashealth.com/abuse/sabuse.asp

Sexual abuse encompasses any form of degradation, manipulation, force, or control of sex. For the abuser, sex is the way that he or she establishes power and dominance in the relationship. Many sex abusers see their partners as sex objects and they depersonalize their partners. Some sexual abusers can only become sexually excited when they use force, degradation, or violence on their partners. And most are not faithful to their partners.

It is important to understand that sexual abuse in a domestic situation need not imply a forced rape. Though forced rape is sexual abuse, sexual abuse can wear many faces:

- A victim of sexual abuse may find that his or her partner (abuser) is the decision maker in regards to their sexual encounters.
- A victim may be coerced or forced into having sex with an abuser whenever and the abuser want it.
- A victim may find that his or her partner (abuser) uses his or her bodily sensitivities and vulnerabilities against him or her.
- A victim may be made to feel that his or her discomfort is his or her problem and not a result of the partner actions.
- A victim may be forced to engage in sex acts with others.

Sexual abuse will sometimes go hand-in-hand with physical abuse. Sometimes sexual abuse may occur after a physical assault. Sometimes physical abuse occurs as part of sex abuse. Sexual abuse can also be purely emotional or psychological.

Many times a sexual abuser is very jealous he or she may be extremely suspicious of what his or her partner does on a daily basis. A sexual abuser may accuse his or her partner of flirting or infidelity. Sexual abusers may also become jealous with any relationship his or her partner has, be it with a friend, co-worker, clergy, or relative. Sometimes the abuser will torment his or her partner with made up details of the partner's infidelities.

Sexual Harassment — Know Your Rights!

Sexual harassment is any unwanted sexual attention a woman experiences. It includes leering, pinching, patting, repeated comments, subtle suggestions of a sexual nature, and pressure for dates.

Sexual harassment can occur in any situation with men in power over women: welfare workers with clients, doctors with patients, police officers with women members of a police force, or teachers with students. In the workplace it can include a supervisor, co-worker, a client, or a customer. Sexual harassment can escalate; women who are being sexual harassed are at risk of being physically abused or raped.

Sexual harassment is a powerful way for men to undermine and control us. Attitudes of race and class superiority can result in feelings by white men that they are entitled to sexually harass women of color employees from a "lower" class or different background. There is an implicit (and sometimes explicit) message that refusal to comply with the harasser's demands will lead to work-related reprisal. These can include escalation of harassment, poor work assignments, sabotaging of projects, and/or denial of raises, benefits, or promotion, and sometimes loss of job with a poor reference to show for it. Harassment can drive women out of a particular job or out of the workplace altogether.

There is such a taboo in many workplaces and schools against identifying sexual harassment for what it is that many of us who experience it are at first aware only of feeling stressed. We may experience headaches, anxieties, or resistance to going to work in the morning. It may take you a while to realize that these symptoms come from our being sexually harassed. We often respond by feeling isolated and powerless, afraid to say "no," to speak out because we fear either that we somehow are responsible or that we won't receive help facing possible retaliation. But when we take the risk and talk with other women, we often find that they are being harassed also (or have been) and have similar responses to ours.

1. Remember that you are not to blame. Sexual harassment is imposed sexual attention. No matter how complicated the situation is, the harasser is responsible for the abuse.
2. Let the harasser know as directly and explicitly as possible that you are not interested in his attentions. If you do this in writing, keep a copy of your letter.
3. Document what happens. Keep a detailed diary including dates, times, and place. Save any notes or pictures from the harasser — don't throw them away in anger. Keep a record of anyone who witnessed the harassment.

Incest

According to the Broken Spirit Network (**www.brokenspirits.com**):

Child sexual abuse is not a rare occurrence. It is estimated that approximately one in every four females and one in every six males experience some form of sexual exploitation as children. Someone they or the family knows molests eighty percent of molested children. *e.g.* a family member, relative, neighbor, family friend, *etc.*

The role that the offender plays in the child's life may be vital. He or she may be a close family member or someone in the position of trust. The abuse occurring will be very confusing to the child because of the secrecy, shame, lies, and isolation that follow. The child wants the abusive behavior to stop but does not want to lose the hope of protection and caring that are his or her rights.

Children do not have the explicit sexual knowledge necessary to describe phenomena they have not experienced and do not have the cognitive capacities to make up stories of sexual abuse. If children lie about sexual abuse, it is most often to deny that it did occur in order to protect the offender and/or the family unit.

Child sexual abuse typically goes on for quite some time before discovery. It is not confined to one child, but usually involves several children.

Adults often do not talk about child sexual abuse because of their own discomfort with the topic. If adults are not willing to talk about the abuse, the child will probably feel that there is something to be ashamed of, that it is dirty and just too awful to talk about. This attitude will only serve to increase the child's feelings of guilt and shame and of being abnormal, compounding the child's problems.

Children who have been sexually abused feel many different and often overwhelming emotions including:
- **Fear** — of the abuser, of causing trouble, of losing adults important to them, most often, the abuser will tell them if they told someone he would kill that person.
- **Anger** — at the abuser, at other adults around them who did not protect them.
- **Isolation** — because "something is wrong with me" because they feel alone in their experience, because they have trouble talking about the abuse.
- **Sadness** — about having something taken from them, about losing a part of themselves, about growing up too fast, about being betrayed by someone they trusted.
- **Guilt** — for they are not being able to stop the abuse, believing they "consented" to abuse.

If you have experienced any form of sexually abuse, are in a relationship where you have been battered, or have been abused in any way, *please get help* **now**. There are all kinds of resources out there: domestic violence shelter programs, hotlines, and other services that can be found in your local telephone book, or your local police department. They will help and advise you on locating emergency shelter until you're ready to move into permanent housing for yourself and your children. These people also provide information about your legal rights. Most of these are free of charge, or fees are adjusted according to your income.

If your believe that you are being sexually harassed in the workplace, refer to the interaction in the resource information and be sure to file an in-house grievance so that it can be proven that you followed the chain of command within your company. The next step, if the previous one is unsuccessful, is to file a claim with the EEOC in your state.

Mothers, I can't stress enough how important it is that you listen to your children and ask questions if you notice behaviors that are not appropriate. Women, we must rise up and take responsibility for ourselves and our children. Before we can do that, we must keep our eyes open and our minds clear by healing ourselves first. We can't do that if we are still in an abusive relationship and abusing drug or alcohol. When we have healed ourselves, we must rise up and protect our children.

I have first-hand experience of what could happen if, as mothers, we don't take responsibility for our children. The pain and heartaches can drag you down in the long run. I didn't protect my daughter. Because of alcohol abuse and staying in the relationship, I was responsible for what happened to my daughter. In that process I lost my daughter — for a long time she resented me and rebelled against me. But, I thank God, that through counseling and crying out to God and asking Him for His tender mercies and forgiveness, I found comfort. I was able to win my daughter back through love, kindness, and compassion, without condemning, one day at a time.

The healing process begins with forgiving ourselves and those who've trespassed against us.

Mark 11:25–26 tells us that when ye are praying, forgive, if ye have ought against any, that your Father also which is in Heaven may forgive your trespasses. But if ye do not forgive, neither will your Father who is in Heaven forgive you.

Psalm 103:1–5 says, "Bless the LORD, O my soul: and all that is within me, *bless* His holy name. Bless the LORD, O my soul, and do not forget all his benefits: who forgives all your iniquities; who heals all thy diseases; who redeems your life from destruction; who crowns you with loving kindness and tender mercies; who satisfies your mouth with good *things; so that* your youth is renewed like the eagle's."

Unforgivness

According to **www.mayoclinic.com/health/forgivness:**

If you are unforgiving, you might pay the price repeatedly by bringing anger and bitterness into relationships and new experiences — your life might become so wrapped up in wrong that you can't enjoy the present. You might become depressed or anxious, you might feel that that your life lacks meaning or purpose, or that you are at odds with your spiritual beliefs. You might lose valuable and enriching connectedness with others.

As you let go of the grudges, you'll no longer define your life by how you've been hurt. You might even find compassion and understanding. Ask God or your higher being forgiveness and forgive yourselves. Let it go, so that we can rise up and be a testimony to help save our children and somebody else's children. If you are an older woman like myself, stay busy and visible so that we can encourage our young women without condemning.

It says in Titus chapter 2:3–5 that the aged women likewise, that *they be* in behavior as becometh holiness, not false accusers, not given to much wine, teachers of good things; shall be your models, for they teach young women to be sober, to love their husbands and to love their children.

Stop saying I am too old to make a difference. Your life isn't over 'til God says it's over.

At age 65, God gave me a vision to unleash my gift to become an artist. As of today I am 73 years old and painting mostly every day. Last year I won an award for the best artistic merit for 2011 at the Red River Revel Art Festival.

Now that we have resources in our hands and the cause to rise again, we know that we are a survivor. You must let your pain go! Get over it! Rise higher than ever before. When we rise together to be whatever we want to be, there is no goal that we cannot achieve.

Rise, women. Rise like you have the wings of an eagle.

Illustrations

To my Mother, Annie Bell Young Edwards	iii
Cotton Queen	iv
Angels watching over the Church	vi
Mary, Joseph, and Baby Jesus	vii
Two Mamas	viii
Claiborne "Jubilee 2008" newspaper ad	x
Dallas Morning News newspaper article	xiii
Bertha Cooper at age three	xiv
Cooper Hill	xvi
Granpa Young at Joe Tuggle's place on "White Lightning Road"	12
My sister Annie	16
Beene Plantaton	20
"Get Up!"	28
Bertha Cooper at age thirteens	32
Lovers at tree swing	34
Family fun time on Cooper Hill	38
Brother Jim hauling cotton on Beene's Plantation	44
Cotton gin (painted directly on wooden cabinet door)	50
Braiding in the Kitchen	59
After a hard day's work	60
Early painting of wagon going up Cooper Hill	64
Downward Spiral	70
Women of the field	73
Old Man Cotton	74
Baptism near Cooper Hill	80
Hanging laundry	88
Mama I remember	90
Bertha's hand-made dolls	92
Grandma smoking a pipe	96
Love	102
"This is all I have."	114
Milking cows at Mr. Hunter's place	120
Bertha and her agents at the insurance company award banquet	122
Bertha receiving insurance company award for Top Staff Manager	126
"Dance, children! Dance!"	134
Jimmy, James, Odell, Eddie, Bertha, Ella, and Annie	148
Milk time on Cooper Hill	153
Bertha & Alce Harris	154
"Claiborne Jubilee to Feature Parish Native" newspaper article	161
"Claiborne Jubilee Draws Large Crowd" newspaper article	161
"Painting from the Heart and Soul" *Louisian Road Trips* magazine article	162
Bertha Cooper Harris at work	162
Rise, women. Rise like you have the wings of an eagle!	169

Rise, women. Rise like you have the wings of an eagle!